THE ECONOMIC THEORY OF THE LEISURE CLASS

THE ECONOMIC THEORY *of the* LEISURE CLASS

NIKOLAI BUKHARIN

Introduction by Donald J. Harris

Monthly Review Press
New York

Library of Congress Catalog Card Number: 72-81775

First Modern Reader Paperback Edition 1972

ISBN: 978-0-85345-261-4

Monthly Review Press
146 West 29th Street Suite 6W
New York, NY 10001
www.monthlyreview.org

CONTENTS

CHAPTER IV

CHAPTER V

CHAPTER VI

APPENDIX

INTRODUCTION

by Donald J. Harris

The Economic Theory of the Leisure Class is not, as its title might suggest, an economic analysis of the conditions which give rise to the existence of a leisure class, in the manner of Veblen's earlier work, *The Theory of the Leisure Class*. The titles are close enough but the subject matter is quite different. It would have been better to have entitled this book "A Marxist Critique of Bourgeois Economic Theory," for that is what it is. In the tradition of Marxist critiques, it is a significant contribution. But there has really been nothing in this area to compare with the monumental work of Marx himself, *Theories of Surplus Value* (or even the shorter treatise, *A Contribution to the Critique of Political Economy*). The standard attained by Marx's performance would in any case be hard to equal. That work still remains the definitive and most "systematic *resumé* of the whole complex of political economy" (in Engels' words) as it had taken shape up to Marx's time. It continues to have direct relevance as well to contemporary theory.

Bukharin's critique is more narrowly focused; its particular object is the Austrian School and the work of its chief spokesman, Eugen von Böhm-Bawerk. But Bukharin situates the ideas of this school in the broader context of marginal theory, and it is to the latter that his critique is addressed. In the process he gives a good account also of some of the essential features of Marxian economic theory through a sharp confrontation of the two theoretical systems. It is a polemical essay. Originally published in Russian in 1917 (in English in 1927), it fell out of use for some time. It is particularly appropriate that it should be made available in paperback at a time when interest is once again aroused in a confrontation of Marxian theory with that of the orthodox schools of economics.

The emergence of marginal utility theory in the late nineteenth century represented a revolution of sorts in economic thought. It marked a basically different approach to economic theory and analysis in comparison with the established tradition of classical political economy and the political economy of Marx which had already gained some headway. A major substantive difference lay in the approach to the theory of value where the chief distinguishing feature of the new school was its introduction of the concept of utility as the basis of a value theory.[1]

"The problem of value," as Bukharin indicates in this book, "has constituted a fundamental question of political economy since the earliest days of the science." (P. 59.) At an initial and preliminary level, common to all approaches to this question, the problem centers around the quantitative ratios at which commodities exchange in the market. It is a problem of the relation of commodities in exchange, or the *exchange value* of commodities. One of the purposes of a theory of value is to adduce some principle that explains this relation.[2] The classical economists found such a principle in the quantity of labor expended in production: commodities exchange at ratios that are determined by the quantity of labor directly and indirectly employed in producing them. This conception provided the organizing principle with which they sought to explain the major movements of the economy in regard to prices, production, distribution, and accumulation.

Starting from this conception, Marx proceeded to broaden

---

1. The term "marginal revolution" is sometimes used to draw attention to the concept of the margin as an element in the analytical system of this school. But this concept is ultimately less important as a distinguishing feature than that of utility. The term "neoclassical" often applied to this school is also somewhat of a misnomer because of the tenuous connection of the new system of ideas with that of the classics. Whatever the name, the system of ideas provided the foundations upon which was built the orthodox ("neoclassical") theory of today. For an exposition of the modern version, see C. E. Ferguson, *Microeconomic Theory,* rev. ed. (Homewood, Ill.: Richard D. Irwin, Inc., 1969); *The Neoclassical Theory of Production and Distribution* (New York: Cambridge University Press, 1969).

2. Most expositions of the orthodox theory, in its modern version, tend to stop at exhibiting the mechanism of operation of the market through interaction of "supply and demand" so as to bring about an "equilibrium price." But, as Bukharin points out here, "this formal aspect of the matter is less interesting than its content, the quantitative determination of the exchange process." (P. 104.)

and deepen it in a number of directions. The basis of his reformulation was the perception that the complex of exchange relations existing in the market is but a reflection of the link between the productive labor of individuals, a link which arises from the social or collective nature of the labor process: "A relation of commodities as exchange-values is nothing but a mutual relation between persons in their productive activity." Like the classical economists, he was thus concerned to explain exchange values in terms of production, labor viewed as being at the center of production. To this extent, the labor theory of value was seen as correctly incorporating the determining role of the "real relations of production." But in addition, Marx sought to bring the *social* relations of production to the forefront of the analysis, emphasizing that these relations have a definite historical character. The problem of value theory therefore becomes not only a matter of explaining quantitative exchange ratios or "prices of production" but, more fundamentally, a matter of exhibiting the nature of the social relations, the manner of their operation through the working of the economy, and the way in which they evolve over time.

The perspective here is that of viewing the production system as a whole and in perpetual historical motion. From this perspective, Marx saw capitalism as an historically specific form of commodity production; its characteristic feature is that "labour-power itself becomes a commodity" and ownership of the means of production is concentrated in the hands of a class of capitalists who are thereby able to appropriate a part of the product of labor in the form of surplus value. The Marxian theory of capitalism, developed on these foundations by Marx and subsequent writers in the Marxist tradition, constitute a distinctive theory with its own method of analysis and specific formulation of "the economic laws of motion" of capitalism.[3]

The marginal utility school represented a major shift, in terms of both method and substance, away from these tradi-

3. For summary treatments, see L. B. Boudin, *The Theoretical System of Karl Marx,* reprint ed. (New York: Monthly Review Press, 1967); Paul M. Sweezy, *The Theory of Capitalist Development* (New York: Monthly Review Press, 1953); John Eaton, *Political Economy: A Marxist Textbook,* rev. ed. (New York: International Publishers, 1966).

tions. For Marx and the classics, *use value* (the objective relation of commodities to human needs) was taken only as a condition for the existence of exchange value. In marginal utility theory, subjective satisfaction is made a determinant of the magnitude of exchange value; specifically, the psychological satisfaction (or utility) derived at the margin from the consumption of different commodities is regarded as determining their exchange ratios. For Marx and the classics, exchange was necessarily connected with the social division of labor in production. Some versions of marginal utility theory are set out in terms of pure exchange, *without* production, a scheme which has been likened to the economics of a prisoner-of-war camp. It is often expounded in terms of a Robinson Crusoe economy where trade is between Crusoe and himself (until Friday comes along). When production is introduced, it is the subjective *disutility* of work which enters into the determinaton of exchange value. The difference carries over to, and appears sharpest in, the theory of profit (or interest). Marx saw the origin of profit in an excess of the total value which the workers produce over the value of the wage goods which sustain and reproduce their labor power. This surplus is appropriated by the capitalists on account of their monopoly, as a class, of the means of production. Marginal utility theory sees profit as arising out of individuals' presumed preferences for present over future consumption.

Some of the originators and practitioners of the new ideas felt it necessary to trace their roots back to the classics. Marshall, in England, was especially prone to this; and it must be granted that there was room for making such a connection, particularly in the work of Adam Smith. Others, at a time when the European labor movement was increasingly adopting Marxism, turned to an attack on Marx. Foremost among these were Wicksteed in England, Pareto in Italy, and in Austria, Böhm-Bawerk and Wieser, the leading figures (along with Menger) of the Austrian School.[4] Of these efforts, Böhm-Bawerk's critique of Marx's analysis soon came to be regarded as the definitive statement from the viewpoint of marginal utility theory. The

4. In America, a similar effort was represented in O. D. Skelton, *Socialism: A Critical Analysis*, 1911; and W. J. Blake, *An American Looks at Karl Marx*, 1939.

substantive charges, directed mainly at the logical connection between labor values and prices of production in Marx's system (the so-called transformation problem) were ably refuted by Bortkiewicz and Hilferding.[5] Against this background, Bukharin's book could be viewed as providing what amounted to a counteroffensive from the Marxist side. It is a striking feature of this period (*circa* 1880-1920) that such a confrontation on theoretical questions should have occurred, paralleling the great social movements taking place across Europe.

Bukharin's approach in this book follows that which Marx had adopted in *Theories of Surplus Value,* which is to give an "exhaustive criticism" not only of the methodology and internal logic of the theory, viewed as a complete system of analysis, but also of the sociological and class basis which the theory reflects.

So far as the sociological criticism is concerned, it is helpful to recall Marx's general characterization of the role of "bourgeois political economy" and its relation to Marxian political economy: In the early phase of capitalist development bourgeois political economy, by championing the interests of the emerging bourgeoisie in its struggle against the pre-existing dominant class, performs a radical scientific role in exposing the true nature of commodity-producing precapitalist society. In the later phase of capitalism, however, bourgeois political economy turns to justification of the system in which the bourgeoisie has become ascendant and is threatened by the growing workers' movement. It thereby loses its scientific role, a role which is to be taken by Marxian political economy rooted in the interests of the working class. In this connection Bukharin points out that "Marxism claims its general validity precisely for the reason that it is the theoretical expression of the most advanced class, whose 'needs' of knowledge are far more audacious than those of the conservative and therefore narrow-minded mode of thought of the ruling classes in capitalist society." (P. 8.)

---

5. The main works in this controversy have been reprinted in a single volume and are worth reading as a supplement to the present work. See Eugen von Böhm-Bawerk and Rudolf Hilferding, *Karl Marx and the Close of His System,* ed. Paul M. Sweezy, reprint ed. (New York: Augustus Kelley, 1966). The formal solution of the "transformation problem" is by now well established. On this, see F. Seton, "The Transformation Problem," *Review of Economic Studies,* June 1957.

This is the broad framework which informs the present work. Since a brief summary cannot adequately represent the underlying conception of the social origins of theory, the reader is referred to Bukharin's ***Historical Materialism,*** where the analytical basis of his position is more systematically developed. One may note also that the conception involved here differs sharply from that of, say, Schumpeter (in ***History of Economic Analysis***). The latter, while recognizing that ideology (or "vision") enters into economic theory and social science in general ("In fact it enters on the very ground floor . . ."), nevertheless viewed economic theory as advancing independently through continual refinement and elaboration of techniques of analysis.[6]

Within his chosen framework, Bukharin seeks to characterize the specific form that marginal utility theory takes and its basis in the concrete conditions of the time. His central thesis is that the new theory is the ideological expression of a particular class, the class of rentiers who have been "eliminated from the process of production" and are interested solely in disposing of their income from holdings of securities and bonds—who have become, simply, "coupon-cutters." He argues that the unhistorical character of the theory, its starting from consumption, and its preoccupation with individual psychology derives from the objective position and interest of this class in contemporary capitalism. The outline of the thesis is sharply drawn and Bukharin is careful to indicate that it is "merely an *outline* . . . ignoring all subsidiary factors." (P. 177, n. 14.) It has roots in the work of Werner Sombart, the well-known historian of capitalism. Some commentators have tried to dismiss the thesis offhandedly.[7] Others grant, for instance, that "it has a certain force."[8] The thesis, as presented, can perhaps be faulted for giving too mechanical an interpretation of the relation between economic

6. For a useful critique of this view see R. L. Meek, *Economics and Ideology and Other Essays* (London: Chapman & Hall, 1967), pp. 196-209; and M. H. Dobb, *Theories of Value and Distribution Since Adam Smith: Ideology and Economics* (Cambridge: Cambridge University Press, forthcoming).

7. See Erich Roll, *A History of Economic Thought,* 3d ed. (Englewood Cliffs: Prentice-Hall, 1956), pp. 369-70.

8. Mark Blaug, *Economic Theory in Retrospect,* rev. ed. (Homewood, Ill.: Richard D. Irwin, Inc., 1968), p. 306.

theory and ideology where a dialectical interpretation is called for. But no one, to my knowledge, has so far attempted an examination of it through a more detailed analysis of the historical facts. It remains a potentially fruitful area of research with direct relevance to current interest in the nature of scientific revolutions in the social sciences.

The criticism of the logic and method of subjective value theory is set out in terms of a direct confrontation with the Marxian system on each and every issue so that the line of demarcation between them is clearly drawn. The discussion relies in part on arguments earlier put forward by Stolzman, Hilferding, and Bortkiewicz (who are properly acknowledged) and is to that extent not entirely original. Bukharin scores the familiar points against particular elements of the theory, for instance, that utility is not measurable, that Böhm-Bawerk's concept of an "average period of production" is "nonsensical," that the theory is static, and so on. Such criticisms of the technical apparatus of the theory have no doubt been better stated elsewhere. The student who has been trained in the techniques of the modern version of the theory can also readily recognize certain weaknesses in Bukharin's presentation, such as an apparent confusion between marginal and total utility, and a misconception of the meaning of interdependent markets. But these are matters that were not well understood at the time, even by exponents of the theory. Besides, as Bukharin emphasizes, they are matters of lesser importance. What is crucial is "the point of departure of the . . . theory, its ignoring the social-historical character of economic phenomena." (P. 73.) This criticism is applied with particular force to the treatment, or lack of it, of the problem of capital, the formation of demand, and the process of economic evolution. In anticipation of developments in mathematical economics, Bukharin notes pointedly: "The unhistorical character of the objectivism of the 'mathematicians' and the 'Anglo-Americans' causes them to accept a purely mechanical view which in reality does not recognize society at all, but only a congeries of moving objects." (Pp. 185-86, n. 52.)

Today many economists would claim that controversy over some of these issues has long ago been put to rest. There is an element of truth in this claim. Value as a category distinct from market price is hardly mentioned these days. The concept of utility as a measurable quantity has been demoted in favor of "revealed preference." As long as "factors of production" are paid according to their "marginal products," it cannot be that profit constitutes exploitation. And so on. The truth is that the main line of recent developments in economics has been in the direction of increasing formalization of theory such as to make of it essentially an elaboration of the problem of rational choice —a problem supposed to be of universal significance—and so, at the same time, to empty it of any real economic content. By a happy coincidence, the central theorems also turn out to provide an ideological justification for laissez-faire capitalism. But the substantive theoretical issues have merely been suppressed. This is readily apparent from their re-emergence in recent controversies on the theory of capital and growth and in recent discussions of the solution of Marx's "transformation problem" and of Ricardo's "invariable standard of value."[9] To this one might add what is perhaps the most telling criticism made by Bukharin:

> . . . the latest theory of the bourgeois scholars fails precisely in the most important fundamental questions of our day. The enormous and speedy accumulation of capital, its concentration and centralisation, the uncommonly rapid progress in technology, and finally, the regular recurrence of industrial crises . . . all these things are a "book with seven seals" . . . And just where the philosophy of the learned bourgeois ceases, the Marxian theory comes into its own, to such an extent, in fact, that mutilated fragments of the Marxian doctrine are accepted as the last word of wisdom even by the bitterest enemies of Marxism. (P. 57.)

Nikolai I. Bukharin (1880-1938) is commonly acknowledged

9. For a review of these controversies, see Joan Robinson, "Capital Theory Up to Date," *Canadian Journal of Economics,* May 1970, and the papers collected in G. C. Harcourt and N. F. Laing, eds., *Capital and Growth: Theory* (Baltimore: Penguin, 1971). The paper by Bharadwaj in this collection clarifies the nature of the solution proposed by Sraffa to Ricardo's problem. Discussion of Marx's "transformation problem" has been revived recently by Samuelson in *Journal of Economic Literature,* June 1971.

to have been one of the most brilliant theoreticians in the Bolshevik movement and an outstanding figure in the history of Marxism. Born in Russia, he studied economics at Moscow University and (during four years of exile in Europe and America) at the universities of Vienna and Lausanne (Switzerland), in Sweden and Norway, and in the New York Public Library. While still a student, he joined the Bolshevik movement and was thrice arrested for his revolutionary activities. His political activities continued in exile and so did his arrests. Upon returning to Russia in April 1917, he worked closely with Lenin and participated in planning and carrying out the October Revolution. After the victory of the Bolsheviks he assumed many high offices in the Party—he became a member of the Politbureau in 1919—and in other organizations. In these various capacities he came to exercise great influence within both the Party and the Comintern. Under Stalin's regime, however, he lost most of his important positions. Eventually, he was among those who were arrested and brought to trial on charges of treason and he was executed on March 15, 1938.

At the peak of his career Bukharin was regarded as the foremost theoretician and authority on Marxism in the Party.[10] Lenin is supposed to have called him "the most valuable and biggest theoretician."[11] He was a prolific writer. There are more than five hundred items of published work in his name. Only a few have been translated into English, and these are the works for which he is now most widely known.[12]

---

10. His contribution to the evolution of Communist revolutionary thought is reviewed in Sidney Heitman, "Between Lenin and Stalin: Nikolai Bukharin," in Leopold Labedz, ed., *Revisionism* (New York: Praeger, 1962).

11. Lenin's estimate was qualified, however, by the remark that "Bukharin's views can only with the very greatest doubt be regarded as fully Marxian, for there is something scholastic in him (as he has never learned and, I think, never fully understood the dialectic)." Quoted by Heitman, ibid., p. 79.

12. These works are available in reprint editions: *Imperialism and World Economy* (New York: Howard Fertig, Inc., 1966); *The ABC of Communism* (Baltimore: Penguin Books, 1966); *Historical Materialism* (Ann Arbor: University of Michigan Press, 1969); *Economics of the Transformation Period* (New York: Bergman Publishers, 1971); *Imperialism and the Accumulation of Capital* (New York: Monthly Review Press, 1972). For a comprehensive bibliography, see Sidney Heitman, *Nikolai I. Bukharin: A Bibliography* (Stanford: Hoover Institution, 1969).

In *Imperialism and World Economy* (1918) he formulated a revision of Marx's theory of capitalist development and set out his own theory of imperialism. This was written in 1914-1915, a year before Lenin's own *Imperialism,* and is credited with having been a major influence on Lenin's formulation.

The ABC of Communism (1919), written with E. Preobrazhensky and used as a standard textbook in the twenties, is a clear and comprehensive statement of the principles of Marxism-Leninism and the practical problems of building socialism in the context of the Russian experience.

Historical Materialism: A System of Sociology (1921) is his major philosophical work. In it he set out a system of sociological analysis in the framework of historical and dialectical materialism and sought to meet the sociological criticisms of Marxism.

A translation of his *Economics of the Transformation Period* has recently become available; and his *Imperialism and the Accumulation of Capital* (combined with Rosa Luxemburg's *The Accumulation of Capital—An Anti-Critique*) is being published in the fall by Monthly Review Press.

April 1972

PREFACE TO THE RUSSIAN EDITION

THIS book was completed in the fall of 1914. The Introduction was written in August and September of that year.

I had long been occupied with the plan of formulating a systematic criticism of the theoretical economy of the new bourgeoisie. For this purpose, I went to Vienna after succeeding in making my escape from Siberia; I there attended the lectures of Professor Böhm-Bawerk (1851-1914), of the University of Vienna. In the library of the University of Vienna, I went through the literature of the Austrian theorists. I was not permitted, however, to finish this work in Vienna, since the Austrian Government had me imprisoned in a fortress just before the outbreak of the World War, while its arguses were entrusted with the task of subjecting my manuscript to careful examination. In Switzerland, to which I repaired after my deportation from Austria, I had an opportunity to study the Lausanne School (Walras), as well as the older economists, at the library of the University of Lausanne, and thus to trace the theory of marginal utility to its roots. At Lausanne, I also made an exhaustive study of the Anglo-American economists. Political activities took me to Stockholm, where the Royal Library and the special economic library of the Higher Commercial School (*Handelshögskolan*) afforded me an opportunity to continue my study of the later bourgeois political economy. My arrest in Sweden and my deportation to Norway brought me to the library of the Nobel Institute at Christiania; after reaching the United States, I was enabled to study the American economic literature even more thoroughly in the New York Public Library.

For a long time the manuscript of this book could not be found in Christiania (now Oslo), where I had left it, and it is only due to the most painstaking efforts of my friend, the Norwegian communist, Arvid C. Hansen, that it was found and brought to Soviet Russia in February, 1919. I have since added but a few notes and observations, concerned chiefly with the Anglo-American School and the most recent publications.

So much for the *external* history of this book. As to its substance, I should like to make the following observations: Hitherto two types of criticism of the latest bourgeois political economy have been practiced in the Marxian camp, either an exclusively sociological criticism, or an exclusively methodological criticism. For instance, it was ascertained that the theoretical system in question was the outgrowth of a specific class psychology, which definitely disposed of it; or, it was pointed out that certain methodological bases, certain approaches to the problem were incorrect, and it was therefore considered unnecessary to proceed to an exhaustive criticism of the *internal* phases of the system.

No doubt, if we start with the fact that it is only a class theory of the proletariat that can be objectively correct, a mere revelation of the bourgeois character of any specific theory, is, strictly speaking, sufficient to justify its rejection. At bottom, this is a correct attitude, for Marxism claims its general validity precisely for the reason that it is the theoretical expression of the most advanced class, whose "needs" of knowledge are far more audacious than those of the conservative and therefore narrow-minded mode of thought of the ruling classes in capitalist society. Yet it is quite clear that the correctness of this assumption should be proved precisely in the struggle between the ideologies themselves, and particularly, by a logical criticism of the theories of our opponents. A sociological characterization of a certain theory, therefore, does not relieve us of the responsibility of waging war against it even in the field of a purely logical criticism.

The same is true also of a criticism of method. To be sure, to prove that the point of departure of the methodological bases is a false one is equivalent to overthrowing the entire theoretical structure erected on those bases. Yet the struggle between ideologies requires that the incorrectness in method be proved by the fallacious partial inferences of the system, in which connection we may point out either the internal contradictions of the old system, or its incompleteness, its organic inability to embrace and explain a number of important phenomena to the advantage of the discipline in question.

It follows that Marxism must give an exhaustive criticism of the latest theories, which must include not only a methodological criticism, but also a sociological criticism, as well as a criticism of the entire system as pursued to its furthest ramifications. It was thus that Marx formulated the problem presented by bourgeois political economy (in his *Theorien über den Mehrwert,* edited by Karl Kautsky, fifth edition, 1923, 3 vols.).

While Marxists have as a rule contented themselves with a sociological and methodological criticism of the Austrian School, the bourgeois opponents of this school have criticised it chiefly from the point of view of the incorrectness of certain specific inferences. Only R. Stolzmann, who stands almost alone in this work, has attempted to furnish a complete criticism of Böhm-Bawerk. In so far as certain fundamental ideas of this author are in close theoretical agreement with Marxism, our criticism of the Austrians resembles that made by Stolzmann. I have considered it my duty to point out agreements between these two criticisms even in cases in which I had arrived at the same conclusions before I became acquainted with Stolzmann's work. However, in spite of his talents, Stolzmann bases his work on an entirely incorrect conception of society as a "purposeful structure". It is not without reason that R. Liefmann, a very important adherent of the Austrian School, whose profundity he has enhanced and whose peculiarities he presents in a more emphatic form, defends himself against Stolzmann by the method of attacking the latter's teleology. This teleological point of view, coupled with his most pronounced apologetic tone, prevents Stolzmann from constructing a suitable theoretical frame for his criticism of the Austrian School. Only Marxists can perform this task; it is to do this that I have written the present book.

Our selection of an opponent for our criticism probably does not require discussion, for it is well known that the most powerful opponent of Marxism is the Austrian School.

It may appear unusual that I should publish this book at a moment when civil war is rampant in Europe. Marxists, however, have never accepted any obligation to discontinue their theoretical work even at periods of the most violent class struggle, so long as any physical possibility for the performance of such work was at hand. More serious is the objection that it is at least foolish to refute the capitalist theory at a moment when both the object and subject of this theory are being destroyed by the flames of the communist revolution. But even such a contention will not hold water, since a criticism of the capitalist system is of the utmost importance for a proper understanding of the events of the present day. And, in so far as a criticism of the bourgeois theories may smooth the path for such an understanding, such criticism has an abstract theoretical value.

Now for a few words as to the form of presentation. I have aimed at the utmost brevity, which probably is the reason for the comparative difficulty of my exposition. On the other hand, I have made many quotations from the Austrians as well as from the mathematical economists, the Anglo-Americans, etc. There is considerable prejudice against this mode of presentation in our Marxist circles, which consider such treatment to be a mark of a merely "bookish" erudition. Yet I have considered it necessary to present evidence from the literature of the history of the subject, which may introduce the reader to the subject and make it easier for him to find his bearings. It is by no means a superfluous matter to learn to know one's enemy, the less in our country, where he is so little known. My notes in the Appendix also provide a sort of parallel systematic criticism of the other ramifications of bourgeois theoretical philosophy.

At this point I should like to express my gratitude to my friend Yuryi Leonidovich Pyatakov, with whom I have often discussed questions of theoretical political economy and who has given me valuable suggestions.

I dedicate this book to Comrade N. L.

N. Bukharin.

Moscow, February 28, 1919.

PREFACE TO THE AMERICAN EDITION

This book was written many years ago. Had the author had more time he would doubtless have rewritten the book with the aid of the many publications that have since appeared. Unfortunately he has not the time. Yet he considers it fortunate that this book is now appearing in the United States, since it is the only Marxist work presenting a systematic criticism of the fundamental tendency of bourgeois theoretical philosophy in the field of economics. From this point of view, the book is by no means out of date, and in our opinion is still perfectly valid from the theoretical standpoint. Thoughtful Marxist readers will find in this book a guide to an understanding of the ideologists of the modern bourgeoisie. It will be a comparatively easy matter to fit the most recent bourgeois writers into the scheme outlined in our treatment.

MOSCOW, SPRING, 1927. N. BUKHARIN.

THE ECONOMIC THEORY OF THE LEISURE CLASS

INTRODUCTION

Bourgeois Political Economy since Marx

1. The Historical School in Germany; sociological characterisation of the Historical School; logical characterisation of the Historical School.

2. The Austrian School; sociological characterisation of the Austrian School; brief logical characterization of the Austrian School.

3. The Anglo-American School.

4. The Predecessors of the Austrians.

It is more than thirty years since the inspired words of the great thinker of the nineteenth century, whose thoughts were to become the lever of the proletarian movement throughout the world, ceased to flow from his lips; the entire economic evolution of the last few decades—the mad concentration and centralization of capital, the elimination of petty operation even in the most remote districts, the rise, on the one hand, of powerful captains of industry crowned with crowns of gold, and the formation, on the other hand, of the proletarian army which, as Marx says, has been trained, united and organized by the mechanism of capitalist production itself—completely confirms the correctness of the economic system of Karl Marx. It was Marx's object to reveal the economic law of motion of present-day capitalist society. The prognosis made by him, first in the *Communist Manifesto* and then in more complete and developed form in *Capital,* has already been nine-tenths confirmed.

One of the most important portions of this prognosis, the theory of concentration, has now become a common possession, a generally admitted scientific truth. To be sure, it is generally served in some other theoretical sauce, thus depriving it of the simplicity so characteristic of the Marxian theory. But the "economic romanticists", who beheld in this theory only a Utopian's imaginings, had lost the ground under their feet when the tendencies revealed and pronounced by Marx recently developed in so swift a manner and on so magnificent a scale that only blind men could fail to observe the victorious advance of large-scale industry. While certain good-natured persons considered the stock corporations to be merely an evidence of a "democratisation of capital" and regarded them, in their fond delusion, as a guarantee of social peace and general prosperity (unfortunately such persons were to be found even in the labour movement), the "economic reality" of the present is destroying this petty bourgeois ideal in the rudest manner. Capital in shares has become a tremendous instrument in the hands of a small band of usurpers to suppress ruthlessly the advance of the "Fourth Estate". This alone is sufficient to show how important an instrument of knowledge is the theoretical structure raised by Marx.

But further, even such phenomena in capitalist development as have only now become evident can be grasped only with the aid of the Marxist analysis. (Rudolf Hilferding's *Das Finanzkapital* will be found very useful in this connection.) The rise of enormous producing organizations, of syndicates and trusts, the establishment of banking organizations, of hitherto unknown immensity, the penetration of banking capital into industry, and the hegemony of financial capital in the entire economic and political life of the advanced capitalist countries—all these are merely a combination of the development of the tendencies pointed out by Marx. The domination of financial capital merely accelerates tenfold the tendency toward concentration and transforms production into social production, already mature for its subjection to social control. To be sure, bourgeois scholars recently declared that the organization of industrial trusts would put an end to the anarchy in production and eliminate crises. But, alas, the capitalist organism continues to be subject to its periodical convulsions, and only very simple people can still believe that capitalism can be cured with the aid of reformist patchwork.

The historical mission of the bourgeoisie has already been fulfilled all over the world. It is now approaching its end. There is now ensuing a period of great performances of the proletariat, in which the struggle has already gone beyond the national boundaries of the state, assuming more and more the forms of a mass pressure on the ruling classes, and already in sight of the final goal. The time at which Marx's prophecy, namely, that the last hour of capitalist property will have struck, will be fulfilled, is no longer far off. And yet, however emphatically the correctness of Marx's conception is borne out by the facts, its acceptance among official scholars is not only not advancing, but even declining. While formerly, in backward countries—Russia and to a certain extent Italy, for example—even university professors occasionally flirted with Marx, of course always interpolating their own more or less "significant corrections", the entire social evolution, the sharpening of class contrasts and the consolidation of all the shades of bourgeois ideology are now causing all to take up the struggle against the ideology of the proletariat, by eliminating these "transition types" (of economic scholars) and substituting for them the "purely European", "modern" scholar, his theoretical garment patterned according to the latest Prussian, Austrian, or even Anglo-American fashion.[1]

The bourgeoisie presented two fundamental tendencies in the economic doctrine which it devised to oppose the ironclad Marxian system: the so called Historical School (Wilhelm Roscher, Eduard Hildebrandt, Karl Knies, Gustav Schmoller, Karl Bücher, etc.), and the Austrian School (Karl Menger, Eugen von Böhm-Bawerk, Friedrich von Wieser); the latter has recently found many adherents. Both tendencies, however, merely express the bankruptcy of bourgeois political economy, but they express this bankruptcy in two quite opposite forms. While the former tendency of bourgeois theory went to pieces because it denied the validity of any abstract theory at all, the other tendency sought to construct merely an abstract theory and therefore arrived at a number of extremely ingenious meretricious exceptions, which failed to hold water just at the point where Marx's theory is particularly strong, namely, in questions as to the dynamics of present-day capitalist society. The classical school of political economy, as is well known, attempted to formulate the general, *i.e.*, the "abstract" laws of economic life, and its most prominent representative, David Ricardo, affords astonishing examples of this abstract-deductive mode of study. The Historical School, on the other hand, makes its appearance as a reaction to this "cosmopolitanism" and "perpetualism" of the classical economists.[2]

There are profound social-economic causes for this difference. The classical theory, with its free trade doctrine, was extremely "national" in spite of its "cosmopolitanism"; it was the necessary theoretical product of *English* industry. England, obtaining exclusive hegemony in the world market by reason of a number of causes, was not afraid of any competitors and had no need of artificial, *i.e.,* legislative, measures, in order to assure it the victory for its competitors. Therefore English industry was not obliged to make reference to specifically English conditions as an argument for the erection of customs barriers of any kind. The theorists of the English bourgeoisie, therefore, had no need to turn their attention to the specific peculiarities of English capitalism; although they represented the interests of *English* capital, they spoke of the *general* laws of economic evolution. Quite different is the picture presented by the economic development of the European continent and America.[3]

Germany, the cradle of the Historical School, was a backward and—for the most part—an agricultural country as compared with England. The rising German industries suffered perceptibly from English competition, particularly in the metallurgical industry; while the English bourgeoisie did not need to emphasize national peculiarities in any way, the German bourgeoisie was obliged to give exceptional attention to precisely the peculiarities and the independence of the German evolution, in order to use them as a theoretical foundation for proving the necessity of "nursery tariffs". The theoretical interest was concentrated precisely on making clear the concrete historical situation and the national limitations; the selection and emphasis of precisely these phases of the economic life was made by theory itself. Considered from a sociological point of view, the Historical School was the ideological expression of this process of growth of the German bourgeoisie, which was afraid of English competition, which therefore demanded protection for the national industries, and consequently emphasised the national and historical peculiarities of Germany, later—in a more general form—of other countries also. Considered from a social-genetic standpoint, both the Classical and the Historical School are "national", since both are the products of an evolution within historical and territorial limitations; viewed from a logical point of view, however, the classical economists are "cosmopolitan", while the historical economists are "national". Thus, the German protective tariff movement was the cradle of the Historical School. In its further development, this movement produced a number of nuances, the most important of which, headed by Gustav Schmoller (the so called "Younger Historical" or "Historical-Ethical" School), assumed an agrarian-conservative tinge. Idealization of the transition form in production, particularly of the "patriarchal" relations between landholders and farm workers, the fear of the "proletarian pestilence" and the "red peril" are constantly unmasking those "objective professors" and revealing the social roots of their "pure science".[4] This sociological designation of the Historical School also affords us the corresponding logical characterization.

From the logical point of view, the Historical School is characterised particularly by its negative attitude toward abstract theory. All abstract investigations move this School to profound aversion; it doubts, occasionally denies outright, any possibility of undertaking such investigations; the word "abstract", as used by this School, means "nonsensical". Many of these scholars even assume a skeptical attitude toward the most important concept of science as a whole, namely, the concept of "law", recognising at most the so called "empirical laws" established by the aid of historical, economical and statistical investigations.[5]

There resulted a narrow-minded empiricism, which recoiled from any generalisation at all. The extreme representatives of this School made it their watchword to collect concrete historical material and postpone indefinitely the work of generalising and of theory. Thus, Gustav Schmoller, the recognised head of the Historical School, characterises the "younger generation" as follows: "The difference between the Younger

Historical School and him [Roscher.—*N.B.*] is in that they refuse to generalise so swiftly, that they feel a need to advance from a polyhistorical gathering of facts to special investigations of the various epochs, opinions, and economic conditions. They demand, in the first place, economic monographs. They would rather explain, to begin with, the history of the individual economic institutions than that of political economy or world economy as a whole. They start with a severe method of investigation of legal history, but wish to supplement their book knowledge by travel and by means of their own understandings, to which they add the results of philosophical and psychological science." (Gustav Schmoller: *Grundriss der Allgemeinen Volkswirtschaftslehre,* Leipzig, 1908, p. 119.) This attitude, opposed in principle to all abstract method, is still dominant in Germany. In 1908, Schmoller again declared: "We are still largely concerned with preparatory work and with the collection of material." (Schmoller, *ibid.*, p. 123.)

Another peculiarity of the "historical tendency" is also connected with its demand for concrete facts: This School does not separate the social-economic life at all from the other phases of the process of life, particularly from law and custom, in spite of the fact that the purposes of knowledge would be best served by such a division.[6] This point of view is again a result of their aversion to all abstraction; for, as a matter of fact, the life process of society is a *single* stream; there is in reality only *one* history, not a number of histories—a history of law, of economy, of customs, etc. It is only with the aid of the abstractions of science that we can divide this single life into parts, artificially emphasising certain series of phenomena and grouping them according to specific traits. Logically, therefore, he who is opposed to abstraction in general should also be opposed to a division between economy and law and custom. But this standpoint would, of course, be untenable. No doubt the social life is a unit; it must not be forgotten, however, that no knowledge is possible at all without generalisation: even *conception* as such is an abstraction from the "concrete"; likewise, all description presupposes a certain selection of phenomena according to traits considered important for one reason or other, and abstraction is therefore only a necessary attribute in the acquisition of knowledge; it is to be rejected only when the process of generalisation from concrete traits results in an absolutely empty abstraction, which is therefore useless for the purposes of science.

Science requires the analysis of the indissoluble life process. The latter is so complicated that it must be divided, for purposes of investigation, into a number of series of phenomena. Whither should we be led by an investigation of economy if we should seek, for example, to include in this investigation also things constituting the object of the science of philology—attempting to justify ourselves with the statement that economy is a human structure and that humans are united by their language? It is obvious that any given science may use the results attained by another science where these results may give assistance to the subject of the first; yet these extraneous elements may then be regarded only from the point of view of the given science and may serve only the purpose of an auxiliary device in the investigation.

The accumulation of material of many kinds therefore leads rather to obstructing than facilitating the gathering of knowledge. We must add that the "psychological-ethical consideration" on the part of the Younger Historical School has assumed the form of moral evaluations and inculcations. The object of science is to reveal causal relations, and here we find the absolutely extraneous element of ethical standards introduced into science, whence this school obtains its name: the Historical-Ethical School.[7]

A number of descriptive historical works have been published as a result of the activity of the Historical School: the histories of prices, of wages, of credit, of money, etc.; yet these works contribute not in the slightest degree toward advancing the *theory* of price or of value, the *theory* of wages, of money circulation, etc. But it must be clear to everyone that the two fields are quite distinct. "It is one thing to set up statistics of *prices* in the Hamburg or London markets during the last thirty years and quite a different thing to construct a general *theory of value and price* as is contained in the works of Galiani, Condillac, and David Ricardo." (Luigi

Cossa: *Introduzione allo Studio dell' Economica Politica*, Milano, 1892, p. 15.)

It is precisely this negation of a "general theory" that would deny the right of political economy to be called an independent theoretical discipline.

Science in general may pursue either one of two goals; it either describes things actually existing at a certain time and in a certain place, or it attempts to derive the laws of phenomena when such are capable of expression in the formula: if A, B and C are present, D must follow. In the first case, science is idiographic in character; in the second, it is nomographic.[8]

It is clear that the *theory* of political economy is of the second type of science; its object is chiefly to solve nomographic tasks, but since the Historical School scorns to set up general laws, it practically destroys political economy as a science and replaces it with a "mere description" of idiographic type; in other words, it makes this science identical with economic history and economic statistics, with idiography *par excellence*. This science was unable to find a place for its only correct idea—evolution—within the framework of *theoretical* investigation, and therefore the science, like the Biblical fig-tree, has remained unfruitful. Its positive importance is to be found only in the collecting of materials for theoretical treatment, and in this sense the labours of the Historical School are quite valuable. It is sufficient to point out only the important works issued by the *Verein für Sozialpolitik* on the subjects of handicraft, petty trade, and the agricultural proletariat.[9]

Karl Menger, the father of the Austrian School, has given an excellent characterisation of this School: "The point of departure, as well as the highest achievement of its [the Historical School's.—*N.B.*] evolution, is an external combination of solid *historical* knowledge and a careful but leaderless eclecticism in the domain of *our* science." (Karl Menger: *Die Irrtümer des Historismus in der deutschen Nationalökonomie*, Vienna, 1884, *Vorwort*, p. IV.)

Quite different is the picture presented by the Austrian School, which entered the field of science as a pronounced opponent of historicism. In the polemical conflict which was fought most bitterly between Karl Menger and Gustav Schmoller, the new theorists of the bourgeoisie rather thoroughly unmasked the fundamental errors of their predecessors; they demanded, in turn, a recognition of "typical phenomena", of "general laws" (in fact, of "exact laws", according to the terminology of Karl Menger). After carrying off a number of victories over the Historical School, the Austrian School, represented by Böhm-Bawerk, proceeded to demolish Marxism, and announced the complete theoretical fallacy of the latter. The Marxian theory is "not alone incorrect, but, when examined as to its theoretical value, must be assigned to one of the last places among all theories of interest." (Böhm-Bawerk, *Kapital und Kapitalzins,* p. 517.) Such was the judgment of Böhm-Bawerk.

It is no cause for surprise, therefore, that this new effort of bourgeois ideologists [10] should have come into a sharp clash with the ideology of the proletariat. The bitterness of this conflict is a necessary result of the *formal* similarity between this new attempt at abstract theory and Marxism, in so far as Marxism makes use of abstract method, while in *essence* the new system is in complete opposition to Marxism. This may be explained, furthermore, by the fact that the new theory is a child of the bourgeoisie on its *last legs*—a bourgeoisie whose experience of life, and therefore whose ideology, is far removed from the experience of life of the working class.

We shall not dwell at length in this chapter on the logical characterisation of the Austrian School, since we intend to revert to it later. We shall here make only the attempt to present the fundamental outlines of a *sociological* description of the Austrian School.

In his last work on the origin of the "capitalist spirit", Werner Sombart (*Der Bourgeois,* 1913) investigates the characteristic traits of the *entrepreneur* psychology, depicting, however, merely the ascending phase in the evolution of the bourgeoisie; he does not investigate, he has no eyes for, the bourgeois psychology in its decline. Yet interesting examples of this psychology may be found in his book, though they do not deal with the latest period. Thus, Sombart characterises the *haute finance* in France and England during the seventeenth and eighteenth centuries as follows: "These were extremely wealthy persons, mostly of bourgeois origin, who had enriched themselves as tax farmers or creditors of the nation and who now floated on the surface of the broth as circles of fat, completely removed, however, from the economic life." (*Ibid.*, p. 46.)

As the "capitalist spirit" in Holland declines in the course of the eighteenth century, the "bourgeois" is not "feudalised", as was the case in other countries; he simply lays on adipose tissue, grows "fat". "He lives on his revenues. *All interest in capitalistic enterprises of any type whatsoever diminishes more and more.*" (*Ibid.*, p. 188; italics mine.—*N.B.*)

Another example: Daniel Defoe, the well-known English journalist-romancer (1661-1731), describes the process of the evolution of merchants into coupon-cutters as follows: "Formerly it had been necessary for him [the merchant.—*N.B.*] at any rate to be diligent and active in order to acquire his fortune; but now he has nothing else to do than to determine to be indolent and inactive. National rents and land ownership are the only proper investment for his savings." (*Der Bourgeois*, p. 201.)

It should not be assumed that no such psychology is possible in the present day; in fact, precisely that is the case. The capitalist evolution of the last few decades involved a swift accumulation of "capital values". As a result of the development of the various forms of credit, the accumulated surplus flows into the pockets of persons having no relation whatever to production; the number of these persons is constantly increasing and constitutes a whole class of society—that of the *rentier*. To be sure, this group of the bourgeoisie is not a social class in the true sense of the word, but rather a certain *group* within the ranks of the capitalist bourgeoisie; yet it displays certain traits of a "social psychology" that are characteristic of it alone. With the evolution of stock corporations and banks, with the rise of an enormous traffic in securities, this social group becomes more and more evident and intrenched. The field of its economic activity is predominantly that of a circulation of financial paper—the Stock Exchange. It is characteristic enough that within this group, living on the income from securities, there are a number of different shades; the extreme type is the stratum which is not only independent of production, but also independent of the circulation process altogether. These are, above all, the owners of gilt-edged securities: national bonds, secure obligations of various kinds. Furthermore, there are persons who have invested their fortunes in real estate and draw permanent and secure incomes from the latter. These categories are not even troubled by the disturbance of the Stock Exchange, while shareholders, being closely connected with the ups and downs of speculation, may, in a single day, either lose everything or become rich men. While these persons are thus living the life of the market, beginning in the morning with attendance at the Exchange and ending in the evening with a perusal of the quotations and the commercial supplements, the groups enjoying the income of gilt-edged securities have severed this bond connecting them with the social-economic life and have emerged from the sphere of circulation. Furthermore, the more highly developed the credit system, the more elastic it has become, the greater is the possibility of "growing fat" and becoming "indolent and inactive". The capitalist mechanism itself takes care of this matter; by making the organisational functioning of a considerable number of *entrepreneurs* socially superfluous, it simultaneously eliminates these "superfluous elements" from the immediate operations of the economic life. These elements are secreted to the surface of the economic life like the "circles of fat on the surface of the soup"—to use Sombart's apt expression.

And it must be remembered that the owners of gilt-edged securities do not represent a decreasing stream of the bourgeoisie of coupon-cutters, but that, on the contrary, this stream is constantly increasing. "The bourgeoisie is being transformed into *rentiers* who have about the same relation to the great financial institutions as they have to the State whose obligations they acquire; in both cases, they are paid their interest and have nothing else to worry about. As a result, this tendency of the bourgeoisie to transfer their fortunes to the State obviously must now be really increasing . . . since . . . the State presents the admitted advantage of greater security.

A company share no doubt offers chances of gain not afforded by the State obligations, but also immense possibilities of loss. It must be borne in mind that the bourgeoisie annually produces a considerable surplus of capital; but even in periods of industrial booms only a small part of this surplus capital is absorbed by new issues of shares; by far the greater part is invested in national loans, municipal obligations, mortgages, and other securities affording fixed interest." (Parvus: *Der Staat, die Industrie und der Sozialismus*, Dresden, pp. 103-4.)

This stratum of the bourgeoisie is distinctly parasitical; it develops the same psychological traits as may be found in the decayed nobility at the end of the *ancien régime* and the heads of the financial aristocracy of the same epoch.[11] The most characteristic trait of this stratum, one which sharply distinguishes it both from the proletariat and the other bourgeois types is, as we have already seen, its removal from the economic life. It participates directly neither in the activities of production nor in trade; its representatives often do not even cut their own coupons. The "sphere of activities" of these *rentiers* may perhaps be most generally termed the *sphere of consumption.* Consumption is the basis of the entire life of the *rentiers* and the "psychology of pure consumption" imparts to this life its specific style. The consuming *rentier* is concerned only with riding mounts, with expensive rugs, fragrant cigars, the wine of Tokay. A *rentier,* if he speaks of work at all means the "work" of picking flowers or calling for a ticket at the box office of the opera.[12] Production, the work necessary for the creation of material commodities, lies beyond his horizon and is therefore an accident in his life. There is no mention of genuine active work for him; his whole psychology presents only passive shades; the philosophy, the æsthetics of these *rentiers,* is purely descriptive in character; they completely lack the active element so typical of the ideology of the proletariat. For the proletariat lives in the sphere of production, comes in direct contact with "matter", from which it is transformed into "material", into an object of labour. The proletariat is an eye-witness to the gigantic growth of the production forces of capitalist society, of the new and more and more complicated machine technology, making possible the throwing of larger and larger quantities of commodities on the market, with prices going lower and lower, the more the process of technical perfection progresses. The psychology of the *producer* is therefore characteristic of the proletarian, while the psychology of the *consumer* is characteristic of the *rentier*.

We have already seen that the class of society here discussed is a product of the decline of the bourgeoisie. This decline is closely connected with the fact that the bourgeoisie has already lost its functions of social utility. This peculiar position of the class within the production process, or, to put it more correctly, without the production process, has led to the rise of a peculiar social type that is characterised particularly by its asociality. While the bourgeoisie as such is individualistic from its very cradle—for the basis of its existence is the economic *cell* which is engaged in the bitter struggle of competition for independent existence with other cells—this individualism in the case of the *rentier* becomes more and more pronounced. The *rentier* knows nothing of the social life at all; he stands apart from it; the social bonds are loosed; even the general trials of the class cannot weld together the "social atoms". There disappears not only the interest in capitalist enterprises, but any interest in the "social" altogether. The ideology of a stratum of this type is necessarily strongly individualistic. This individualism expresses itself with particular sharpness in the æsthetics of this class. Any treatment of social themes appears to it *eo ipso* as "inartistic", "coarse", "tendencious".

Quite different is the evolution of the psychology of the proletariat. The proletariat swiftly discards the individualistic garb of the classes from which it takes its origin, the urban and rural petty bourgeoisie. Held captive within the stone walls of great cities, concentrated in the centres of a common labour and a common struggle, the proletariat develops the psychology of collectivism, of a keen sense of the social bonds; only in its very earliest stages of development, when it has not yet evolved into a specific class, does it still present individualistic tendencies, which soon disappear without leaving a trace. And thus the proletariat evolves in a direction that is just the opposite of that taken by the bourgeoisie of *rentiers*. While the proletariat has a collectivist psychology, the evolution of individualistic traits is one of the fundamental traits of the bourgeoisie. *An outspoken individualism is the significant characteristic property of the rentier.*

The third characteristic trait of the *rentier,* as of all the bourgeoisie in general, is the fear of the proletariat, the fear of impending social catastrophes. The *rentier* is not capable of looking forward. His philosophy of life may be resolved into the maxim: "Enjoy the moment", *Carpe diem;* his horizon does not extend beyond the present; if he thinks of the future, he thinks of it only after the pattern of the present; in fact, he cannot imagine a period in which persons of his type will not be collecting interest on paper securities; his eyes close in horror at such a possibility; he hides his face at the prospect of coming things and tries not to see in the present the germs of the future; his thinking is thoroughly unhistorical. Quite different is the psychology of the proletariat, which presents none of these elements of conservative thought. The class struggle, as it unfolds, confronts the proletariat with the task of surmounting the existing social-economic order; the proletariat is not only not interested in the maintenance of the social *status quo,* but it is interested precisely in its destruction; the proletariat lives chiefly in the future; even the problems of the present are evaluated by it from the point of view of the future. Therefore its mode of thought may be declared outright—and particularly its scientific thought—as distinctly and pronouncedly dynamic in character. *This is the third antithesis between the psychology of the rentier and that of the proletariat.*

These three earmarks of the "social consciousness" of the *rentier,* which arise directly from his "social being", also influence the highest stages of his consciousness, namely, his scientific thought. Psychology is always the basis of logic; feelings and moods determine the general course of thought, the points of view from which reality is viewed and later logically manipulated. While it may not in every case be possible, even after the most exhaustive analysis of a specific isolated sentence in some theory, to expose its social substructure, this substructure always makes itself clearly obvious as soon as the distinguishing marks of the great theoretical system, its general points of view, have been pointed out; now each individual sentence acquires a new meaning, becomes a necessary link in an entire chain embracing the life experience of a specific class, a specific social group.

Turning to the Austrian School and to its most prominent representative, Böhm-Bawerk, we shall find that the psychological traits of the *rentiers,* as described above, here present their logical equivalents.

In the first place, we here find for the first time a consistent carrying out of the point of view of *consumption.* The initial stage in the development of bourgeois political economy, which arose during the rule of commercial capital (mercantilism), is characterised by the fact that it considers economic phenomena from the point of view of exchange. "It is quite characteristic of the bourgeois horizon, which is entirely bounded by the craze for making money," says Karl Marx, "not to see in the character of the mode of production the basis of the corresponding mode of circulation, but vice versa." [13]

The following stage corresponded to an epoch in which capital had become the organizer of production. The ideological expression of this condition was the Classical School which considered economic problems from the point of view of production (the "labour theories" of Adam Smith and David Ricardo) and placed the emphasis on their theoretical investigation of production. This point of view was taken over from the classics by the proletarian political economy. On the other hand, the bourgeois *rentier* finds his task in a solution of the problem of consumption. And it is this point of view which constitutes the fundamental, most characteristic, and the *newest* theoretical position of the Austrian School, as well as of those tendencies related to it. Even though the Austrian theory may merely be a continuation of a theoretical tendency of earlier origin, there is no doubt that the theories which made the consumption and the consumption value of "commodities" the basis of their analysis, never found such ready acceptance in the official strata of the science as did the

Austrian School. It is only the latest stage of evolution that has created, in the *rentier* psychology of the modern bourgeois, a firm foundation for those theories.[14]

This crass individualism is likewise neatly parallelled in the "subjectivist-psychological" method of the new tendency. To be sure, the theorists of the bourgeoisie had assumed an individualistic attitude even in earlier periods; they always enjoy making references to Robinson Crusoe. Even the representatives of the "labour value theories" based their position on individualistic references: their labour value was not, as one might perhaps expect, the social *objective law of prices,* but the subjective *evaluation* of the "economic subject" (*the economic man*) who evaluates the commodity variously, depending on whether the expenditure of labour has been connected with greater or less inconveniences (for example, Adam Smith). It is not until Marx that the labour value assumes the character of a "natural law", making the exchange of commodities independent of the will of the agents of the modern order of society. Nevertheless, it was only now, and precisely in the doctrine of the Austrian School, that psychologism in political economy, *i.e.,* economic individualism, attained its justification and its completely renewed formulation in political economy. (*Cf.* Albert Schatz: *L'Individualisme économique et sociale,* 1907, p. 3, *note.*)

Finally, the fear of revolution is expressed in the representatives of the theory of marginal utility in their most pronounced aversion towards everything historical. Their economic categories (according to the opinion of these authors) are declared to be various for all times and epochs; they never even consider the possibility of an investigation of the laws of evolution of modern capitalist production as a specific historical category, as is the Marxian point of view. On the contrary, such phenomena as profit, interest on capital, etc., are considered eternal attributes of human society. Here we already find the attempt to justify the present conditions. But the weaker the elements of a theoretical knowledge, the louder resounds the voice of the apologist of the capitalist order of Society. "There is nothing in the *essence* of interest [*i.e.,* of profit.—*N.B.*] that would make it appear unreasonable or unrighteous *per se,"*—such is the final conclusion (and, in our opinion, the object) of all of Böhm-Bawerk's huge treatise. (*Positive Theorie des Kapitals,* third edition, vol. i, p. 574.)

We consider the Austrian theory as the ideology of the bourgeois who has already been eliminated from the process of production, the psychology of the declining bourgeois, who has thus immortalized, in his scientifically fruitless theory—as we shall see later—the peculiarities of his failing psychology. It is no contradiction of this statement to find that the theory of marginal utility itself, as formulated by the Austrians, is being supplanted at present by the now even more fashionable Anglo-American School, whose most prominent representative is John Bates Clark. The present period of capitalist evolution is an epoch of the utmost exertion of all the forces of the capitalist world. The economic process of the transformation of capital into "finance capital" [15] is again incorporating in the sphere of production a portion of the bourgeoisie that had held aloof (in so far as banking capital is being absorbed in industry and thus being made an organiser of production)—for instance, the organisers and managers of the trusts, an extremely active type whose political ideology is a militant imperialism and whose philosophy is an active pragmatism. This type is very much less individualistic, for it has been trained in organisations of *entrepreneurs,* which are, after all, a unit in which the personal ambition is to a certain extent relegated to the background. Accordingly, the ideology of this type is somewhat different from that of the *rentier;* it counts on production; it even applies the "social-organic" method of investigation to the entirety of the social economy.[16] The American School is the product of a progressive, and by no means of a declining bourgeoisie; of the two curves now to be observed—that of progressive ascent and that of incipient disintegration—the American School expresses only the former. It is not by accident that this School is permeated with the American spirit, with the spirit of the land of which Sombart, the minstrel of capitalism, declares: "All that the capitalist spirit can express in the way of consequences has to-day been developed to the highest point in the United States.

Here its strength is as yet unbroken. Here, for the present, everything is still in a whirlwind of growth." [17]

It is therefore precisely the *rentier* type which represents the border type of the bourgeoisie, and the theory of marginal utility is the ideology of this border type. From the psychological point of view, this theory is therefore of interest; likewise, from the point of view of logic, since it is obvious, after all, that the American economists view this theory merely as *eclectics*. For the very reason that the Austrian School is the ideology of the border type of the bourgeoisie, it embodies a complete antithesis to the ideology of the proletariat. The methodological difference between Karl Marx and Böhm-Bawerk may be summarized concisely as follows: objectivism—subjectivism, a historical standpoint—an unhistorical standpoint, the point of view of production—the point of view of consumption. The purpose of this exposition is to provide a logical analysis of this methodological difference, both in the bases of the theory in question, as well as in the entire theoretical work of Böhm-Bawerk.

A few words should be said concerning the forerunners of the Austrian School.

In Condillac's work we already find a presentation of the fundamental ideas of what was later to be the theory of marginal utility. Condillac lays great stress on the "subjective" character of value, which in his opinion is not a social law of prices, but the individual judgment, based on the one hand on usefulness (*l'utilité*), and on the other on rarity (*rareté*). This writer comes so close to the modern formulation of the problem as to distinguish even between "present" and "future" needs (*besoin présent, besoin éloigné*) [18] which, as the reader knows, is precisely the main point in the transition from the theory of value to the theory of interest, as formulated by the principal representative of the Austrian School, Böhm-Bawerk.

Similar ideas may be encountered at about the same period in Count Verri, an Italian economist,[19] who also considers value as a resultant of utility and rarity.

In 1831, there appeared a book by Auguste Walras, the father of the famous Léon Walras, entitled *De la Nature de la Richesse et de l'Origine de la Valeur*, in which the author derives value from the rarity of useful commodities and seeks to refute those economists who turn their attention *only* to the utility of the commodities of which "wealth" consists. Owing to the clarity of this fundamental doctrine, the work really is deserving of more attention from the representatives of the new tendency than they have bestowed upon it.

In 1854, Hermann Gossen (1810-1858) presented an exact and lucid defence of the theory of marginal utility, which he formulated mathematically in his work, *Entwicklung der Gesetze des menschlichen Verkehrs und der daraus fliessenden Regeln für menschliches Handeln.* Hermann Gossen was not only seeking "new paths", but also imparted a carefully devised and finished form to his theory. Many theses ascribed chiefly to the Austrians (Karl Menger) are to be found in Gossen already in perfect formulation, so that we really should regard Gossen as the father of the theory of marginal utility. Gossen's work passed entirely unnoticed; the author would have fallen into complete oblivion if he had not been rediscovered in the seventies; the later representatives of the ideas that resemble Gossen's at once recognized him as the father of the school. Gossen himself had a very high opinion of his work and called himself the Copernicus of political economy.

At approximately the same time, a firm foundation for the new tendency was laid in three countries, England, Switzerland, and Austria, by the labours, respectively, of W. Stanley Jevons, Léon Walras and Karl Menger. It was these men, furthermore, who again called attention to the work of their forgotten predecessor Gossen.[20] The importance of Gossen is perhaps best to be judged from the tributes bestowed upon him by Stanley Jevons and Léon Walras. After expounding Gossen's theories, Jevons adds: "It is apparent from this exposition that Gossen anticipated my work both in his general principles as well as in the method of economic theory. As fas as I can judge, his manner of treating the fundamentals of the theory is actually more general and more profound than mine."

The opinion of Léon Walras is quite similar: *Etudes d'économie sociale,* Lausanne and Paris, 1896; particularly the section: "Un Economiste inconnu", p. 360.) "We are dealing with a man who lived entirely unnoticed and who was one of the greatest economists that ever lived." (Pp. 354-5.) Yet Gossen did not succeed in establishing a new school of thought. The school did not arise until the activities of the later economists began; only at the beginning of the decade 1870-80 did the theory of marginal utility find a sufficient prop in the "social public opinion" of the ruling scientific circles and rapidly become *communis doctorum opinio.* The school of Jevons, and more particularly Walras, who laid stress on the mathematical character and the mathematical method in political economy, elaborated a cycle of ideas diverging somewhat from the Austrian theory; so did the American School, headed by Clark. The Austrians, on the other hand, devised a theory of subjectivism (psychologism) on the basis of an analysis of consumption. In this process, Böhm-Bawerk became the crassest spokesman of the Austrian theory. He published one of the best motivated theories of value, from the point of view of this School, and finally, starting with the theory of marginal utility, set up an almost entirely new theory of distribution. He is the acknowledged head of the School, which is at bottom not *Austrian* at all, any more than it ever has been Austrian (as we have already been able to show by a cursory reference to its predecessors), and which has actually become the scientific implement of the international bourgeoisie of *rentiers,* regardless of their domicile. It was only the development of this bourgeoisie that gave the "new tendencies" serious support; up to that time, there had been only learned "individual scholars". The rapid evolution of capitalism, the shifting of social groupings and the increase in the number of the class of *rentiers,* all these produced in the last decades of the nineteenth century all the necessary social-psychological presuppositions for bringing these delicate plants to efflorescence.

It was the international *rentier* who found his learned spokesman in Böhm-Bawerk; in Böhm-Bawerk's theory, he found a scientific weapon not so much in the struggle against the elemental forces of capitalist evolution, as against the ever more menacing workers' movement. We are therefore delivering a criticism of this new weapon as embodied in the person of Böhm-Bawerk.

CHAPTER I

Methodological Foundations of the Theory of Marginal Utility and of Marxism

1. Objectivism and subjectivism in political economy.
2. The historical point of view and the unhistorical point of view.
3. The point of view of production, and the point of view of consumption.
4. Conclusions.

Any fairly well organized theory must present a definite whole whose parts are united by a sound logical bond. Therefore a consistent criticism must inevitably deal with the basis of the theory, with its method, for it is this and nothing else which unites the various parts of the theoretical structure. We are therefore beginning with a criticism of the methodological presuppositions of the theory of marginal utility, by which we do not understand its *deductive* character, but its *characteristic* traits within the frame of the abstract deductive method. In our opinion, any theory of political economy—if it be a theory at all—is an abstract thing; to this extent Marxism completely agrees with the Austrian School.[21] But this agreement is only formal in character; if there were no such agreement, there would be no means of comparing the Austrian theory with that of Karl Marx. For we are interested here in the concrete contents of the abstract method peculiar to the Austrian School, and making it so strikingly different from Marxism.

Political economy is a *social* science and its presupposition —whether the theorists of political economy are conscious of this fact or not—is some conception or other as to the essence of society and its laws of evolution. In other words, any economic theory depends on certain presuppositions having a sociological character and serving as the basis of an investigation of the *economic* phase of social life. Such presuppositions may be clearly expressed or may remain unformulated; they may be enunciated as an orderly system, or they may remain an "indefinite general view"—but they cannot be absent. The political economy of Karl Marx possesses such a basis in the sociological theory of historical materialism. The Austrian School, however, possesses no well-rounded or even fairly defined sociological basis; it is necessary for us to reconstruct the vestiges of such a basis out of the economic theory of the Austrians. In this process, we repeatedly encounter contradictions between general fundamental thoughts as to the nature of "political economy" and the *actual* basis of the Austrian economic theory.[22] It is the latter, therefore, that will receive our chief attention. The following sociological bases of economic science are characteristic of Marxism: recognition of the priority of society over the individual; recognition of the historical, temporary nature of any social structure; and finally, recognition of the dominant part played by production. The Austrian School, on the other hand, is characterised by extreme individualism in methodology, by an unhistorical point of view, and by its taking consumption as its point of departure. In our Introduction, we have attempted to furnish a social-genetic explanation for this fundamental difference between Marxism and the Austrian School; this difference, or rather, this opposition, we have characterised as a social psychological contrast. We shall now analyse this contrast from the point of view of *logic.*

1. Objectivism and Subjectivism in Political Economy.

Werner Sombart, in the well known article in which he reviewed the third volume of Marx's *Capital,* after having contrasted the two methods of political economy, the subjective method and the objective method, designates Marx's system as an outgrowth of "extreme objectivism"; while the Austrian School, in his opinion, was "the most consistent development in the opposite direction."[23] We consider this characterisation perfectly accurate. It is true that the study of social phenomena in general and of economic phenomena in particular may be approached in either one of two ways: we may assume that science proceeds from the analysis of society as a whole, which at any given moment determines the manifestations of the individual economic life, in which case it is the task of science to reveal the connections and the causal chain obtaining between the various phenomena of *social* type and determining the *individual* phenomena; or, it may be assumed that science should proceed from an analysis of the causal nexus in the individual life, since the social phenomena are a certain resultant of individual phenomena—in which case it would be the task of science to begin with the phenomena of the causal relation in the individual economic life from which the phenomena and the causation of the social economy must be derived.

No doubt Marx is an "extreme objectivist" in this sense, not only in sociology, but also in political economy. For this reason, his fundamental economic doctrine—the doctrine of value—must be sharply distinguished from that of the classical economists, particularly Adam Smith. The latter's labour value theory is based on an individual estimate of commodities, corresponding to the quantity and quality of the used labour. This is a subjective labour value theory, as compared with which Marx's theory of value is objective; *i.e.*, Marx's theory is a social law of prices. Marx's theory is accordingly an objective theory of labour value, based by no means on any individual evaluation, but expressing only the connection between the given social productive forces and the prices of commodities as the latter are determined on the market.[24] In fact, it is with the example of the theory of value and price that Sombart best shows the difference between the two methods. "Marx does not for a moment concern himself," says Sombart, "with the individual motives of those engaging in the exchange, or with assuming as his starting point considerations as to production costs. No, his reasoning is as follows: prices are made by competition; how they are made, that is another matter. But competition, in turn, is regulated by the rate of profit; the rate of profit by the rate of surplus value; the rate of surplus value by the value, which is itself the expression of a socially conditioned fact, the social productive forces. Marx's system now enumerates these elements in the reverse order: value—surplus value—profit—competition—prices, etc. If we must formulate the situation in a single crisp sentence, we may say that Marx is never concerned with motivating, but always with defining (limiting) the individual caprice of the economic person." (Werner Sombart, *op. cit.*, p. 591.) Quite different is the subjective school. We find "nothing but 'motivation' everywhere, for each [individual] economic transaction." (*Ibid.*, p. 592.)

The difference is here beautifully expressed. As a matter of fact, while Marx considers "the social movement as a process of natural history governed by laws not only independent of the human will, consciousness and intelligence, but rather, on the contrary, determining that will, consciousness, and intelligence",[25] the point of departure for Böhm-Bawerk is an analysis of the individual consciousness of the economic person.

"The social laws," writes Böhm-Bawerk, "whose investigation is the task of political economy, depend on coinciding transactions of individuals. Such uniformity of action is in turn a consequence of the operation of like motives determining action. Under these circumstances, it is not easy to admit a doubt as to the propriety of explaining social laws by tracing them back to the impelling motives determining the actions of individuals, or, by starting with these motives."[26] The difference, therefore, between the objective and the subjective method is nothing more nor less than the contrast between the social and the individualist methods. (R. Stolzmann: *Der Zweck in der Volkswirtschaftslehre,* Berlin, 1909, p. 59.) Yet the above quoted definition of the two methods needs still to be amplified. We must emphasise above all the unimportance of the will, the consciousness or the intentions of men, of which Marx speaks. In the second place, the "economic individual" must be more clearly defined, since it is the point of departure of the Austrian School. "These determined social relations are as much produced by men as are the cloth, the linen, etc." (Karl Marx: *The Poverty of Philosophy, Chicago,* Charles H. Kerr, p. 119.) It by no means follows, however, that the social consequences, that "social product" of which Marx speaks, is contained within the consciousness of these individuals as a goal or an impelling motive. Modern society, with its anarchic structure (the theory of political economy makes precisely *this* society the object of its study); with its market forces and their elemental action (competition, fluctuation of prices, stock exchange, etc.), offers numerous illustrations in favour of the assumption that the "social product" predominates over its creators, that the result of the motives of the individual (yet not isolated) economic men, not only does not correspond to these motives, but at times even enters into direct opposition to them.[27] This may best be explained by the example of the formation of prices. A number of buyers and sellers go to market with a certain (approximate) idea of the value of their own goods as well as of each other's goods; the result of their struggle is a certain market price, which will not coincide with the individual estimates of the great majority of the contracting parties. Furthermore, in the case of a number of "economic individuals" the established price may actually operate with destructive effect; low prices may force them to go out of business; they are "ruined". This phenomenon is even more striking on the stock exchange, where gambling is the rule. In all these cases, which are typical for the modern social-economic organisation, we may speak of the "independence" of social phenomena of the will, the consciousness and the intentions of men; yet this independence should by no means be understood as involving two different phenomena, completely independent of each other. It would be absurd to assume that human history is not being made *by* the will of men, but regardless of this will (this "materialist conception of history" is a bourgeois caricature of Marxism); precisely the opposite is the case. Both series of phenomena—individual transactions and social phenomena—are in the closest genetic relation with each other. This independence must be understood only in the sense that such results of individual acts as have become objective are supreme over all other partial elements. The "product" dominates its creator; at any given moment, the individual will is determined by the already achieved resultant of the clash of wills of the various "economic individuals". The entrepreneur defeated in the competitive struggle, the bankrupt financier, are forced to clear the field of battle, although a moment ago they served as active quantities, as "creators" of the social process which finally turned against them.[28] This phenomenon is an expression of the irrationality of the "elemental" character of the economic process within the frame of the commodities economy, which is clearly expressed in the psychology of commodities fetishism, as first exposed and brilliantly analysed by Marx. It is precisely in a commodities economy that the process of "objectivism", of relations between human beings, takes place, in which these "thing-expressions" lead a specific "independent" existence by reason of the elemental character of the evolution, an existence subject to a specific law of its own.

We are thus dealing with various series of individual phenomena and with a number of series of social types; no doubt a certain causal connection obtains both between these two categories (individual and social) and between the various series of the same category, particularly between the various series of *social* phenomena dependent on each other. Marx's method consists precisely in ascertaining the causal law of relations between the various *social* phenomena. In other words, Marx examines the causal nature of the resultants of the various individual wills, without examining the latter in themselves; he investigates the laws underlying *social* phenomena, paying no attention to their relation with the phenomena of the individual consciousness.[29]

Let us now turn to the "economic subjects" of Böhm-Bawerk.

In his article on Karl Menger's book (*Untersuchungen*, etc.), Böhm-Bawerk, in agreement with the opponents of the Austrian School and with Menger himself, admits that the "economic subjects" advanced by the representatives of the new School are nothing more nor less than the atoms of society. The task of the new School is "the elimination of the historical and organic methods as the dominant methods of theoretical investigation in the social sciences . . . and . . . the restoration of the precise atomistic tendency." (Böhm-Bawerk: *Zeitschrift für Privat- und öffentliches Recht der Gegenwart*, Vienna, 1884, vol. XI, p. 220.)

The starting point of the analysis is evidently not the individual member of a given society, in his social relations with his fellow men, but the isolated "atom", the economic Robinson Crusoe. The examples chosen by Böhm-Bawerk in order to clarify his views are also of this type. "A man is seated by a spring of water which is gushing profusely"—such is Böhm-Bawerk's introduction to his analysis of the theory of value. (Böhm-Bawerk: "Grundzüge der Theorie des wirtschaftlichen Güterwerts." Hildebrandt's *Jahrücher für Nationalökonomie und Statistik,* vol. XIII, p. 9.) He then introduces: a traveller in the desert *(ibid.,* p. 9), a farmer isolated from all the rest of the world *(ibid.,* p. 9), a colonist, "whose log-cabin stands lonely in the primeval forest" *(ibid.,* p. 30), etc. We encounter similar examples in Karl Menger: "the inhabitant of the forest primeval" (Karl Menger: *Grundsätze der Volkswirtschaftslehre,* Vienna, 1871, p. 82), "the dwellers in an oasis" *(ibid.,* p. 85), "a nearsighted individual on a lonely island" *(ibid.,* p. 95), "an isolated farmer" *(ibid.,* p. 96), "shipwrecked people" *(ibid.,* p. 104).

We here find the standpoint once so neatly formulated by Bastiat, the "sweetest" of all economists. In his *Economic Harmonies,* Bastiat says: "The economic laws operate in a uniform manner, whether we are dealing with a totality of lonely persons or with only two persons, or with a single individual, obliged by circumstances to live in isolation. If the individual could live for a period in isolation, this individual would simultaneously be a capitalist, an *entrepreneur,* a worker, a producer, and a consumer. The entire economic evolution would be realised in him. By reason of his opportunity to observe every step in this evolution, namely: the need, the effort, the satisfaction of the need, enjoying the free use of profit of labour, he would be able to form an idea of the entire mechanism, even though it might be in its simplest form." (Frédéric Bastiat, *Harmonies économiques,* Bruxelles, 1850, p. 213.)

Earlier in the same book, Bastiat says: "I maintain that political economy would attain its goal and fulfill its mission if it had finally proved the following fact: that which is right with regard to one person is also right with regard to society." *(Ibid.,* p. 74.) [30]

Jevons makes an equivalent declaration: "The general form of the laws of economy is the same in the case of individuals and nations." [31]

However venerable this point of view may have become by reason of its age, it is nevertheless entirely fallacious. Society (as is consciously or unconsciously assumed) is not an arithmetical aggregate of isolated individuals; on the contrary, the economic activity of each specific individual presupposes a definite social environment in which the social relation of the individual economies finds its expression. The motives of the individual living in isolation are entirely different from those of the "social animal" (*zoon politikon*). The former lives in an environment consisting of nature, of things in their pristine simplicity; the latter is surrounded not only by "matter" but also by a peculiar *social milieu.* The transition from the isolated human to society is possible only by way of the social milieu. And indeed, if we were dealing only with an aggregate of individual economies, without any points of contact between them, if the specific milieu which Rodbertus has so appropriately termed the "economic community" should be absent, there would be no society. Of course, it is theoretically quite possible to embrace a number of isolated and remote economies in a single conception, to force them into a "totality" as it were. But this totality or aggregate would not be a society, a system of economies closely connected with each other with constant interaction between them. While the former aggregate would be one we had artificially constructed, the second is one that is truly present.[32] Therefore the individual economic subject may be regarded only as a member of a social economic system, not as an isolated atom. The economic subject, in its actions, adapts itself to the given condition of the social phenomena; the latter impose barriers upon his individual motives, or, to use Sombart's words, "limit them".[33] This holds true not only of the "economic structure of society," *i.e.*, of the production conditions, but also of the social-economic phenomena arising on the basis of a given structure. Thus, for example, the individual estimates of price always start with prices that have already been fixed; the desire to invest capital in a bank depends on the interest rate at the time; the investment of capital in this industry or that is determined by the profit yielded by the industry; the estimate of the value of a plot of land depends on its rent and on the rate of interest, etc. No doubt, individual motives have their "opposite effects"; but it must be emphasised that these motives from the start are permeated with a social content, and therefore no "social laws" can be derived from the motives of the isolated subject.[34] But if we do not begin with the isolated individual in our investigation, but consider the social factor in his motives as given, we shall find ourselves involved in a vicious circle: in our attempt to derive the "social", *i.e.*, the "objective", from the "individual", *i.e.*, the "subjective", we are actually deriving it from the "social", or doing somewhat worse than robbing Peter to pay Paul.

As we have seen above, the motives of the isolated individual constitute the point of departure for the Austrian School (Böhm-Bawerk). To be sure, the works of the representatives of this School sometimes present quite correct conceptions of the essence of the social structure as a whole. But, as a matter of fact, this School begins at once with an analysis of the motives of the economic subjects, disregarding any social connection between them. This point of view is quite characteristic of the latest theorists of the bourgeoisie. And it is precisely this point of view that the Austrian School consistently applies in all its development. It follows that the School will be inevitably obliged to smuggle the notion of the "social" into the individual motives of its "social atoms", as soon as it attempts to derive any social phenomena at all. But this situation will force it into an inescapable and monstrous *circulus vitiosus*.

In fact, this inevitable logical fallacy is already apparent in the analysis of the Austrian School's theory of subjective value, that cornerstone of the entire theoretical structure of which its representatives are so proud. Yet this fallacy alone is sufficient to destroy the significance of this scientific economic ideology of the modern bourgeoisie, constructed with so much ingenuity, "for", as Böhm-Bawerk himself rightly observes, "it is a mortal sin of method to ignore that which one should explain, in a scientific investigation." [35]

We thus arrive at the conclusion that the "subjectivism" of the Austrian School, the intentional isolation of the "economic subject", the ignoring of the social relations,[36] must inevitably lead to a logical bankruptcy of the entire system; this system is as unsatisfactory as the ancient theory of the costs of production, which also revolved helplessly in its magic circle.

There now arises the question whether it is possible to set up a theoretical formulation of the economic life, to determine its causal laws, without involving the causal laws of individual motives; in other words, is the "objectivism" possible which constitutes the basis of the Marxian theory?

Even Böhm-Bawerk admits this possibility: "Not, to be sure, causally conditioned actions without causal motivation, but indeed a recognition of causally conditioned actions without a recognition of the attending motivation!"[37] But Böhm-Bawerk assumes that "the objectivistic source of knowledge . . . can contribute at best only a very small part, and one especially insufficient for its own purposes, or the total attainable knowledge, since we are concerned in the economic field particularly with conscious, calculated human actions." (*Zum Abschluss des Marxschen System*, p. 202, translated into English under the title: *Marx and the Close of His System*,—references are to the German edition).

We have already seen, as opposed to the above, that it is precisely the individualistic psychological abstractions promulgated by the Austrian School that yield so sparse a harvest.[38] And we are speaking here not of abstraction as such. In fact we have emphasised above that abstraction is a necessary element in any acquisition of knowledge. The fallacy of the Austrians consists in their ignoring precisely the social phenomena which they are studying. This condition is excellently formulated by R. Stolzmann: "The types of economy may be simplified by means of isolation and abstraction as much as you like, *but they must be social types;* they must be concerned with a social economy". (R. Stolzmann, *op. cit.*, p. 63; also his *Soziale Kategorie*, pp. 291, 292; *cf.* also D. Lifschitz: *Zur Kritik der Böhm-Bawerkschen Werttheorie*, Leipzig, 1908, chapter iv, particularly pp. 90, 91.) For it is not possible to proceed from the purely individual to the social; even if there had once existed in reality such an historical process of transition, *i.e.*, even if human beings had actually passed out of an isolated condition into that of "social being", the only possibility—even in this case—would be an historical and a concrete description of this process, a purely idiographic (cinematographic) solution of the problem. Even in this case, it would be impossible to set up a nomographic theory. Let us assume, for example, that certain isolated producers enter into relations with each other, are united in an exchange of goods and gradually construct a society of exchange on the modern model. Now let us examine the subjective evaluations made by modern man. These evaluations are based on prices formerly established (as will be shown in detail below); these prices would, in turn, be shaped out of the motives of the economic subjects of some former epoch; but those prices also have been dependent on prices established at a still earlier period; these again have been the result of subjective evaluations based on still more ancient prices, etc. We thus finally encounter the evaluations of the individual producers, evaluations which in reality no longer involve any element of price, since all social bonds, all society itself, are lacking in them. But such an analysis of subjective evaluations, beginning with modern man and ending with an hypothetical Robinson Crusoe, would mean nothing more or less than a simple historical description of the process of transformation of the motives of isolated man into the motives of modern man, with the difference that the process proceeded in the opposite direction. Such an analysis is merely a description; it is just as impossible to base a general theory of prices or a theory of exchange on such foundations. Any attempts at such a construction of a theory must inevitably lead to fallacious circles in the system, for so long as we wish to remain within the framework of a general theory, we must—instead of explaining the social element—begin with it as the given quantity. To advance beyond this quantity would be equivalent, as we have seen, to a transformation of theory into history, *i.e.*, to entering into an entirely different field of scholarly work. There remains for us, therefore, but a single mode of studying, namely, a combination of abstract deduction and objective method; this combination is extremely characteristic of the Marxian political economy. Only by this method will it be possible to set up a theory that will not involve repeated self-contradictions, but will actually constitute a means of examination of capitalist reality.

2. The Historical Point of View and the Unhistorical Point of View.

Karl Marx, in his *Theorien über den Mehrwert* (vol. I, p. 34 said about the Physiocrats: "It was their great achievement to have conceived these forms [*i.e.*, the forms of the capitalist mode of production] as physiological forms of society: as forms emanating from the natural necessity of production itself, and independent of the will, politics, etc. They are material laws; the fallacy of the Physiocrats consists in having conceived the material law of a specific historical stage of society as an abstract law dominating all the forms of society in a uniform manner."

This is an excellent formulation of the difference between the purely social point of view and the historico-social point of view. It is possible to consider the "social economy as a whole" and yet misunderstand the entire significance of the specific forms of society as they have developed historically. Of course, the unhistorical point of view in modern times frequently appears coupled with a lack of understanding for social connections; yet, we must distinguish between these two methodological questions, for the possibility of "objective treatment" alone affords no guarantee that problems are to be put historically. An example of this is furnished by the Physiocrats. The case recurs, in modern economic literature, in Tugan-Baranovsky, whose "social distribution theory" is applicable to any society built up of classes (and therefore explains nothing at all).[39]

Marx strictly emphasises the historical character of his economic theory and the relativity of its laws. "According to his opinion, each historical period has its own laws. . . . As soon as life has gone beyond a given period of evolution, has passed from one given stage into another, it also begins to be guided by other laws."[40] Of course it does not necessarily follow that Marx denied the existence of any general laws dominating the course of social life in all its various evolutionary phases. The materialist theory of history, for example, formulates certain laws intended as explanations of the social evolution at every point. But they do not exclude the specific historical laws of political economy, which, as opposed to the sociological laws, express the essence of a specific social structure, namely, that of capitalist society.[41]

We shall here anticipate an objection that might be raised; it might be urged that the acceptance of the historical principle would lead directly to an idiographic, purely descriptive type of theory, *i.e.*, precisely the point of view defended by the so called Historical School. But this objection would be equivalent to a confusion of a number of things. Let us take at random any general method of the idiographic sciences *par excellence,* for example, statistics: we have the "empirical law" of population statistics that there are between 105 and 108 male births to every 100 female births. This "law" is purely descriptive in character; it indicates no causal relation. On the other hand, any theoretical law of political economy must be capable of formulation as follows: if $A, B, C,$ are present, D also must ensue; in other words, the presence of certain conditions, "causes", involves the appearance of certain consequences. It is obvious that these "consequences" may also be of historical character, *i.e.*, they may actually supervene only at the given time. From a purely logical point of view, it is quite immaterial where and when these conditions actually occur, even more immaterial whether they occur at all—in this case "we are dealing with eternal laws"; but, insofar as they occur in reality, they are "historical laws", for they are connected with "conditions" occurring only at a certain stage in historical development.[42] But once these conditions are present, their consequences are also indicated. Precisely this character of the theoretical economic laws makes possible their application to countries and epochs in which the social evolution has already attained a corresponding level; it was possible, therefore, for the Russian Marxists to prophesy correctly the "destinies of capitalism in Russia", although the Marxian analysis was actually based on concrete empirical material gathered with reference to England.[43]

In other words, the "historical" character of the laws of political economy by no means transforms the latter into a science of the idiographic type. On the other hand, only the historical point of view can be of any scientific value in this field.

Political economy as a science can have as its object only a commodities society,—a capitalist society. If we were dealing with an economy organised in any way at all, for instance, with the *oikos* economy of Rodbertus, or with the primitive communist society, with feudal landholding or with the organised socialised economy of the socialist "state", we should not encounter a single problem whose solution could be found in the domain of theoretical political economy. These problems are connected with the commodities economy, particularly with its capitalist form: the problems of value, price, capital, profits, crisis, etc. This is of course no accident; it is just at this moment, in view of the more or less pronounced prevalence of the system of "free competition", that the elemental nature of the economic process obtains particularly striking expressions, the individual will and the individual purpose being relegated entirely to the background as opposed to the objectively developing chain of social phenomena. It is only to commodities production as such, and to its highest form, capitalist production, that we may apply the phenomenon described by Marx as the "fetishism of commodities" and analysed by him in *Capital*. Just at this point the personal relation of human beings themselves in the production process becomes an impersonal relation between things, whereby the latter assume the form of a "social hieroglyphic" of value (Karl Marx: *Capital*, vol. I, p. 85). Thence the "enigmatical" character peculiar to the capitalist mode of production and the characteristic traits of the problems here for the first time subjected to theoretical investigation. The analysis of capitalist society affords particular interest and bestows a special logical form on economic science, which investigates the causal connections in the elemental life of modern society, formulates laws that are independent of the human consciousness, "regulative natural laws", similar to the law of gravitation "when one's house comes tumbling down about one's ears".

"not because of the *caractère typique de la liberté économique,* but because of the epistemological peculiarity of the competitive system, involving, as it does, the greatest number of theoretical enigmas, as well as the greatest difficulty in their solution". (Heinrich Dietzel: *Theoretische Sozialökonomik,* p. 90.)

This rudimentary character, a consequence of extremely complicated conditions, is itself a historical phenomenon peculiar to commodities production alone.[44] Only unorganised social economy presents such specific phenomena in which the mutual adaptation of the various parts of the production organism proceeds independently of the human will consciously turned to that end. In a planful guidance of the social economy, the distribution and redistribution of the social production forces constitute a conscious process based on statistical data. In the present anarchy of production, this process takes place through a transfer mechanism of prices, by means of the fall and rise of prices, by their pressure on profits, by a whole series of crises, etc., in a word, not by a conscious calculation by the community, but by the blind power of the social element, evidencing itself in a whole chain of social-economic phenomena, particularly in the market price. All these are characteristic of modern society and constitute the subject of political economy. In a socialist society, political economy will lose its *raison d'être*: there will remain only an "economic geography"—a science of the idiographic type; and an "economic politics"—a normative science; for the relations between men will be simple and clear, the fetishist objective formulation of these relations will disappear and the causal consequences in the life of the unbridled elements will be replaced by the causal consequences of the conscious performances of society. This fact alone is sufficient to show that an investigation of capitalism must take into account its fundamental traits, those distinguishing the capitalist "production organism" from any other; for the study of capitalism is the study of that which distinguishes capitalism from any other social structure. Once we ignore the typical peculiarities of capitalism, we arrive at general categories that may be applied to any social production conditions and may therefore not explain the historically conditioned peculiar evolutionary process of "modern capitalism". It is precisely in their ability to forget this principle, says Marx, that there "lies the entire wisdom of modern economists, who prove the eternity and harmony of the existing social conditions."[45] It must also be noted that capitalism is the developed form of commodities production, characterised not by exchange *per se*, but by *capitalist* exchange. In this system, labour power appears on the market as a commodity, and the production conditions ("the economic structure of society") include not only the relations among the producers of commodities, but also those between the capitalist class and the wage-earning class. An analysis of capitalism therefore involves not only an investigation of the general conditions of the commodities economy (this element unmodified would be equivalent to the theory of simple commodities production) but also an investigation of the specific structure of capitalism itself. A truly scientific economic theory cannot be devised unless the questions be formulated as above. Only if the object is to glorify and perpetuate the capitalist conditions, and not investigate them theoretically, may one omit an analysis and emphasis of their typical characteristics. Accordingly, Marx introduces his *Capital* with the following words: "The wealth of those societies in which the capitalist mode of production prevails presents itself as 'an immense accumulation of commodities', its unit being a single commodity. Our investigation must therefore begin with the analysis of a commodity." (*Capital*, vol. I, p. 41.)

From the outset, therefore, Marx's investigation proceeds along the historical path; his subsequent analysis shows that all the fundamental economic concepts are historical in character.[46] "Every product of labour," says Marx on the subject of value, "is, in all states of society, a use-value; but it is only at a definite historical epoch in a society's development that such a product becomes a commodity, *viz.*, at the epoch when the labour spent on the production of a useful article becomes expressed as one of the objective qualities of that article, *i.e.*, as its value." (*Capital*, vol. I, p. 71.)

Marx's words on capital are similar: "But capital is not

a thing. It is a definite interrelation in social production belonging to a definite historical formation of society. This interrelation expresses itself through a certain thing and gives to this thing a specific social character. Capital is not the sum of the material and produced means of production. Capital means rather the means of production converted into capital, and means of production by themselves are no more capital than gold or silver are money in themselves." (*Capital,* vol. III, part VII, pp. 947, 948.)

It will be interesting to compare with this the definition of capital offered by Böhm-Bawerk:

"*Capital as such is the term we assign to a sum total of products serving as means for the acquisition of commodities.* The narrower concept of *social capital* may be detached from this general conception of capital. We assign the term social capital to a congeries of products serving as a means for the acquisition of social-economic commodities; or, in short, a group of intermediate products."[47]

It is obvious that these two definitions proceed from entirely different points of departure. While Marx emphasises the historical character of a certain category as its principal trait, Böhm-Bawerk ignores the historical element entirely; while Marx is concerned with historically determined relations between men, Böhm-Bawerk presents universal forms of the relations between men and things. In fact, once one ignores the relations between men, subject as they are to historical change, there remain only the relations between men and nature; in other words, in place of the social-historical categories, we have left only the "natural" categories. Yet it is clear that the "natural" categories cannot in any way explain the social-historical categories, for, as Stolzmann very properly observes, "the natural categories may only afford technical possibilities for the development of economic phenomena." (R. Stolzmann: *Der Zweck in der Volkswirtschaftslehre,* 1909, p. 131.)

And as a matter of fact, the labour process, the process of production and distribution of commodities, always assumes certain varying historical forms, alone capable of producing specific social-economic phenomena. Quite untenable is the point of view of such men as "Colonel Torrens" and Böhm-Bawerk, who regard the "stone of the savage as the origin of capital" [48] and the savage himself as a capitalist. Only after the means of production resulting on the basis of the commodities production,[49] have been monopolised by a single class as opposed to the only commodity still remaining in the possession of the workers—their labour power—do we have the peculiar phenomenon known as capital; and of course the "profit of the capitalist" begins only at this point. The same is true of rent. The fact of a varying yield of the soil in various parcels of land, or, as the famous formula puts it, "the law of diminishing returns from the soil" should by no means result (even if met with in the form favoured by the most radical Malthusians), in the phenomenon of land rent. Rent begins only after real estate, built up on the foundation of the commodities production, has been monopolised in the form of property by the class of landed proprietors. As for the difference in the yield of the various parcels and for the "law" in question, they are merely technical conditions, since it is they which *make possible* [50] the social phenomenon of *rent*. Therefore Böhm-Bawerk's laments over many of his critics, whom he upbraids for failing to distinguish the "essence of the matter" from its "manifestation", are without foundation. The essence of capitalism is not in the fact that it constitutes an "aggregate of intermediate products" (the "essence" of the means of production), but in its constituting a peculiar social relation resulting in a number of economic phenomena entirely unknown to other epochs. It may, of course, be maintained that capital is a manifestation of the means of production in present-day society, but it may not be maintained that modern capital is the universal manifestation of capital and that the latter is identical with the means of production.

Even the phenomenon of value is historical in character. Even if we admit the correctness of the individualistic method of the Austrian School, and seek to derive value outright from "subjective value", *i.e.*, from the individual evaluations of various persons, we must also consider the fact that in modern economy the psyche of the "producer" has an entirely different content from the psyche of the producer in a natural economy (particularly, from the psyche of the man "sitting by the brook" or "starving in the desert"). The modern capitalist, regardless of whether he be a representative of industrial or of commercial capital, is not at all interested in the consumption value of products; he "works" with the aid of "hired hands" for profit exclusively; he is interested only in exchange value.

It is obvious that even the fundamental phenomenon of political economy, that of value, cannot be explained on the basis of the circumstance common to all times and peoples, that commodities satisfy some human need; yet this is the "method" of the Austrian School.[51]

We therefore reach the conclusion that the Austrian School is pursuing an absolutely erroneous methodological course in ignoring the peculiarities of capitalism. A political economy aiming to explain the social-economic relations, *i.e.*, the relations between men, must be an historical science. "Any one attempting to class the political economy of Tierra del Fuego," Engels observes with appropriate malice, "under the same laws with those of present-day England, would obviously arrive at nothing but the most trivial commonplaces." [52] These "commonplaces" may be constructed on a more or less ingenious foundation, but even this cannot explain the peculiarities of the capitalist order of society, once they have been eliminated in advance. And thus the "hypothetical economy", "constructed" by Böhm-Bawerk, whose "laws" he investigates, is so far removed from our sinful reality that it refuses to yield to any yardstick of reality.

And the creators of this new tendency are not entirely unconscious of this condition. For example, Böhm-Bawerk, in the latest edition of his book, says: "I should particularly have liked to fill the gap still left in the investigation of the nature and importance of the influences of the so called 'social category', of the relations of power and authority flowing from social institutions. . . . This chapter of social economy has not yet been satisfactorily written . . . not even by the theory of marginal utility." (Preface to the third edition of *Kapital und Kapitalzins*, vol. II, pp. 16, 17.)

Of course, we may predict that this "chapter" cannot be

written "satisfactorily" by the representatives of the theory of marginal utility, since they do not consider the "social category" as an organic ingredient of the purely "economic category", but regard it as a foreign substance outside of economy.

Böhm-Bawerk is here again opposed by Stolzmann, one of the representatives of the "social-organic" method, to whom we have repeatedly referred: "The so-called 'objectivism' thus enters into a new stage, becoming not only social but also 'historical'; there is no longer any gulf between the systematic-logical science and the historical-realistic science; they now have a common field of labour; both are concerned with the study of historical *reality*." [53] But this task of uniting the abstract classical method with "objectivism" and "historicism" was solved long before Stolzmann's day by Karl Marx and without any ethical trimmings.

It would appear that the "antiquated" theory of the proletariat is superior to all others on this point also.[54]

3. The Point of View of Production and the Point of View of Consumption.

"The first theoretical treatment of modern modes of production," says Karl Marx, "started out necessarily from the superficial phenomena of the process of circulation . . . The real science of modern economy does not begin, until theoretical analysis passes from the process of circulation to the process of production". (*Capital*, vol. III, p. 396.) On the other hand, Böhm-Bawerk and the entire Austrian School take consumption as the point of departure in their analysis.

While Marx considers society above all as a "production organism" and economy as a "production process", Böhm-Bawerk relegates production to the background entirely; for him the analysis of consumption, of the needs and desires of the economic man, takes first place.[55] We are therefore not surprised to find him taking as his point of departure not the economic commodities considered as products, but a given quantity of such products *a priori*, a "supply" as to the origin of which one is very uncertain. This also fixes the entire value theory as the central point of the entire theoretical system.

Since the factor of production is excluded from the outset, it is obvious that the resulting theory of value must be entirely independent of production. Quite similar is the peculiar application of the method of "isolating abstraction"; for instance, instead of having his Robinson Crusoes—in his analysis of value—produce commodities, he has them lose them, "dispense with them". This causes the possibility of production or reproduction to be regarded not as a phenomenon requiring analysis above all, but as a disturbing factor.[56] It is therefore only natural that "utility" should become the fundamental concept of the Austrian School, from which the concept of subjective, later also objective, value, is derived in due course. The concept of utility really implies neither an "expenditure of labour" nor production; it expresses no active relation to things, but a passive relation; no "objective activity" but a certain relation to a uniform given state. It is for this reason that this concept of utility may be so successfully applied in such important situations as those involving as their active agents: castaways, "near-sighted persons on uninhabitated islands", "starving travellers" and other monstrous constructions of the professorial imagination.

But it is quite clear that this point of view precludes in advance any possibility of grasping social phenomena or their evolution. The motive force in the latter is the increase in the production forces, in the productivity of social labour, the extension of the productive functions of society. Without consumption there is no production; no one doubts this; needs are always the motive for any economic activity. On the other hand, production also has a very decisive influence on consumption. Marx explains this influence as making itself felt in three ways: first, in that production creates the *material* for consumption; second, in that it determines the *mode* of the latter, *i.e.*, its qualitative character; third, in that it creates *new* needs.[57]

Such are the facts if we consider the mutual relations between production and consumption *in general*, without reference to a specific historically given structure. In the study of capitalism, an added factor must be considered, namely, in the words of Karl Marx: " . . . The 'social demand,' in other words, that which regulates the principle of demand, is essentially conditioned on the mutual relations of the different economic classes and their relative economic position, that is to say, first, on the proportion of the total surplus value to the wages, and secondly, on the proportion of the various parts into which surplus-value is divided (profit, interest, ground-rent, taxes, etc.)." (*Capital,* vol. III, Part 1, p. 124.) This relation between the classes is in turn, however, shaped and altered under the influence of the growth of the productive forces.

We thus observe chiefly: *the dynamics of the requirements are determined by the dynamics of production.* It follows first, that the point of departure in an analysis of the dynamics of requirements must be the dynamics of production; second, that the given quantity of products necessary to secure a static production also involves a static consumption, in other words, a static condition in the aggregate of the economic life, therefore of life altogether.[58]

Marx gave first place to the "evolution of the productive forces"; for the goal of all his huge theoretical labours was, to use his own words, "to lay bare the economic law of motion of modern society." (*Capital,* vol. I, p. 14.) Of course, it must be rather difficult to reveal the "law of motion" where there is no motion, where an aggregate of products is assumed as "descending from the sky".[59] It may therefore be assumed in advance that the point of view of consumption which underlies the whole Austrian system will turn out to be entirely unfruitful in all questions involving social dynamics, *i.e.,* the most important problems of political economy. "They [the representatives of the Austrian School.—*N.B.*] are incapable of even formulating, to say nothing of solving, such fundamental questions as the evolution of technique in a capitalist society, the origin of capitalist profit, etc.," says Charasoff.[60] In this connection, the confessions of one of the principal representatives of the Austrian School, Josef Schumpeter, will be found of interest. Schumpeter was courageous enough to state frankly that the Austrian School has nothing to contribute in all cases dealing with evolutionary processes. "We see, therefore, that our static system," says Schumpeter, "does not by any means explain all economic phenomena, *e.g.*, interest and the profit of the *entrepreneur*." (Josef Schumpeter: *Das Wesen und der Hauptinhalt der theoretischen Nationalökonomie*, Leipzig, 1908, p. 564.)

" . . . Our theory breaks down, in spite of its firm foundations, before the most important phenomena of the modern economic life." (*Ibid.*, p. 587.)

"It again breaks down in the face of any phenomenon that can . . . be understood only from the point of view of evolution. Among these are the problems of the formation of capital, and other problems, particularly that of economic progress and crises." (*Ibid.*, p. 587.)

It is apparent that the latest theory of the bourgeois scholars fails precisely in the most important fundamental questions of our day. The enormous and speedy accumulation of capital, its concentration and centralisation, the uncommonly rapid progress in technology, and finally, the regular recurrence of industrial crises—this specifically capitalistic phenomenon which shakes the social-economic system to its foundations—all these things are a "book with seven seals", according to Schumpeter's admission. And just where the philosophy of the learned bourgeois ceases, the Marxian theory comes into its own, to such an extent, in fact, that mutilated fragments of the Marxian doctrine are accepted as the last word of wisdom even by the bitterest enemies of Marxism.[61]

4. *Conclusions*

We have investigated the three initial fallacies of the Austrian School: its subjectivism, its unhistorical point of view, its beginning with consumption. These three logical points of departure, connected, as they are, with the three basic mental traits of the bourgeois *rentier*, inevitably involve also the three fundamental errors in the theory of the Austrian School, which are found repeated again and again in the various sections of the general theoretical "system": the "vicious circles" resulting from the subjectivist method; their inability to explain the specifically historical forms of capitalism, because of their unhistorical point of view, and, finally, their complete failure in dealing with all the problems of economic evolution—a ailure necessarily connected with their consumption philosophy. But it would be erroneous to assume that all these "motives" operate independently; both their psychic and logical systems are complicated quantities in which various elements are variously united and fused, their effects becoming now stronger, now weaker, depending on the other concomitant factors.

Therefore every concrete fallacy to be unveiled in the subsequent exhaustive analysis of Böhm-Bawerk's theory will not be the result merely of a single "thought-motif" of the new theoreticians of the *rentiers*, but always of several simultaneously. Yet this must not prevent us from selecting out of all the related factors the three fundamental factors constituting in their various composition a source of Böhm-Bawerk's countless "blunders". These "blunders" are an evidence of the complete incapacity of the *fin de siècle* bourgeoisie for theoretical thinking.

CHAPTER II

The Theory of Value

1. The importance of the problem of value.
2. Subjective and objective value; definitions.
3. Utility and value (subjective).
4. The measure of value and the unit value.

1. *The Importance of the Problem of Value.*

The problem of value has constituted a fundamental question of political economy since the earliest days of the science. All other questions, such as wage-labour, capital, rent, accumulation of capital, the struggle between large-scale and petty operation, crises, etc., are directly or indirectly involved in this fundamental question.

"The theory of value stands, as it were, in the centre of the entire doctrine of political economy," Böhm-Bawerk rightly observes. (*Grundzüge der Theorie des wirtschaftlichen Güterwerts,* p. 8.) This is not hard to understand; price, and therefore the standard determining price—which is value—is the fundamental all-embracing category in the production of commodities in general and in the capitalist production of commodities in particular, whose child is political economy. The prices of commodities regulate the distribution of the production forces of capitalist society; the form of exchange, whose presupposition is the category of price, is the form of distribution of the social product among the various classes.

The movement of prices leads to an adaptation of the supply of goods to demand, since the rise and fall of the rate of profit causes capital to flow from one branch of production to another. Low prices are the weapon by which capitalism cuts its path and finally conquers the world; it is low prices that enable capital to eliminate artisan production, to supplant petty operation with large-scale operation.

The contract between the capitalist and the worker—the first condition for the enrichment of the capitalist—assumes the form of a *purchase* of labour power, *i.e.*, the form of a price relation. Profit, the expression in terms of money-value, but not the natural "expression" of surplus product, is the driving motive of modern society; on this precisely rests the entire process of the accumulation of capital, which destroys the old forms of economy and is distinguished sharply from them in its evolution as an entirely specific historical phase of the economic evolution, etc. Therefore the problem of value has again and again attracted the attention of economic theorists in far higher measure than any other problem of political economy. Adam Smith, David Ricardo, Karl Marx—all took the analysis of value as the basis of their investigations.[62] The Austrian School also made the theory of value the cornerstone of its system; having undertaken to oppose the classics and Marx and to create their own theoretical system, they necessarily concerned themselves chiefly with the problem of value.

It follows that the theory of value in reality still occupies the central position in present day theoretical discussions, although John Stuart Mill already considered this question disposed of. (John Stuart Mill, *ibid.*, p. 209.) As opposed to Mill, Böhm-Bawerk believes that the theory of value has still remained "one of the most unclear, most confused, and most disputed sections of our science"; (Böhm-Bawerk, *Grundzüge*, etc., p. 8), yet he hopes that the studies of the Austrian School will put an end to this confused state. "It seems to me that certain labours performed in recent and very recent days," he says, "have introduced the creative thought into this confused ferment, from a fruitful development of which we may expect complete clearness." (*Ibid.*, p. 8.)

We shall attempt below to subject this "creative thought" to the necessary examination; but let us state at the outset that the critics of the Austrian School often point out that the latter has confused value with use-value; however, that its theory belongs rather to the domain of psychology than to that of political economy, etc. No doubt this objection is fundamentally correct. Yet we do not think our judgment should end here. We must rather proceed from the point of view of the representatives of the Austrian School, we must grasp the whole system in its internal relations, and only then reveal its contradictions and insufficiencies, the products of its *fundamental* fallacies. For instance, value has been variously defined. Böhm-Bawerk's definition will necessarily differ from that of Karl Marx. But it is not sufficient to declare simply that Böhm-Bawerk does not touch the essence of the matter, *i.e.*, that he does not treat that which should be treated; rather, we must show *why* his treatment is wrong. Furthermore, it must be shown that the presuppositions from which the theory in question proceeds lead either to contradictory constructions or fail both to include and explain a number of important economic phenomena.

But where is there any point of departure for criticism in this case? If the conception of value is completely different even in the most varied tendencies, *i.e.*, if, according to Marx, it has no points of contact at all with that of Böhm-Bawerk, how will it be possible to formulate a criticism at all? In this situation, however, we are aided by the following circumstance: great as are the differences between the definitions of value, though they may even contradict each other in places, they nevertheless have something in common, namely, in conceiving *value as a standard of exchange,* in that the conception of value serves to explain price.[63] Of course, the explanation of prices alone is not sufficient, or, more properly, we have no right to limit ourselves to an explanation of prices; yet the theory of value is the *direct* basis for the theory of *price.* If the corresponding theory of value solves the question of price without internal contradictions, it is a correct theory; if not, it must be rejected.

These are the considerations from which we shall proceed in our criticism of Böhm-Bawerk's theory.

We have seen in the preceding section that price is considered by Böhm-Bawerk to be the resultant of individual evaluations. His "theory" therefore is divided into two parts: the first part investigates the laws of the formation of individual evaluations—"the theory of subjective value"—the second part investigates the laws of the origin of their resultant— "the theory of objective value".

2. *Subjective and Objective Value; Definitions.*

We already know that according to the views of the subjectivist school, we must seek the basis of social-economic phenomena in the individual psychology of men. In the case of price, this demand requires us to begin our analysis of price with the *individual evaluations*. Comparing the Böhm-Bawerk mode of treatment of the question of value with that of Karl Marx, the difference in principle between them at once becomes clear: in Marx the value concept is an expression of the *social* connection between two *social* phenomena, between the productivity of labour and price; in capitalist society (as opposed to a simple commodities society) this connection is very complicated.[64]

In Böhm-Bawerk, the value concept is an expression of the relation between the *social* phenomenon of price and the *individual-psychological* phenomenon of the various evaluations.

The individual evaluation presupposes an evaluating subject and an object to be evaluated; the resultant of the relations between these is subjective value. For the Austrian School, subjective value is therefore not a specific character inherent in commodities as such, but rather a specific psychological state of the evaluating subject itself. When we speak of an object, we mean its significance for a given subject. *Therefore "value in the subjective sense is the significance possessed by a commodity or group of commodities for the purposes of the well-being of a subject."*[65] This is the definition of subjective value.

Quite different is Böhm-Bawerk's concept of objective value: *"Value in the objective sense, on the other hand, is the virtue or capacity of a commodity to bring about a certain objective result.* In this sense there are as many kinds of value as there are external consequences to be brought about. We may speak of the nutritive value of foods, of the fuel value of wood and coal, of the fertilizing value of various fertilizers, of the ballistic value of explosives. *In all these expressions we have eliminated any relation to the weal or woe of a subject from the concept of value."*[66] [The last italics are mine.—*N.B.*]

Among these objective values, thus declared neutral as to

"weal or woe of the subject", Böhm-Bawerk also enumerates the values of economic character, such as, "exchange value", "the yield value", "production value", "rent value", and the like. The greatest importance is assigned to *objective exchange value.* Böhm-Bawerk defines the latter as follows: " . . . *The objective validity of commodities in exchange,* or in other words, *the possibility of acquiring in exchange for them a quantity of other economic commodities, viewing this possibility as a function or quality of the former commodities.*"[67] This is the definition of objective exchange value The last definition is neither correct in its essence, nor would it be correct if Böhm-Bawerk had applied his point of view consistently. The exchange value of commodities is here enumerated as "their objective quality" similar to their physical and chemical qualities. In other words, "the utility effect", in the *technical* sense of the word, is made identical with the economic concept of exchange value. This evidently is the point of view of crass commodities fetishism so characteristic of the vulgar political economy. As a matter of fact, "the existence of the things quâ commodities, and the value relation between the products of labour which stamps them as commodities, have absolutely no connection with their physical properties and with the material relations arising therefrom." (Karl Marx: *Capital,* vol I, p. 83.)

Even from the point of view of Böhm-Bawerk, his assertion could not be defended, at bottom. If the objective value is nothing more or less than a resultant of the subjective evaluations, it *must* not be grouped with the chemical and physical properties of commodities. On the other hand, it differs from them in principle: it contains not an "atom of matter", being descended from and shaped by immaterial factors, namely, the individual evaluations of the various "economic subjects". However peculiar this may sound, we must nevertheless point out that the pure psychologism so characteristic of the Austrian School and of Böhm-Bawerk is perfectly compatible with a vulgar, excessively materialistic fetishism, in other words, with a point of view essentially naïve and uncritical. Böhm-Bawerk of course protests against an understanding of *subjective* value, which would ascribe the latter to commodities as such, without any relation between the commodities and the evaluating subject, but Böhm-Bawerk himself, when he defines the concept of objective value, enumerates it altogether with the technical properties of objects independent or neutral as to "weal or woe of the subject", forgetting that he has thus destroyed the genetic relation between the subjective and the objective value which is after all the basis of his theory.[68]

We are therefore dealing with two categories of value; one represents a basic quantity, the other a derived quantity. It is therefore necessary first to test the theory of *subjective* value. Besides, it is in this portion of the Austrian theory that the most originality is displayed in the attempt to lay a new foundation for the theory of value.

3. Utility and Value (Subjective).

"The central conception (of the Austrian School) . . . is utility." (Werner Sombart: *Zur Kritik des ökonomischen Systems von Karl Marx,* in Braun's *Archiv,* vol. VII, p. 592.) While with Marx utility is only the *condition* for the origin of value, without determining the degree of value, Böhm-Bawerk derives value from utility entirely and makes it the direct expression of the latter.[69]

Böhm-Bawerk distinguishes, however (differing, he thinks, with the old terminology, which made utility and consumption value always synonymous), between usefulness *in general* and value, which is, as it were, of certificated usefulness. "The relation to human welfare," says Böhm-Bawerk, "expresses itself in two essentially different forms; the lower form is present whenever a commodity in general has the capacity of serving human welfare. The higher form, on the other hand, requires a commodity to be not only an efficient cause but simultaneously an indispensable condition of a resultant well-being. . . . The lower stage is termed (by language) *usefulness;* the higher one, *value.*"[70] Two examples are given by Böhm-Bawerk to clarify this difference: the first example is a "man", sitting by "a spring that affords an abundant supply of good drinking water"; the second example, "another man, a traveller in the desert". It is obvious that a cup of water is of quite different significance for the "welfare" of these two persons. In the former case, the cup of water may not be regarded as an indispensable condition; but in the latter case, its utility is of "extreme" degree, since the loss of a single cup of water may have serious consequences for our traveller.

From this, Böhm-Bawerk derives the following formulation of the origin of value: "Commodities achieve value when the available total supply of commodities of this type is so slight as to suffice not at all to cover the demands made for them, or to cover them so insufficiently as to make necessary absolutely the utilization of the specific commodities mentioned, in order that there may be any hope of fulfilling the demand at all." [71]

In other words, the "certified" utility of commodities is taken as the point of departure for an analysis of the prices of commodities since any theory of value serves chiefly to explain prices, *i.e.*, Böhm-Bawerk takes as his point of departure what Marx excludes from his analysis as an irrelevant quantity.

Let us now consider this question in more detail. We must not forget that the point of departure of the Austrian School is the motives of the economic subjects in their "pure", *i.e* simplest, form. "It will now be our task to hold the mirror before the casuistic selecting practice of life, as it were, and to formulate the rules which are applied so surely and instinctively by the common man in action, to formulate them as principles of equal certainty and with the added quality of being conscious." (Böhm-Bawerk: *Grundzüge*, etc., p. 21.) Now let us see how the theoretical "mirror" manipulated by the head of the Austrian School reflects this "practice of life."

It is characteristic of the modern mode of production above all, that it does not produce for the producer's own needs, but for the market. The market is the last link in a chain of varied forms of production, in which the evolution of the productive forces, and the corresponding evolution of the exchange relations have destroyed the old system of natural economy and called forth new economic phenomena. We may distinguish three stages in this process of transformation from a natural economy to a capitalist commodities economy.

At the first stage, the centre of gravity lies in production for one's own consumption; the market receives only the surplus of products. This stage is characteristic of the initial forms of exchange. Gradually the evolution of the productive forces and the threatening of competition leads to a shifting of the centre of gravity in the direction of production for the market. But a small number of the products turned out are consumed in the producer's establishment (such conditions may still be observed frequently in agriculture, particularly in peasant agriculture). Yet this does not involve a cessation of the process of evolution. The social division of labour continues to advance, finally achieving a level at which *mass production for the market becomes a typical phenomenon, none of the products turned out being consumed within the establishment producing them.*

What are the alterations in the motives and in the "practice of life" of the economic subjects, alterations that must parallel the process of evolution described above?

We may answer this question briefly; the importance of the subjective evaluations based on utility lessens: "One sets up (to retain our present-day terminology) no exchange values as yet (determined in a purely quantitative manner), but merely consumption commodities, in other words, objects with qualitative differences." (Werner Sombart, *Der Bourgeois,* p. 19.) But for the higher stages of evaluation we may set up the rule: "A good family head should be concerned more with the *profit* and the durability of objects than with momentary *satisfaction* or with immediate utility." [*Ibid.,* p. 150; italics mine.—*N.B.*]

And indeed, a natural economy presupposes that the *commodities* produced by it will have use value for *this economy.* At the next stage in evolution, the *surplus* loses its significance as use-value; furthermore, the *greater portion* of the products turned out are not evaluated by the economic subject in accordance with utility, the latter being non-existent for the economic subject; finally, and this is the last stage, the entire product turned out within the individual establishment has no "utility" for this establishment. It is therefore precisely the complete absence of evaluations based on the utility of commodities which is characteristic of the economies producing them.[72] Yet it must not be assumed that the state of affairs is thus for the seller alone; the buyer's case is no different. This is particularly manifest in the analysis of evaluation on the part of tradesmen. No business man, from wholesaler down to peddler, ever has the slightest thought of the "utility" or "use-value" of his commodity. In his mind, the content so vainly sought by Böhm-Bawerk is simply non-existent. In the case of purchasers who buy the products for their own use, the matter is a little more complicated; we shall speak below of the purchase of means of production. Here again the path pursued by Böhm-Bawerk leads nowhere. For any "housewife", in her daily "practice", begins both with the existing prices and with the sum of money at her disposal. It is only within these limits that a certain evaluation based on utility can be practiced. If for a certain sum of money, *x*, we may obtain commodity *A*, or, for the sum of money *y*, commodity *B*, or, for money *z*, commodity *C*, each purchaser will prefer the commodity having the greater utility for him. Yet such an evaluation presupposes the existence of market prices. Furthermore, the evaluation of each individual commodity is by no means conditioned by its utility. A plain example is that afforded by objects in daily use; no housewife who must shop in the market estimates the value of bread by its immense subjective worth, on the contrary, her evaluation fluctuates about the market prices already established; the same holds good for any other commodity.

Böhm-Bawerk's isolated man (and it matters very little whether he be seated by a spring or travel over the burning sands) can no longer be compared—from the point of view of "economic motives"—either with the capitalist bringing his wares to market, or with the merchant acquiring these wares to sell them again, or even with the plain purchaser who lives under the conditions of a money commodities economy, whether he be a capitalist or a trader. It follows that neither the concept of "use-value" (Karl Marx) nor that of "subjective use-value" (Böhm-Bawerk) may be taken as the basis of an analysis of price. Böhm-Bawerk's point of view is in sharp contradiction with reality, and yet he had made it his task to explain reality.

The result at which we have arrived, namely, that use-value is not a possible basis for an analysis of prices, also applies to that stage of commodities production in which not all of the product is brought to market, but only the "surplus of the product", since we are dealing not with the value of the product consumed in the original establishment but precisely with the value of this surplus part. Prices originate not on the basis of evaluations of products as such, but of commodities; the subjective evaluations of the products consumed in the establishment itself are without effect on the formation of commodities prices. But insofar as the product becomes a commodity, the use-value ceases to play its former rôle.[73] "The fact that this commodity is useful for others is the necessary condition for its exchangeability; but being useless for me, the use-value of my commodity is not a *measure* even for my own individual evaluation, not to mention any objective value level." (R. Hilferding: *Böhm-Bawerk's Marx-Kritik*, p. 5.)

On the other hand, when exchange conditions have been sufficiently developed, the evaluation of products according to their *exchange* value extends even to that group of products which covers the needs of the producer himself. As W. Lexis very appropriately observed, "in a money commodities exchange system, all goods are regarded and reckoned as *commodities*, even though they be intended for the consumption of the producer." (W. Lexis: *Allgemeine Volkswirtschaftslehre*, 1910, p. 8.)

This is the explanation for Böhm-Bawerk's efforts to represent the modern social-economic organization as an *undeveloped* commodities production; " . . . under the domination of the production based on division of labour and exchange, chiefly surplus products are put on sale." (Böhm-Bawerk: *Grundzüge*, etc., p. 35); in the case of the modern organisation of labour, "each producer produces only a few articles, but far more of these than he needs for his personal uses." (*Ibid.*, p. 491.)

Such is Böhm-Bawerk's presentation of the capitalist "political economy". Of course, it will not hold water; yet it appears again and again in the authors that base their theory of value on the foundation of utility. We may therefore apply literally to Böhm-Bawerk the words Marx uttered on Condillac: "We see in this passage, how Condillac not only confuses use-value with exchange value, but in a really childish manner assumes that in a society, in which the production of commodities is well developed, each producer produces his own means of subsistence, and throws into circulation only the excess over his own requirements." [74]

Marx is therefore perfectly right in refusing to accept use-value as the foundation of his analysis of prices. On the other hand, it is a fundamental error of the Austrian School that "the central principle" of their theory has nothing in common with the capitalist reality of the present day.[75] As will be seen later, this circumstance inevitably influences the entire structure of the theory.

4. *The Measure of Value and the Unit of Value.*

Whereby can we determine the level of the subjective value? In other words; on what does the level of the individual evaluation of "the commodity" depend? It is in their answer to this question that the "newness" of the doctrine advanced by the representatives of the Austrian School, as well as their adherents in other countries, chiefly consists.

Since the utility of a commodity is its capacity of satisfying some need, it is obviously necessary to analyse these needs. According to the doctrine of the Austrian School, we must observe: first, the *variety* of needs; second, the *urgency* of the needs for a specific object of a specific type. The various needs may be classified according to the order of their increasing or decreasing importance for the "welfare of the subject". On the other hand, the urgency of the needs of a particular kind is dependent on the degree in which the satisfaction takes place. The more the need has been satisfied, the less "urgent" is the need itself.[76] It was on the basis of these considerations that Menger set up his famous "scale of needs", which appears in some form or other in all the works on value issued by the Austrian School. We reprint this scale in the form in which Böhm-Bawerk communicates it.

I	II	III	IV	V	VI	VII	VIII	IX	X
10	–	–	–	–	–	–	–	–	–
9	9	–	–	–	–	–	–	–	–
8	8	8	–	–	–	–	–	–	–
7	7	7	7	–	–	–	–	–	–
6	6	6	6	6	–	–	–	–	–
5	5	5	5	5	5	–	–	–	–
4	4	4	4	4	4	4	–	–	–
3	3	3	3	3	3	–	3	–	–
2	2	2	2	2	2	–	2	2	–
1	1	1	1	1	1	–	1	1	1
0	0	0	0	0	0	0	0	0	0

The vertical series, those headed by Roman numerals, represent the various kinds of needs, beginning with the most basic ones. The numbers in each vertical series indicate the decreasing urgency of a need in accordance with the degree of satisfaction.

The table shows, among other things, that the concrete need of an important category may be less in volume than the concrete need of a less important category, according as the need has been satisfied. "Satiation in the vertical series[77] may depress the level of need in the first series down to 3, 2, or 1, while a lower degree of satiation in the series VI may cause this requirement, *theoretically* less important, to be *actually* raised to the degrees 4 or 5."[78]

In order to determine what concrete need is fulfilled by a specific commodity (it is this condition which determines its subjective utility value), we must learn "what need would remain unfulfilled if the commodity to be evaluated were not available; the need is in this case obviously a dependent variable." (Böhm-Bawerk: *Grundzüge,* etc., p. 27.)

On the basis of this method, Böhm-Bawerk arrives at the following result: since all persons prefer to permit less important needs to remain unsatisfied, a commodity will be evaluated in accordance with the least need that it may satisfy. "The value of a commodity is measured by the importance of that concrete requirement or partial requirement which is the least important among the requirements capable of fulfillment by the available stock of commodities of this type." Or, to put it more simply: "the value of a commodity is determined by the degree of its marginal utility." (*Ibid.*, pp. 28, 29.). This is the famous doctrine of the entire School, from which this theory has received its designation, "the Theory of Marginal Utility"; [79] it is the general principle from which all other "laws" are derived.

The above-indicated method of determining value presupposes a definite measure of value. As a matter of fact, the value figure is a result of measurement; but this presupposes a fixed unit of measure. What is Böhm-Bawerk's unit of measure?

It is here that the Austrian School encounters a serious difficulty; one it has not yet surmounted and will never surmount. We must first point out how enormously important is the selection of a unit value from the point of view of Böhm-Bawerk. "The fact is that our judgment of value may, with regard to one and the same type of commodities, at the same epoch, and under the same conditions, be of varying degree, depending on whether only a few specimens or great quantities of the commodity as a unit bulk are subjected to evaluation." (Böhm-Bawerk: *Grundzüge*, etc., p. 15.) Not only does the *degree* of value depend on the selection of the unit of measure, but it may be questioned whether value exist at all. If (to use Böhm-Bawerk's example) a farmer consumes ten gallons of water per day and has twenty gallons available, the water has no value for him. But if we choose as our unit a greater bulk than a ten-gallon quantity, the water will have value. Thus, value as such seems to depend on the choice of a unit. Another phenomenon is connected with the above. Let us assume that we possess a number of commodities whose marginal utility declines with the increase in their numbers. Let us assume that this declining value is expressed in the series 6, 5, 4, 3, 2, 1. If we own six specimens of a certain commodity, the value of each specimen is determined by the marginal utility of this specimen itself, *i.e.*, it will be equivalent to 1. If we take as our unit a combination of two of the former units, the marginal utility of these two units will not be 1×2, but $1 + 2$, *i.e.*, not 2, but 3;

and the value of three units will no longer be 1 × 3, but 1 + 2 + 3, *i.e.*, not 3, but 6, etc. In other words, the value of a greater number of commodities does not vary directly with the value of a specific example of these material commodities.[80] The unit of measure plays an important part. But what is the unit of measure? Böhm-Bawerk gives us no definite answer to this question, nor do the rest of the Austrians.[81] Böhm-Bawerk's answer is this: "This objection is not reasonable. For men cannot choose arbitrarily their unit of evaluation. Since external circumstances that are otherwise uniform . . . may imperatively demand that one quantum rather than another be considered as a unit in the evaluation." (Böhm-Bawerk: *Grundzüge*, etc., p. 16.) Yet it is clear that this unit of measure may be present particularly in the cases in which the exchange of commodities is an accidental phenomenon of economic life, and not its typical phenomenon. On the contrary, the mediators in the exchange of commodities in a developed commodities production do not feel themselves bound to imperative standards in the selection of their "unit value". The manufacturer selling linen, the wholesaler buying and selling linen, a great number of middlemen—all these may measure their goods by the metre and centimetre, or by the piece (a certain large number of metres taken as a unit), but in all these cases there is no difference in evaluation. They dispose of their goods (the modern form of sale is a regular process of disposing of goods by the producer or by any of his confederates); they are indifferent as to the physical unit of measure by which the goods sold are measured. We encounter the same phenomenon in an analysis of the motives of purchasers buying for their own consumption. The matter is quite simple. Present-day "economic subjects" evaluate commodities according to their market prices, but the *market prices* by no means depend on the selection of the unit of measurement.

Another point. We have already seen that the total value of the units according to Böhm-Bawerk is not at all equivalent to the value of a single unit multiplied by the number of units. In the case of series 6, 5, 4, 3, 2, 1, the value of these six units (the value of the entire "supply") is equivalent to 1 + 2

$+ 3 + 4 + 5 + 6$. This is a perfectly logical conclusion from the fundamental assumptions of the theory of marginal utility; yet it is entirely fallacious. The blame lies with the point of departure of the Böhm-Bawerk theory, its ignoring the social-historical character of economic phenomena. As a matter of fact, no one concerned in present-day production and exchange, either as a buyer or a seller, calculates the value of the "supply", *i.e.*, the aggregate of commodities, according to the Böhm-Bawerk method. Not only does the theoretical mirror manipulated by the head of the new school distort the "practice of life", but its image presents no corresponding facts at all. Every seller of n units regards the sum of these units as n times as much as a single unit. The same may be said of the purchaser. "A manufacturer regards the fiftieth spinning machine in his factory as having the same importance and the same value as the first, and the whole value of all fifty is not $50 + 49 + 48 \ldots + 2 + 1 = 1275$; but, quite simply, $50 \times 50 = 2500$." [82]

This contradiction between Böhm-Bawerk's "theory" and actual "practice" is so striking that even Böhm-Bawerk was unable to ignore the difficulty. He has this to say on the subject: "In our ordinary practical economic life, we do not frequently have occasion to observe the above-described casuistic phenomenon [*i.e.*, the absence of a proportional relation between the value of the sum and that of the unit.—*N.B.*]. This is due to the fact that under the system of production of division of labour, commercial sales are drawn chiefly [!] from a surplus [! !] which was originally not intended for the personal needs of the owner. . . . " (Böhm-Bawerk: *Grundzüge, etc.*, p. 35). This is very well, but the question is precisely this: if this "casuistic phenomenon" cannot be ascertained in the present-day economic life, it is obvious that the theory of marginal utility may be whatever you like, but it cannot be a law of capitalist reality, because precisely this "phenomenon" is a logical consequence of the theory of marginal utility in which it takes its logical birth and with which it falls.

We thus see that the absence of proportion between the value of the sum, and the number of added units is, as far as present-day economic conditions are concerned, a pure fiction. It is so emphatically in contradiction with reality that Böhm-Bawerk himself is unable to pursue his own point of view to a logical conclusion. Referring to the great number of indirect evaluations, he states: "But if we are capable of judging that an apple has for us precisely the value of *eight* plums, while a pear has precisely the value of *six* plums, we are also capable of judging, after making a conclusion from these two premises, as our third judgment, that an apple is precisely one-third more valuable to us than a pear." (*Ibid.*, p. 50.) (Böhm-Bawerk is discussing *subjective* evaluations.) This observation is essentially quite correct, but it is not a correct application of Böhm-Bawerk's point of view. For, how do we arrive in this case at the "third judgment" that an apple is one-third "dearer" than a pear? Merely because eight plums are evidently one-third more than six plums. We are here presupposing a proportion to exist between the value of the sum and the number of units; the value of eight plums can only be one-third greater than the value of six plums, if the value of eight plums is eight times the value of one plum, and the value of six plums, six times the value of one plum. This example again shows us how slight is the agreement between Böhm-Bawerk's theory and the economic phenomena of reality. His presentation is perhaps acceptable as an explanation of the psychology of the "wanderer in the desert", the "colonist", the "man" sitting "by the spring", and in these cases only insofar as these "individuals" have no opportunity to produce. In a modern economy motives like those postulated by Böhm-Bawerk are psychologically impossible and absurd.

CHAPTER III

The Theory of Value (Continued)

1. THE THEORY OF UTILITY BY SUBSTITUTION.
2. THE AMOUNT OF MARGINAL UTILITY AND THE QUANTITY OF COMMODITIES.
3. THE FIXING OF THE VALUE OF COMMODITIES IN VARIOUS TYPES OF CONSUMPTION; SUBJECTIVE EXCHANGE VALUE; MONEY.
4. THE VALUE OF COMPLEMENTARY COMMODITIES (THE THEORY OF IMPUTATION).
5. THE VALUE OF PRODUCTIVE COMMODITIES. PRODUCTION COSTS.
6. CONCLUSIONS.

1. *The Theory of Utility by Substitution.*

We now arrive at a point where the new theory runs up against a terrible snag and sails inevitably into destruction, from which not even so skilled a mariner as Böhm-Bawerk can save it.

We have hitherto considered only the simplest cases of an evaluation of commodities. Together with Böhm-Bawerk, we have assumed that the evaluation of commodities depended on the marginal utility of the commodity in question. As a matter of fact, the matter is not quite so simple; Böhm-Bawerk himself says:

"The existence of a developed exchange system may here produce serious complications, for, by making it possible to transform commodities of a certain type into commodities of another type at any moment, it also makes possible the filling of a lack in commodities of one type by means of commodities of another. . . . The lack therefore influences the marginal utility of the substituted new commodities, the marginal utility of the group of commodities of another type here used as a substitute." Böhm-Bawerk: *Grundzüge*, etc., pp. 37, 38.)

The following example is offered by Böhm-Bawerk:

"I have only one winter overcoat, which some one steals

from me. I cannot immediately substitute another unit of the same type for it, having possessed only one winter overcoat. I shall also have but little inclination to bear the loss consequent upon this theft where the loss is felt most directly. . . . I shall therefore seek to transfer the loss to other types of commodities, which I do by acquiring a new winter overcoat in exchange for commodities that might otherwise have been differently applied." (*Ibid.*, p. 38.) Böhm-Bawerk will sell such commodities as have least "importance". Besides direct sale, other cases may occur, depending on the material situation of the "economic subject". If the latter is a wealthy man *"the forty florins that he may have to pay for the new winter overcoat"* [Italics mine.—*N.B.*] may be taken from his available cash, which may result in a corresponding decrease in expenditures for luxuries; if he is neither wealthy nor impoverished, this decrease in his cash supply will oblige him to do without a number of things for a time. Should this also be impracticable, he will sell or pawn a number of articles of household furniture; only in cases of extreme poverty will it be impossible to transfer the loss to other types of needs, and therefore necessary to dispense altogether with a winter overcoat. In all these cases, except the last, the evaluation of the commodities is therefore not an isolated evaluation, but is closely related with the evaluation of other commodities. "I am inclined to believe," says Böhm-Bawerk, "that most of the subjective evaluations that are formed at all are ascribed to *such combined evaluations.* For we hardly ever estimate . . . commodities indispensable to us, by their direct utility, but almost always by the 'substitution utility' of other types of commodities." (*Ibid.*, p. 39; [italics mine.—*N.B.*].)

This discussion approaches reality more closely than the author's preceding statements; but they have a great negative "value" for the "welfare" of the entire theory of Böhm-Bawerk and his adherents. For instance, where does Böhm-Bawerk get his "forty florins", and why forty; why not fifty or one thousand? It is clear that in this case Böhm-Bawerk simply accepts the *market prices* as given. Assuming purchase and sale, or even only purchase, as a necessary condition, he simultaneously also presupposes the objectively given *price.* (*Cf.*

R. Stolzmann: *Der Zweck in der Volkswirtchaftslehre*, 1909, p. 723.) Nor does Böhm-Bawerk ignore this fact, for he formulates this point of view quite clearly. "Yet I should like to emphasise expressly," he observes, "that even in the midst of a developed commercial life . . . we have not always occasion to apply the latter mode of evaluation [*i.e.*, that by "substitution utility".—*N.B.*]. We apply it only . . . when the prices of commodities and simultaneously the cessation of the various types of needs are so situated that a loss occurring within the specific type itself would cause relatively more important requirements to go unsatisfied, than if the purchase price of a replacing specimen should be taken from the satisfaction of other needs." [83]

Böhm-Bawerk therefore admits that in our *subjective* evaluation (he modestly grants that this means *in a majority of cases*) an *objective* real value is assumed. But since his task consists precisely in deriving this value figure from subjective evaluations, it is obvious that the entire doctrine of substitutional utility developed by our author is simply a *circulus vitiosus*: objective value is traced back to subjective evaluations, which in turn are explained by objective value. And Böhm-Bawerk was guilty of this theoretical outrage at the very moment when he was directly faced with the problem of explaining some hypothetical economy having no point of contact with reality, with an actual real economy, characterised by "a developed exchange system." [84] It is interesting to note that Böhm-Bawerk himself recognizes the "serious theoretical difficulty" this point involves for the theory of marginal utility. Yet he attempts to make his escape from this maze of contradictions. Here is his method of saving the face of his theory: the assumption of the winter overcoat at forty florins is based on the "anticipation of a condition which can only be created later on the market." [85] Therefore, "such subjective evaluations have no other influence on their [men's] practical actions on the market than would any general expectation of being able to purchase the necessary commodity at a certain price, for example, forty florins. If the article is obtained at this price, very well; if it is not obtained, one need not go home empty-handed, but may abandon the expectations thus frustrated by reality and consider whether the *general state of one's circumstances* will permit one to continue bidding to a higher level." (*Ibid.*, p. 517.) Böhm-Bawerk makes the decision depend on whether a single market or a number of markets are available to the purchaser. In the former case: "If there is no other market, the purchaser will no doubt continue to bid, if necessary up to the full level of the direct marginal utility he expects from the commodity to be secured." (*Ibid.*, p. 518.) "The purchaser will therefore," concludes Böhm-Bawerk (and this is the result which is important for our theory of prices), "contribute to the formation of the price resultant not in accordance with the lower *direct marginal utility,* constructed on the assumption of a certain market price, *but in accordance with the higher indirect marginal utility.*" In the second case: "the hypothetical evaluation . . . may at any rate [!] cause the customer to transfer his purchase from one part of the market to another; but it cannot prevent him from applying the full pressure of his evaluation, up to the indirect marginal utility, to some part of the entire market." (*Ibid.*, p. 518.) There follows the conclusion: "Subjective evaluations, based on the conjecture that it will be possible to purchase the desired commodity at a certain price, constitute a noteworthy psychical step in our attitude in the market in which this conjecture is to be realised but not a final law of conduct. The latter can only be based on a consideration of the degree of indirect marginal utility." (*Ibid.*, pp. 518, 519.)

This is Böhm-Bawerk's method of disposing of the above-mentioned "theoretical difficulty". Yet his explanation is only imaginary and is made of whole cloth. Let us take the crassest example, that of foodstuffs. Their subjective value, based on utility (let us take a unit corresponding to the lowest limit of satisfaction and the highest limit of utility) is boundless. Let us assume, furthermore, that the evaluation based on an anticipation of market conditions is two rubles. When is the decision to be made, which Böhm-Bawerk assumes? In other words, when will our "individual" decide to pay any price at all, to give "all for a piece of bread"? Obviously this condition may occur only in very unusual market situations.

Not even abnormal situations, but altogether exceptional states must supervene, *i.e.*, where there is no social production at all, no social economy, etc., in the common sense of the word. Such a case may perhaps occur in a "besieged city" (one of Böhm-Bawerk's favourite examples) or on a ship that has run aground on a deserted island, or to the man who wanders in the desert. But *no such thing can occur* in modern life while the social production and reproduction are engaged in their normal course. The process here is quite different. Between the subjective evaluation according to utility and the presumable figure of the market price (in the present case, therefore, between infinity and two rubles) there is a great series of various possible prices (ignoring, for the moment, a possible descent *under* two rubles). As a rule, each single concrete transaction will be concluded on a basis very close to the anticipated prices, and in some cases they will completely coincide, as in a one-price shop. But be this as it may, one thing is plain: assuming a normal course of social production, the relation between the *social* demand and the *social* supply is such as to prevent individual evaluations as to utility from playing any dominant part, in fact, they do not even appear on the surface of the social life at all. (Wilhelm Scharling, *op. cit.*, p. 29; also Lewin: *Arbeitslohn und soziale Entwicklung*. Appendix.)

Our example is appropriate for both of the cases cited above by Böhm-Bawerk. We have still to analyse another case treated by him, namely, purchase for the purpose of resale, in which "a purchaser estimates the commodity entirely according to its (subjective) *exchange* value, and not at all by its use value." [86] In such cases, Böhm-Bawerk represents the condition in the following words: "The market price is first influenced by the (exchange) *evaluation of the trader;* this is based on the conjectured *market price of a second market,* and this, in turn, among other things [!!] on the *evaluation* of prospective purchasers in this second market field." (*Ibid.*, p. 519.) Here the condition is even more complicated. Böhm-Bawerk maintains that the purchaser evaluates the useful article on the basis of the sum of money "one hopes to obtain in another market (allowing also for cost of transportation and handling) for it". This sum of money he analyses into the evaluations of the purchasers (evaluations according to *utility*) in the second market. But the matter is by no means so simple. The trader aims to secure as large a profit as possible, the amount of which depends on a number of circumstances. Böhm-Bawerk himself points out a few: transportation cost, handling expenses (overhead). But this means to Böhm-Bawerk merely the introduction of new series (each having their varying constituent elements) of commercial prices, as quantities requiring no explanation. But actually each ingredient of these costs must be explained. Furthermore, Böhm-Bawerk imagines he has reached the final stage in his explanation when he comes to the evaluations of the purchasers in the second market. Here he deludes himself mightily. For these evaluations may be further subdivided. Surely they cannot be based on pure "utility" alone. For again there are *new* traders who are purchasing the commodity for other markets; on the other hand, even the purchasers for direct use do not evaluate the commodity directly, but also by its "substitution utility". The presence of middlemen obliges us to set forth for a third market also, and since middlemen may again be found there, we may have to travel to a fourth, a fifth market, etc., *ad infinitum.* Furthermore, we have also seen that a further series of trading *prices* and evaluations by substitution utility have been smuggled in by Böhm-Bawerk as *given.* The final fact is that the total phenomenon is really divided into a host of elements of which none can be explained with even a fair degree of satisfaction.

Let us dwell for a moment on a defence offered by Böhm-Bawerk, since it is of general importance; it appears in his attempt to meet the objection that his theory constitutes a *circulus vitiosus.*

"The essential point in the question of such a circle is always that those subjective evaluations based upon the conjectured formation of a concrete market price are different from the evaluations on which this market price itself is based, and vice versa. The apparent circle is due merely to the dialectic similarity of the words used in both cases—'subjective evaluation'—whereas it should actually be explained and emphasised that the same name in these two cases does not indicate one and the same phenomenon, but different phenomena, both being covered by the same general term." (Böhm-Bawerk: *Kapital und Kapitalzins,* vol. II, part I, p. 403, *footnote.*) Böhm-Bawerk attempts to clarify this by the following example: "A parliamentary caucus has adopted the unit rule; its members must vote according to the decision of the majority in the caucus meetings. Obviously the decisions of the caucus are to be correctly explained as the result of a vote of the various members of the caucus, and the later votes of the members in the parliament are to be just as correctly explained by the decision of the caucus; yet this explanation involves no circle at all." (*Ibid.,* p. 403.)

In other words, Böhm-Bawerk seeks to justify himself for having explained *one* set of subjective evaluations by *another* set of subjective evaluations. We may add that the "other" set also has a "third", a "fourth", etc., set after it. The situation is not saved by the fact that these evaluations are *different,* for the theory of production costs, so vigorously combated by the representatives of the theory of marginal utility, also proceeds from *one* cost group to *another;* from *one* price group to *another,* which did not save it from the perpetration of a *circulus vitiosus.* The reason is quite clear; we are not merely tracing phenomena to other phenomena of the same type, but explaining one *category* of phenomena by a different *category* of phenomena. In the former case, we are limited only by the boundlessness of time and space, with the result that any evaluation will lead far beyond the bounds of the present time; we should be practically projecting an endless moving picture in the reverse direction, which would be far from constituting a solution of a *theoretical* problem, but rather an endless retracing of steps. Such a situation is of course not an accident. As has been already stated, Böhm-Bawerk could not help becoming involved in this circle, an inevitable consequence of the individualistic position of the Austrian School. The Austrians do not understand that the individual psychology is conditioned by the social milieu, that the "individual" characteristics of man in society are for the greater part a "social characteristic", that the "social atom" is a figment of the Austrian imagination, similar to Wilhelm Roscher's "feeble proletarian of the primeval forests."[87] The matter proceeds quite smoothly as long as the analysis of "motives" and "evaluations" is concerned only with the make-believe Robinson Crusoe. But as soon as we reach the present day, insurmountable difficulties are met with; we cannot construct a theoretical bridge from the psyche of the "isolated subject" to that of man in an economy of commodities production. But if we proceed from the psychology of the latter, the "objective" elements of the economic phenomena of the commodities economy are already given; consequently they may not be derived exclusively from individual-psychical phenomena without incurring the accusation that one is thus explaining *idem per idem.*

In the theory of substitution utility, the incorrectness of the methodological bases of the Austrian School, and their theoretical insufficiency, become quite clear. The fundamental fallacy of Böhm-Bawerk is his determining of subjective value by objective value, which in turn is derived from subjective value; many solutions of parts of the problem again and again present this same fallacy.[88]

2. *The Amount of Marginal Utility and the Quantity of Commodities.*

In investigating the question as to the level of value, we found that Böhm-Bawerk made it depend on the level of marginal utility. We may now proceed to the further question as to the factors defining this level.

"Here," says Böhm-Bawerk, "we must mention the relation between *demand* and *supply.*" In his analysis of this relation, Böhm-Bawerk discovers the following simple "law", intended as an expression of the relation between "consumption" and "commodities": "The greater and the more important the needs requiring satisfaction, and the less the quantity of commodities available for the purpose . . . the higher 'must' therefore be the marginal utility." (Böhm-Bawerk: *Grundzüge,* etc., p. 40.) In other words, the level of marginal utility is determined by two factors: a subjective factor (needs, requirements), and an objective factor (quantity of commodities). But how is this quantity itself determined? The theory of the Austrian School has no answer to this question.[89] It simply assumes a certain number of products to be present, it presupposes a certain degree of "rarity" to be given for all time. But this point of view is theoretically weak, for the "establishment" whose phenomena are analysed by political economy includes an economic activity and above all the production of economic commodities. The concept of a "supply" of commodities, as A. Schor has quite correctly observed, presupposes a preliminary process of production,[90] a phenomenon which in one way or other must have enormous influence on the evaluation of commodities. Production becomes still more important when we proceed from the static to the *dynamic*. It is obvious that the Austrian theory, starting with the *given* supply of commodities, cannot explain the most elementary phenomena of elementary dynamics, as for example, the movement of prices, not to mention more complicated phenomena. Closely related to this fact is the peculiarity that Böhm-Bawerk's explanation as to the question of the level of value at once calls forth new questions. "Pearls and diamonds happen to exist in such small quantities [!] that the need for them can be satisfied only in small measure, and the marginal utility possessed by its satisfaction is relatively high, while fortunately bread and iron, water and air, are as a rule available in such large quantities as to assure the satisfaction of all the more important needs for these substances." (Böhm-Bawerk: *Grundzüge*, etc., p. 32.)

"Exist,"—"are as a rule available,"—what would Böhm-Bawerk say of the so called "price revolutions", when the increased productivity of labour produces an outright catastrophic fall of prices? We can no longer content ourselves here with the phrase "are as a rule available". The reader has noted with what partiality Böhm-Bawerk chooses his examples. Instead of offering an explanation for the value of typical products, products constituting a commodity, *i.e.* products bearing the stamp of factory production, he prefers to speak of water and air. Even "bread" reveals the insufficiency of our professor's position; we need only recall the sudden drop in grain prices at the beginning of the agricultural crisis caused in the decade 1880-1890 by overseas competition. The "supply of commodities" was altered at once, for the simple reason that new *conditions of production,* never mentioned in a single breath by Böhm-Bawerk, were here concerned.[91] The process of production, however, is not a "complicated circumstance", a "modification of the principal case", as Böhm-Bawerk imagines. On the contrary, production is the basis of the social life in general and of its economic phase in particular. The "rarity" of commodities (except in a few cases which we have a right to ignore) is merely an expression for certain conditions of production, a function of the expenditure of social labour.[92] Therefore an object once "rare" may become very common under altered conditions. "Why . . . are cotton, potatoes and whiskey the fulcra of bourgeois society? Because their production requires least labour and their price is consequently lowest." (Karl Marx: *Poverty of Philosophy.*) But these products do not always play such a rôle. Both cotton and potatoes achieve this importance only on the alteration in the system of social labour, only when the costs of production and reproduction of these products (also of their transportation) have attained a certain level.[93]

In other words, without offering to answer the question as to how the quantum of commodities is determined, Böhm-Bawerk cannot also give an exhaustive answer to the second question as to what determines the various levels of marginal utility.

Together with Böhm-Bawerk, we have thus far been considering the question abstractly. Let us now turn to the "modifying influence" of *exchange* economy. As might have been expected in advance, Böhm-Bawerk's explanations will here be particularly confused.

"The existence of the system of exchange here also produces complications. At any moment, it makes possible a partial fulfilment of a requirement, to be sure at the cost of the fulfilment of other types of needs, which are accordingly abridged. . . . This complicates the circle of factors which influence the level of the marginal utility in the following manner: an influence is exerted, in the first place, by the relation of demand and supply *existing for commodities of the type to be evaluated, throughout the society united by exchange traffic.* For this relation (of demand and supply) influences . . . the level of the price to be paid for the desired replacement specimen, and simultaneously the volume of self-denial that must be practiced as to other types of commodities which must suffer for the replacement. *In the second place,* there is the influence of the relation between demand and supply existing *in the evaluating individual himself, as to the types of needs which must be abridged by reason of the replacement.* For it will depend on this condition whether the abridgment of commodities will affect a low or high level of satisfaction of requirements, in other words, whether it is a small or a large 'marginal utility', that must be dispensed with." (Böhm-Bawerk: *Grundzüge,* etc., pp. 40, 41.) We find, therefore, that the relation between the social demand and the social supply of goods is a factor determining the level of the individual subjective evaluation (or, the level of the "marginal utility"), for it is this relation that determines the price. The higher the price of a certain new object, the higher the subjective evaluation of the old object.

It is not difficult to observe that this question again involves a number of contradictions. In the first place, all we have already said in our analysis of the theory of substitution utility is again applicable here; the subjective evaluation from which price is to be derived really starts from this price. Furthermore, the final circumstance governing price is considered to be the law of demand and supply, which, from the point of view of the Austrians, must be traced back to laws determining the subjective evaluations, in the last analysis to the law of marginal utility. But if price may really be explained satisfactorily by the law of demand and supply, *without further elucidation,* why have a subjective theory of value at all? Finally, since the law of demand and supply may be explained, even according to the theory of marginal utility, only by those laws which determine the subjective evaluations, the "prices" intended as explanations of the subjective evaluations must be themselves explained by the subjective evaluations. In an exchange commodities system, however, even these subjective evaluations are subject to the general law and are dependent on prices.[94] It is the same old song, the old Böhm-Bawerk tune, based on this School's erroneous conception of the relation between the "individual" and the "social aggregate".

3. The Fixing of the Value of Commodities in Various Types of Consumption; Subjective Exchange Value; Money.

We have hitherto considered only cases in which the commodity to be evaluated has satisfied only *one* need; we shall now proceed with Böhm-Bawerk to take up the case in which a single commodity may serve for the satisfaction of *several* needs. "The answer to this question," says Böhm-Bawerk, "is quite simple. The *highest* marginal utility is always the determining one. . . . The true marginal utility of a commodity is identical with the smallest utility *in whose achievement it may be economically used.* Now if various mutually exclusive uses are disputing for an available commodity, it is obvious that a rational economic procedure will assign priority to the most important use. It alone is economically admissible; all less important uses are shut out and can therefore have no influence on the evaluation of the commodity, which is in no case to serve them." (Böhm-Bawerk: *Grundzüge,* etc., p. 52.) From this, Böhm-Bawerk derives the following general formula: *"in the case of commodities alternately permitting of various applications and capable of bringing about a varying level of marginal utility in these uses, the highest of the alternative marginal utility applications is dominant in fixing the level of its economic value."* (*Ibid.,* pp. 52, 53; italics mine.—*N.B.*)

It is the remarkable terminology that most surprises us. "The highest utility of the commodity turns out to be the 'lowest utility' in whose achievement it may be economically used." Why it is just the "smallest" remains completely obscure. But this is not a question touching the essence of the matter. If we apply Böhm-Bawerk's formula to real economic life, we again encounter the fallacy we have met so often, namely, the circle in which his discussions move. As a matter of fact, let us assume a simple case: we have a commodity *A,* with the money obtained from the sale of which we may buy a number of things, *i.e.,* with money *x* we can buy commodity *B,* with money *y,* commodity *C,* with money *z,* commodity *D,* etc. It is obvious that the commodity to be purchased, consequently also the application of the commodity, will depend on the existing market prices; we shall buy this commodity or that, depending on their being dear or cheap at the moment. Similarly, if we are concerned with the choice of the "means of application" of means of production, we make our choice in accordance with the prices of the products of the various branches of production; in other words, the question of "modes of application" presupposes the price, as is rightly observed by Gustav Eckstein. (Gustav Eckstein: "Zur Methode der politischen ökonomie," *Die Neue Zeit,* Vol. XXVIII, part I, p. 371.)

This fallacy reaches its culmination in the theory of *subjective exchange value.*

Böhm-Bawerk distinguishes between two varieties of the "versatility" of commodities, based upon the two varieties of their "application"; namely, the various modes of application are either the result of a "*technical* versatility" of the commodity or that of its capacity of being *exchanged* for another commodity. The latter is the more often the case, the more involved are the exchange relations. The division of subjective value into *subjective use-value* and *subjective exchange-value* [95] is based on this dual significance of the commodity, on its being directly or indirectly a means of satisfying a need, on the one hand (meaning its use as a means of production), or, on the other hand, a means of exchange.

"The magnitude of use-value," says Böhm-Bawerk, "is measured . . . by the level of the marginal utility involved in the commodity to be evaluated, for one's own use. The magnitude of subjective exchange value must therefore be measured by the marginal utility of the commodities to be exchanged for it." (Böhm-Bawerk: *Grundzüge,* etc., pp. 53, 54.) It follows that the magnitude of the subjective exchange value "must depend on two circumstances; first, *on the objective exchange power* (objective exchange value) of the commodity, for the latter determines whether one may obtain many or few commodities in exchange for it; and second, on the condition of the requirements and resources of the owner." (*Ibid.*, p. 54.)

We have quoted Böhm-Bawerk's formulation almost in full, as it is the best expression of the absurdity and contradiction involved in the concept of objective exchange value. Böhm-Bawerk himself tells us that the "measure of the *subjective* exchange value . . . must depend on the *objective* exchange value. . . ." [Italics mine.—*N.B.*]

Here the "objective" world of the market is not smuggled in by a side entrance. On the contrary, the collapse of the theory founded on the sands of the individual psychology becomes apparent in the very *definition* of the standard of subjective exchange value.[96]

It is quite natural that the complete untenability of the Austrian theory should reveal itself most crassly in the question of money.

"The most versatile commodity," says Wieser, "is money. . . . No other commodity affords an opportunity of forming so clear a conception of the notion of marginal utility. . . ." (Friedrich von Wieser, *Der natürliche Wert*, Vienna, 1889, page 13.) This statement by one of the most prominent theoreticians of marginal utility sounds rather ironical when compared with the results attained by the new school in this field. As is well known, money is distinguished from other commodities in being a universal equivalent of commodities. Precisely this property, by virtue of which money is a universal expression of abstract exchange value, makes it extremely difficult to analyse money from the point of view of marginal utility.[97] In actual fact, the agent of the modern capitalist economic order always regards money, in all exchange transactions, exclusively from the point of view of its "purchasing power", *i.e.*, its *objective* exchange value. Not a single "economic subject" would ever think of estimating his available cash supply of gold from the point of view of its ability to satisfy the "need for adornment". In view of the dual use-value of money,[98] namely, as a *commodity* and as *money*, its evaluation touches only the latter function. If, in an analysis of the value of ordinary commodities, it be possible to ascertain the presence of social relations, precluding any individualistic interpretation of economic phenomena (see our analysis of the doctrine of substitution utility, above), these social connections find their fullest expression in the case of *money*. For money is the "commodity" whose subjective evaluation, according to the terminology of the Austrian School, is *subjective exchange* value. In exposing the contradictoriness and the logical untenability of this conception, we have revealed the fundamental error of the entire money theory. Gustav Eckstein ably paraphrases this error: "The objective exchange value of money, therefore, results from its subjective use-value; the latter consists in its subjective exchange value, which in turn depends on its objective exchange value. The final result appears to possess the same cogency and the same value as the famous theorem that indigence is a result of poverty. . . ." [99] In other words, the objective exchange value of money is determined by the objective exchange value of money.

The theory of money and of money circulation may be regarded in a certain sense as a touchstone for any value theory, since money is precisely the most obvious objectivisation of the complicated human relations. Just for this reason, "the enigma of the fetish of gold", which "blinds by its metallic lustre", is one of the most difficult problems for political economy. Karl Marx presented a classic example for the analysis of gold (in *Capital* and in his *Contribution to a Critique of Political Economy*) and those pages of his work concerned with the analysis of money are the finest things ever done in this field. As opposed to this work of Marx, the "theory" of money advanced by the Austrian School plainly reveals the entire theoretical barrenness of all their constructions—their complete theoretical bankruptcy.[100]

4. *The Value of Complementary Goods. (The Theory of Imputation.)* *

One of the most confusing questions treated by the Austrian School is that of the value of the so-called "complementary

* We are using the word "imputation" as an equivalent for the German "*Zurechnung*," following Professor William A. Scott's usage in his English version: *Recent Literature on Interest (1884-1899); a Supplement to Capital*

goods" (Karl Menger) or the "theory of imputation", a term introduced by Wieser.

By complementary goods Böhm-Bawerk understands those goods which mutually complement each other; in this case, "the co-operation of several commodities is required, for the attainment of an economic utility, in such manner . . . that, if one commodity should be missing from the series, the utility could not be attained, or could be attained but imperfectly." (Böhm-Bawerk: *Grundzüge*, etc., p. 56.) Examples of such series of commodities, cited by Böhm-Bawerk, are: paper, pen and ink; needle and thread; the two gloves of a pair, etc. It is obvious that such groups of complementary goods are to be found with particular frequency in production materials, for which the production conditions require the co-operation of a whole series of factors, the omission of even a single factor frequently destroying the total operation and neutralizing the effectiveness of the other factors. In his analysis of the value of complementary goods, Böhm-Bawerk arrives at a series of special "laws", "all operative within the frame of the general law of marginal utility." His point of departure in this analysis is the total value of the entire group, for which he states the following theorem: "The total value of the entire group is determined as a rule by the figure of the marginal utility which they are capable of producing in their combination." (*Ibid.*, p. 56.) If three commodities, *A, B, C,* when used conjointly, are capable of attaining a minimum economic utility of one hundred value units, the whole value of the group will be equal to one hundred. But such simple cases, according to Böhm-Bawerk, are found only "in the general normal case". We must distinguish the special cases from this "normal" one; in the case of the former, the law of substitution is operative, of which we have spoken above (see the analysis of the theory of substitution utility). For example, if the marginal utility in a joint utilisation is 100, "while the substitution value of the three members of the group may individually be only 20, 30, 40, a total of only

and Interest, by Eugen v. Böhm-Bawerk, New York, 1903. A translation of *Capital and Interest* (by Prof. William Smart) appeared in London in 1890.—*Translator.*

90, the attainment of their joint utility of 100 is evidently not dependent on all three taken together, while that of the low utility of 90 is so dependent." (*Ibid.*, p. 57.) Such "subsidiary matters" (matters quite "normal" in capitalist economy, we may add) are apparently of no interest to Böhm-Bawerk; he analyses only the principal case "in which the marginal utility to be obtained by a joint application is simultaneously the true 'value-determining' marginal utility." (*Ibid.*, p. 57.)

In other words, the value of the entire group is assumed as given. The question is merely to determine the proportions according to which the aggregate value is to be distributed to the individual commodities constituting the group. This is the problem of "economic imputation." This economic imputation must be distinguished, according to the Austrian School, from all other economic responsibility: for instance, from legal, moral, and physical responsibility. The earlier theorists, according to Wieser, were guilty of the following fallacy: "They attempt to determine which share of the total product, *physically considered,* has been produced by each factor, or, which share of the effect must be assigned to each physical cause. But it is impossible to determine this." (Friedrich von Wieser: *Der natürliche Wert*, p. 72; also, Peter Struve, *op. cit.*, vol. II, Moscow, 1916, in Russian.) Böhm-Bawerk's attitude is similar; in this matter he agrees thoroughly with Wieser.[101] In distributing values to the various shares in the group, there arise various combinations, which depend, according to the terminology of Böhm-Bawerk, on "the casuistic peculiarity of the case." Let us examine the three fundamental cases distinguished by Böhm-Bawerk.

I. *The given commodities may yield utility only when used together and may not be replaced.* In this case each is the bearer of the total value of the entire complementary group.

II. *The various members of the group may also be put to use elsewhere, outside the given complementary group.* "In this case, the value of the individual article no longer fluctuates between 'nothing' and 'everything' but only *between the magnitude of the marginal utility to which it may give rise unaided, as a minimum, and the magnitude of the total marginal utility of the other members, as a maximum.*" (*Ibid.*, p. 58.) Let us assume that three articles, *A, B, C,* by their joint effect produce a marginal utility of 100; let us assume also that *outside* the complementary group (in another "mode of utilization"), their "isolated values" are: $A = 10$, $B = 20$, $C = 30$; in this case the "isolated value" of *A* is 10. However, the value of *A* as a member of the complementary group (found by assuming *A* to be eliminated and the group consequently destroyed) is equal to $100 - (20 + 30)$, *i.e.*, 50.

III. *Certain members of the group may be replaced.* In this case the law of substitution becomes operative. The general formula covering the case is: "The value of the replaceable members, regardless of their concrete complementary use, is fixed at a specific figure, which determines the degree of their participation when the whole value of the group is distributed to its various members. The distribution is now effected by first assigning their fixed value to the members that can be replaced, to be subtracted from the value of the entire group resulting from its conjoining, and then assigning the remainder—which will vary with the magnitude of the marginal utility—to the non-replaceable members as their individual value." (*Ibid.*, p. 59.) So much for the theory of "economic responsibility" in its general aspect. No doubt the "ascribing" (imputing) of the value of a product to the various production factors constitutes to a certain extent a psychological process that actually takes place.[102] Insofar as we are dealing with *individual* psychological phenomena, such as systems, etc., an ascribing (imputing) of the value of the product to the various "factors" takes place.[103] Of course, whether the study of these phenomena may lead to a satisfactory solution of the problem is another matter. Suffice it here to examine the most typical case, namely, the case in which the introduction of substitution evaluations is a determining factor. Here the question is above all: "What 'value of the product' is to be assigned to the complementary group? What does it represent in the eyes of the capitalist?"

We have seen above that even Böhm-Bawerk puts the evaluations of commodities by their capitalist producers at hardly more than zero. In the eyes of the capitalist, there is no marginal utility of goods as a standard for *his* estimate.

On the other hand, it would be absurd to speak of a "social marginal utility".[104] But it is possible in this case for the capitalist to speak (and he *does* speak) of the *price* of the product, which he imputes now to one operation, now to another operation, of his production capital. It follows that the introduction of one or another production factor for one or another portion of the complementary group depends above all on the *price of the product and by no means on its marginal* utility, as is maintained by Böhm-Bawerk. Furthermore, in our typical case, the portions of the complementary group may be replaced, may at any time be obtained in the market. Nor is it by any means a matter of indifference to our capitalist how much he must pay for this machine or that, or what wages he gives his workers, etc. In other words, he is interested in the *market price of the instruments of production;* on this depends his acquisition of new machinery, his employment of new labour power, his expanding or restricting his production. Finally, there is also another category of objectively given economic quantities—the interest rate. For instance, how shall the peasant evaluate his land? According to Böhm-Bawerk, his estimate takes the following form: "In actual practice, the 'costs' are first deducted from the total yield. The costs are . . . precisely the expenses for the *replaceable means of production of given substitution value.*" (Böhm-Bawerk: *Grundzüge,* etc., p. 60.) The rest the peasant "ascribes" (imputes) to his land. (*Ibid.,* p. 60.) This is what we call rent of land, a capitalisation of which will give the price of the land. There is no need to prove that each parcel of real estate is actually evaluated in this manner, by capitalising the ground rent; any practical instance will confirm this fact. But such an evaluation presupposes the interest rate to be given; the result of the capitalisation depends entirely on the latter.

We thus find that Böhm-Bawerk wrongly describes even the "fetishistic psychology of the producer" since he excludes the "objective" factors always involved as soon as we assume a commodities production and—still more so—a capitalist commodities production.

The theory of "economic responsibility" (imputation) constitutes a direct transition to the theory of distribution, in the representatives of the Austrian School. We shall, therefore, ignore, for the present, a number of questions touched upon by Böhm-Bawerk, since we are to take them up in our analysis of his theory of interest.[105]

5. *The Value of Productive Commodities; Production Costs.*

The classical school of political economy, like Marx, in its analysis of the component elements in the value of consumption commodities, traces this value chiefly to the value of the materials of production that are consumed. Whatever the form of the analysis in a specific case, the underlying idea always was this: the value of the means of production constitutes the determining value factor for commodities that may be reproduced *ad libitum.* But this is not the case with the Austrian theorists. "Their value is equal to the 'prospective value of the prospective yield' in marginal commodities. Just this is the true fundamental idea of the modern system of economy as opposed to the classics. *This idea is that, as we proceed from the value of the articles of consumption, we base our theory of the formation of prices on this value, thus creating the value of the productive commodities, a value* we need in this procedure, by deriving it from that of the consumption commodities." (Joseph Schumpeter: *Bemerkungen,* etc., p. 83; italics mine.—*N.B.*)

Let us examine this fundamental idea more closely. According to Menger's, or rather Gossen's, example, Böhm-Bawerk divides all commodities into categories, depending on their greater or smaller proximity to the consumption process. We thus obtain: (1) consumption commodities; (2) productive commodities, *directly* in contact with certain given consumption commodities, or, "productive commodities of the *first order"*; etc. These latter commodities are called commodities of the "highest" or "remotest" order. How is the value of these commodities of the "highest" order determined? Böhm-Bawerk discusses the matter as follows: each commodity, therefore any commodity of the "highest order", *i.e.,* any instrument of production, may possess a value only when it directly or indirectly satisfies a requirement. Assuming we are dealing with a consumption commodity *A*, a result of the utilisation of the productive commodities G_2, G_3, G_4, (the figures $_2$, $_3$, $_4$ indicating the order of commodities, the degree of their remoteness from the consumption commodity *A*), it is obvious that the marginal utility of commodity *A* will result from commodity G_1. "The marginal utility of *A* will depend on group G_2, as well as on the final product *A* itself." (Böhm-Bawerk: *Grundzüge*, etc., p. 64.) Böhm-Bawerk arrives at the following theorem:

"On all the successive groups of productive commodities of more remote order depends one and the same useful result, namely, the marginal utility of their final product." (*Ibid.*, p. 64.) It follows that: "The magnitude of the marginal utility will express itself first and directly in the value of the final product. The latter then constitutes the guiding line for the value of the group of commodities from which it proceeds; this in turn, for the value of the group of commodities of the third order; the latter, finally, for the value of the final group, that of the fourth order. At each stage, the name of the decisive factor may change; but the same fact is always present under the various names—the marginal utility of the final product." (*Ibid.*, p. 65.) This condition is found whenever we ignore the circumstances that one and the same means of production may serve, and usually does serve, for the production of *various* consumption commodities. Let us assume that the productive commodity G_2 may be utilised in three different branches of production, resulting in the products *A*, *B*, *C*, having respectively marginal utilities of 100, 120, and 200 value units. Böhm-Bawerk resorts to the same reasoning as in the analysis of the value of consumption commodities and infers that the loss of one group of the productive commodities of the category G_2 will lead to a diminishing of that branch of production which furnishes the product having least marginal utility. There results the theorem: "*The value of the unit means of production is determined by the marginal utility and value of that product which among all those commodities for producing which the unit means of production might have economically been used, has least marginal utility.*" (*Ibid.*, p. 69.) This law, according to Böhm-Bawerk, also serves to explain the "classical" law of production costs, in such manner that the value of those commodities whose marginal utility is ***not*** the lowest marginal utility (groups *B* and *C* in our example) are not determined by ***their own*** marginal utility, but by the *value of the means of production* ("production costs"), which depends in turn on the value and marginal utility of the "marginal product", *i.e.*, the product having least marginal utility. In other words, the above-mentioned substitution law becomes operative here. With the exception of the "marginal product", the production costs are, therefore, the determining factor in all the types of "commodities related in production",[106] yet this magnitude itself, *i.e.*, the value of the means of production, is determined by the value of the marginal product, by its marginal utility: " 'In the last analysis' the marginal utility appears as the determining quantity, while the law of production costs appears as a 'particular' law, since the costs are not the final, but always only a medial cause of the value of commodities." (*Ibid.*, p. 71.) So much for the general form of the value of productive commodities according to the new school. Let us now turn to a criticism of this theory, beginning with its fundamental idea, namely, that of the dependence of the value of the means of production on the value of the product.[107] The fall in the price of commodities involved in the progress of industry was the most important empirical fact upon which the "older" theory could work, which stated that the production costs constitute a factor determining the value (or price) of the product. The connection between the decrease in the production costs and the drop in the prices of commodities seemed perfectly clear. We must call Böhm-Bawerk's attention to this phenomenon above all as a touchstone of his own theory. Böhm-Bawerk has the following to say on this subject:

Let us assume, he says, that new deposits of copper have been discovered. This circumstance (unless there should be a great simultaneous increase in the demand for copper) will cause a drop in the value of copper products. The immediate cause of this drop is, therefore, to be found in the field of the productive commodities, which does not mean, as Böhm-Bawerk continues to say, that the original cause is the fall in the value of copper. He represents the process as follows:

the total supply of copper increases; this brings about an increase in copper articles; this circumstance is accompanied by a decreasing value of these products, which, in turn, results in a decrease in the value of the productive commodity (copper).[108]

Let us examine this thesis. In the first place, it is quite clear that each productive commodity may have value so long (whatever be our definition of value: the Marxian objective value, or the Böhm-Bawerk subjective value) as it truly remains a productive commodity, *i.e.*, a means for the production of any *useful* object. Only in *this* sense can we speak of the value of a product as of a "cause" of the value of the productive product.[109] Our assuming the "causal provocation" as precisely the "cause" is quite another matter.

This "causal provocation" emanates, as we have seen, from the field of the productive commodities. The question now is whether we are here dealing only with the total quantity of the means of production—as assumed by Böhm-Bawerk—or whether a lowering of their value is already involved simultaneously with their increased number, as a result of the latter (which would mean that the value of the product is the magnitude to be determined). No doubt we have no reason to *oppose* the total quantity of the means of production to their value.[110] It is particularly clear that a drop in the value, *i.e.*, in the long run, *the price* (see below), of the productive commodities, occurs earlier than the drop in the value of the consumption commodities. Any commodity appearing on the market not only is present in a certain quantity, but also represents a certain magnitude of value. Raw copper, thrown on the market in excessive quantities, will go down in price long before the copper products become cheaper. Böhm-Bawerk finds it possible to urge an objection even here, pointing out that the value of the commodities of "higher order" is not determined by the value of the commodities of "lower order", a value they possess at the moment, but by the value which they *will have* as a result of an increase in the total quantity of the means of production brought about in the total sphere of production.[111] But the distance between the means of production and the consumption commodities is in general so great that even the representatives of the marginal utility theory themselves doubt the dependence of the value of the means of production on the value of the product.[112] It is obvious that an alteration in the quantity of means of production thrown on the market will make it impossible to ascertain any such dependence as is maintained by Böhm-Bawerk. To clarify this question, it is sufficient, in this case, to oppose Böhm-Bawerk's assertions with his own theses, which read: "When we consider what . . . a product of higher, more immediate marginal utility is worth for us, we must confess that it is worth just what the production commodities are worth for us, from which we might at any moment reproduce the product. Continuing in our quest, asking what the means of production themselves are worth, we come to marginal utility. *But time and time again we may spare ourselves this further study. Again and again we are thoroughly aware of the value of the cost commodities without being put to the necessity of evolving it from its foundations in each case. . . .*" In a footnote, he adds: "Particularly, the intervention of the division of labour and of the exchange process contributes much too frequently [!] to causing the value of intermediate products to be fixed independently." (Böhm-Bawerk: *Grundzüge*, etc., pp. 70, 71, *footnote;* italics mine.—*N.B.*)

Unfortunately, Böhm-Bawerk does not pursue this thought; he does not show why the division of labour and exchange should have such a decisive influence on the formation of the "independence" of the value of the productive commodities. As a matter of fact, the process is as follows: Modern society is not a harmoniously developed whole in which production is planfully adapted to consumption; in the present day, production and consumption are isolated from each other, representing two economically opposite poles in the economic life. This severing of production from consumption expresses itself also in economic upheavals, such as crises. The estimates made for products by the agents of production themselves are by no means made in accordance with the "marginal utility"; this holds true, as we have seen, even for consumption commodities; it is even more true in the manufacture of means of production. An anarchically constituted society, in which there is no planful relation at all between the various phases of production, in which the relation is regulated in the last instance by the social consumption, will inevitably lead to a condition of affairs that may in a certain sense be designated as "production for production". This circumstance has its effect, on the one hand, on the psychology of the agents of the capitalist mode of production (an analysis of this psychology is a part of Böhm-Bawerk's task) in a quite different manner than is assumed by Böhm-Bawerk. Let us now begin with the estimates of the sellers of the means of production. They are capitalists whose capital is invested in the branches of production which produce means of production. Whereby is the estimate of the resulting means of production determined on the part of the owner of the specific enterprise? He by no means estimates his commodity ("productive commodities") by the marginal utility of the product manufactured with its aid; rather, he estimates his commodity on the basis of the "price" he can get for it in the market; in Böhm-Bawerk's terminology, he values it according to its subjective *exchange* value[113] Let us now assume that the above-mentioned "producer" introduces a new technique and increases production; he is now in a position to throw a greater number of goods—means of production—on the market. In what direction will the evaluation of the individual unit commodity be altered thereby? It will of course go down. But this decline will not, in his eyes, be effected by the decline in the prices of the products manufactured from his wares, but rather by his own effort to lower prices in order thus to win his competitors' customers and thus attain higher profits.

Let us now turn to the other party to the transaction, the purchasers, in the present instance, the capitalists of the branch of production, producing articles of consumption with the aid of production commodities purchased from the capitalists of the first category (production of production commodities). Their evaluation will of course take into consideration the price at which the product is offered; yet this assumed price of the product may at best serve as an upper limit. Actually the estimate of the production commodities is always lower; and the amount by which the estimate of the production commodities is lessened by the purchasers is in the present instance nothing more nor less than a certain correction of the price, produced by the larger quantity of production commodities thrown on the market. Such is the true psychology of the agents of commodities production. The value of the means of production is in truth fixed more or less independently, and the alteration in the value of the means of production occurs sooner than the alteration in the value of the articles of consumption. In consequence, the analysis must begin with the alterations in the value in the sphere of the production of means of production.

We must again point out a very grave logical fallacy. We saw above that the value of the means of production, according to Böhm-Bawerk, is determined by the value of the product: "In the last instance" the marginal utility of the marginal product is the decisive factor. But what determines the amount of this marginal utility? We already know that the amount of the marginal utility is in inverse ratio to the quantity of the product to be evaluated; the more the units that are available of a certain class of commodities, the lower will go the estimate for each unit in the "supply", and vice versa. The question naturally arises, how is this quantity in turn determined? Our professor tells us: "The total quantity of commodities available in a market region (is) in turn determined . . . in particularly great measure *by the height of the production costs*. For, the higher the production costs of a commodity go, the lower remains, relatively, the number of specimens furnished by production to the demand". (*Ibid.*, p. 521.) This "explanation" may be paraphrased thus: the value of the productive commodities (production costs) is determined by the value of the product; the value of the product depends on its quantity; the quantity of the product is determined by the costs of production, or, in other words, the costs of production are determined by the costs of production. This is another one of the spurious explanations in which the theory of the Austrians is so prolific. Böhm-Bawerk is thus trapped in the same vicious circle in which he rightly observes that the old theory of production is still involved.[114]

In conclusion, let me say a word on Böhm-Bawerk's general formula for the value of means of production. As we have seen, "the value of the unit means of production . . . is determined by the marginal utility and value of that product which, among all those that might have been *economically* used for the production of the unit means of production in question, has the lowest marginal value". (Böhm-Bawerk: *Grundzüge,* etc., p. 69.) Considering, for a moment, the capitalist production, we at once observe that the word "economically", already presupposes the category of *price* as given.[115] This is again an error "immanent" in the entire Austrian School; it arises, as we have shown, from a misunderstanding of the function of the social relations in the formation of the individual psychology of the modern "economic man".

6. Conclusions.

We may conclude our investigation of the subjective theory of value by examining also the *price theory* of the Austrian School, for Böhm-Bawerk considers price, after a fashion, as a resultant of subjective evaluations colliding in the exchange prices on the market. In deriving this resultant, Böhm-Bawerk is obliged to enumerate a number of factors participating in its production, and concerned chiefly with the content, *i.e.,* the quantitative definiteness of the subjective evaluations made by purchasers and sellers contending in the market. In our proof of the contradictions and uselessness of Böhm-Bawerk's assertions concerning these "factors", we shall also recapitulate briefly our previous detailed objections.

Let us first dwell for a moment on Böhm-Bawerk's picture of the mechanism of the exchange process. Böhm-Bawerk considers the exchange process on the basis of its constantly increasing complexity. He recognises four types of the process (1) isolated exchange; (2) one-sided competition between *purchasers* themselves; (3) one-sided competition between *sellers* themselves; (4) "mutual competition", *i.e.,* the case in which both buyers and sellers contend together.

In the first case (isolated exchange), the formula is very simple: *"In the isolated exchange taking place between two persons, the price is fixed within a field whose upper limit is the subjective evaluation of the product by the purchaser, and whose lower limit is its evaluation by the seller.*" (Böhm-Bawerk: *Grundzüge*, etc., p. 493.)

In the second case (competition between buyers) Böhm-Bawerk sets up the following theorem: "*In a one-sided competition between prospective purchasers, the competitor most capable of exchange, i.e., he having the highest estimate of the commodity as compared with the price, will obtain the commodity. The price moves between the evaluation of the obtainer as an upper limit, and that of the most exchange-capable of his excluded competitors as the lower limit, constituting at each moment the purchaser's own evaluation.*" (*Ibid.*, p. 494.)

The case in the third type, namely, in that of one-sided competition between sellers, is similar; here the limits within which the price fluctuates are determined by the *lowest* estimate of the strongest (or, to use Böhm-Bawerk's term, "the most exchange-capable") seller and the estimate of the strongest among his defeated competitors.

Of course, the most interesting case is the fourth, that of competition between all the buyers and sellers. This is the typical example of exchange transactions within any fairly developed exchange economy.

For this type, Böhm-Bawerk presents a case in which ten buyers seek to purchase a horse while eight sellers wish to sell one. The following table gives the individual estimates assumed by Böhm-Bawerk:

BUYERS

A1	estimates	the	value	at	300	florins.
A2	"	"	"	"	280	"
A3	"	"	"	"	260	"
A4	"	"	"	"	240	"
A5	"	"	"	"	220	"
A6	"	"	"	"	210	"
A7	"	"	"	"	200	"
A8	"	"	"	"	180	"
A9	"	"	"	"	170	"
A10	"	"	"	"	150	"

SELLERS

B1	asks	for	his	horse	100	florins.
B2	"	"	"	"	110	"
B3	"	"	"	"	150	"
B4	"	"	"	"	170	"
B5	"	"	"	"	200	"
B6	"	"	"	"	215	"
B7	"	"	"	"	250	"
B8	"	"	"	"	260	"

Let us assume that the buyers begin by offering 130 florins; all of them would be willing to obtain horses at this price, but only two of the sellers (B1 and B2) would consent to meet their price. This being the case, the exchange obviously cannot be realised since the sellers would doubtless utilise the competition between the buyers to bring about a higher price. Likewise the competition among the buyers themselves would prevent the *two* buyers from finishing their transactions at 130 florins per horse. As the price rises, the number of competitors among the purchasers will decrease; for instance, if the price exceeds 150 florins, purchaser A10 also is eliminated, while a price exceeding 170 florins will eliminate purchaser A9, etc. On the other hand, as the number of purchasers decreases, the number of sellers increases, who will be enabled economically to take part in the exchange transaction. At the price of 150 florins, B3 can also sell his horse; at a price of 170 florins, even B4, etc. At a price of 200 florins, there is still competition among the purchasers. But the situation changes if a further increase in price takes place. Let us assume that the price rises above 200 florins. Now supply and demand balance each other. The price cannot rise above 200 florins, for in this case purchaser A5 will be eliminated, with the result that the competition between the *sellers* would lower the price; in the given case, the price could not even rise to 215 florins, for now there would be six sellers and only five purchasers. *The resulting price will be somewhere between 210 and 215 florins.*

It follows, in the first place: the exchange will be effected *"by the most exchange-capable competitors on both sides;*

namely, the purchasers who estimate the unit highest (A1 to A5) and the sellers who estimate it lowest (B1 to B5)." (*Ibid.*, p. 499.)

In the second place, "as many of the competitors on each side will effect an exchange as there are pairs resulting from a juxtaposition of the competitors according to the descending order of their exchange-capacity, within which pairs the prospective purchaser estimates the article at a higher price than the seller." [116]

In the third place: *"In a mutual competition between all parties, the market price will be fixed between an upper limit constituting the evaluations of the last purchaser available for exchange and that of the most exchange-capable of the excluded prospective sellers, and a lower limit fixed by the evaluations of the least exchange-capable of the sellers who effect an exchange and the most exchange-capable of the prospective buyers excluded from exchange."* (*Ibid.*, p. 501.) Taking these pairs as "limiting pairs" we *obtain* the following formulation of the price law: *"The magnitude of the market price is limited and fixed by the magnitude of the subjective evaluations of the two limiting pairs."* (*Ibid.*, p. 501.)

So much for the *mechanism* of competition, *i.e.*, the process of price formation considered from the *formal* aspect. Essentially this is nothing more or less than an amplified formulation of the old law of supply and demand. Therefore this formal aspect of the matter is less interesting than its content, the quantitative determination of the exchange process. But let us insert a third observation. In determining the "general rules" moving those who take part in the exchange, Böhm-Bawerk formulates the following three "rules": "He [the candidate in the exchange process] will in the first place *not exchange at all unless the exchange brings advantage to him;* he will, in the second place, *rather exchange with a large advantage than with a small one;* and in the third place, he will *rather exchange with slight advantage than with none at all."* (*Ibid.*, p. 489.) The first of these three rules is fallacious, for there are cases in which the sellers accept an exchange though it may mean a loss, recognising the principle that a small loss is better than a big one. Such is the case, for instance, when capitalists are obliged by market conditions to sell their goods below cost of production. Böhm-Bawerk himself states, in another passage, that only "a sentimental fool" could under such conditions refuse to sell his goods. In this case the original valuation for which the seller came to market is defeated by the elemental force of the market conditions, which obliged him to accept an exchange involving loss to his business. Let us now touch upon the factors determining the level of prices in accordance with the above formal "price law". Böhm-Bawerk enumerates six such factors: (1) the number of specific demands for the commodity; (2) the absolute magnitude of the subjective value of the commodity for the prospective purchaser; (3) the absolute magnitude of the subjective value of the price money for the prospective purchaser; (4) the number of specimens of the commodity available; (5) the absolute magnitude of the subjective value of the commodity for the sellers; (6) the absolute magnitude of the subjective value of the purchase money for the sellers. Let us note how Böhm-Bawerk considers each of these factors conditioned.

(1) *The number of specific demands for the commodity.* Böhm-Bawerk has the following to say on this point: "Very little that is not self-evident can be said of this factor. It is obviously influenced on the one hand by the extent of the market, and on the other by the character of the need. Furthermore—and this is the sole remark of theoretical interest to be made here—not every one who wishes to *possess* the commodity by virtue of his needs constitutes thereby a *prospective purchaser*. . . . Countless persons who need a commodity and wish to own it nevertheless voluntarily [!] absent themselves from the market because their evaluation of the purchase money, *in view of the presumable level of prices* [Böhm-Bawerk's italics], so far exceeds their evaluation of the goods as to preclude any economic possibility of their effecting a purchase." (*Ibid.*, pp. 514, 515.) In other words, the "number of demands" is fixed as the number of possible demands minus the number of demands that are self-precluded from purchase; the latter depends on the *market prices,* which in turn appear to be determined by the "number of demands".

(2) *The estimation of the commodity by the purchasers.* On this point, Böhm-Bawerk writes: "The magnitude of the value is determined . . . in general by the magnitude of the marginal utility." (*Ibid.*, p. 515.) We have already examined this principle at length and have found that the purchasers by no means evaluate the commodity by its marginal utility. The corrective which Böhm-Bawerk seeks to introduce in the form of his *substitution* theory is merely, however, a theoretical circle.

3) *The subjective value of the commodity for the prospective purchasers.* All of Böhm-Bawerk's elucidations are concentrated in the following sentence: "In general, therefore, the rich man will put a lower subjective value on the unit of money than the poor man." (*Ibid.*, p. 520.) In its essence, the theory of money consists in the fact that the subjective value of money—for sellers as well as for buyers—is its own subjective *exchange value*, which is in turn determined by the market prices of the commodities. Thus, this "determination of prices" is explained by the prices themselves.

(4) *The number of specimens of the commodity available,* The determining factors are (a) purely natural conditions (such as limited available real estate); (b) social and legal conditions (monopolies); (c) "in particularly great extent, however", *the magnitude of the production costs.* But we find no explanation for the latter figure, as pointed out above, in Böhm-Bawerk's theory, since this quantity is determined on the one hand by the product's marginal utility and on the other hand by the product itself.

(5) *The subjective value of the commodity for the seller.* Böhm-Bawerk formulates this matter in two ways: The first is that " . . . the immediate marginal utility and also the subjective consumption value possessed by a single specimen in their [the sellers'] eyes *is usually extremely low*". (*Ibid.*, p. 521.) This formulation, as has been shown in detail, is not in accordance with fact, since there exists no evaluation of the commodities offered for sale, according to their utility, *i.e.*, this evaluation is mathematically equal to zero. On the other hand, it is obvious that the sellers estimate the value of their commodities and do not put it "extremely low". Now let us

see Böhm-Bawerk's second formula. "The magnitude of the market price", he says elsewhere, "to be achieved by each producer for his product is decisive for the magnitude of the subjective (exchange) value which he assigns to it". (*Ibid.*, p. 538.) Yet this formulation is theoretically even less tenable, since the very concept of subjective value constitutes a contradiction in itself; it is sometimes the basis for the formation of prices while at other times it assumes the prices to be given.

(6) *The subjective value of the price money for the sellers.* "On this point," says Böhm-Bawerk," we may again apply, in general, what has been said above on the value of purchase prices for the purchasers. Now, it may be true for the sellers more frequently than for the buyers that the value they place upon the purchase price in money depends not so much on the general condition of their fortune as on a specific need for cash." (*Ibid.*, p. 521.) We have accordingly to distinguish two factors: (a) the evaluation of money in accordance with one's "general condition of fortune"; this evaluation arises under the influence of two factors: the amount of money at the disposal of the owner, and the *prices of commodities;* (b) the evaluation of money in accordance with the "specific need", *i.e.*, the market situation, which again means simply "a specific condition of market prices". We thus find that the peculiar nature of money as an exchange value does not permit this phenomenon to be explained from the point of view of utility, with the result that Böhm-Bawerk's theory inevitably moves in a circle.

"In the whole course of the process of price formation, therefore," Böhm-Bawerk says, "there is indeed . . . not a single phase, not a single trait, that cannot be traced back completely to the condition of subjective evaluations as its cause, and we have every right, therefore, to regard a price as the resultant of the subjective evaluations of commodity and purchase money which come into contact on the market." (*Ibid.*, p. 503) But this view, as we have already shown in our first section, is fallacious; it does not consider the fundamental fact of the social relation between men, a relation given at the outset and determining the individual psyche of each person concerned, by informing it with social content. Whenever the Böhm-Bawerk theory, it appears, resorts to individual motives as a basis for the derivation of social phenomena, he is actually smuggling in the social content in a more or less disguised form in advance, so that the entire construction becomes a vicious circle, a continuous logical fallacy, a fallacy that can serve only specious ends, and demonstrating in reality nothing more than the complete barrenness of modern bourgeois theory. Thus, we have seen in our analysis of his theory of prices, that of the six "determining factors" in the formation of price, not a single one is in reality well supported by Böhm-Bawerk. The Böhm-Bawerk theory of value has been unable to explain the phenomenon of prices. The peculiar fetishism of the Austrian School, which provides its adherents with individualistic blinders and thus shuts off from their view the dialectic relation between phenomena—the social threads passing from individual to individual and alone constituting man a "social animal"—this fetishism precludes any possibility of their understanding the structure of modern society. The Marxian School is still the only one capable of offering a solution to this problem.

CHAPTER IV

The Theory of Profit

1. The Importance of the Problem of Distribution; Formulation of the Question.

We may observe in any specific branch of political economy the peculiarity that it will be developed in a direction depending on who it is that works the field; this is particularly true of the theory of distribution, and more particularly of the theory of profit. For this problem is too closely concerned with the "practice" of struggling classes; it touches their interests too strongly, and we shall naturally expect to find here a more or less crude or delicate—as the case may be—apology for the modern order of society, an apology which it is impossible to conceal. No doubt great importance must be assigned, from the standpoint of logic, to the question of distribution, which Ricardo termed one of the most essential problems of political economy. (David Ricardo: *Principles of Political Economy and Taxation,* Preface.) It is impossible to understand the laws of social evolution—as far as modern society is concerned—without undertaking an analysis of the process of reproduction of social capital. One of the very first attempts to grasp the motion of capital—we refer to Quesnay's famous economic table—necessarily devoted considerable space to the plan of distribution. But even aside from the problem of grasping the mechanism of the entire capitalist production in all its compass, in its "complete social measure", the problem of distribution as such is of immense theoretical interest. What are the laws governing the distribution of goods among the various social classes? What are the laws of profit, of rent, of wages for labour? What is the relation existing between these categories, and what is their magnitude at each given epoch? What are the tendencies of social evolution determining this magnitude? These are the fundamental questions investigated by the theory of distribution. While the theory of value analyses the comprehensive fundamental phenomenon of the production of commodities, the theory of distribution must analyse the antagonistic social phenomena of capitalism, of the class struggle, which assumes new specific forms characteristic of the commodities economy as such. It is the task of a theory of capitalist distribution to show how this class struggle has assumed its capitalist formulation, in other words, how this struggle manifests itself in the form of economic laws.[117] To be sure, by no means all theorists conceive the tasks of a theory of distribution in this manner. Even in the formulation of the problem, two fundamental tendencies may be detected. We find here, says N. Shaposhnikov, one of the latest students in this field, "two diametrically opposed points of view, only one of which can be correct". (Shaposhnikov, *op. cit.*, p. 80.) The difference is in the fact that one group of economists seeks to explain the origin of the so called "income without labour" by means of the eternal and "natural" conditions of human management, while the other views this phenomenon as a consequence of the specific historical conditions, or, in concrete language, as a result of the private property in the means of production. Yet a more comprehensible formulation may be given of this problem, for, in the first place, we are not dealing merely with "income without labour", but also with "income from labour" (for instance, the concept of wages for labour is a correlative to that of profit, standing and falling with the latter); in the second place, the question as to the forms of distribution may be put in general form, *i.e.*, it may concern not only the forms of capitalist distribution, but also the universal dependence of the forms of distribution on the forms of production. An analysis of this question yields the following result: in its functional aspect, the process of distribution is nothing more or less than the process of reproduction of the conditions of production; every historically determined form of production relations presents an adequate form of distribution reproducing the given production relation. Thus, for instance, with capital: "The capitalist process of production is an historically determined form of the social process of production in general. This process is on the one hand the process by which the material requirements of life are produced, and on the other hand a process which takes place under specific historical and economic conditions of production, and which produces and reproduces these conditions of production themselves, and with them the human agents of this process, their material conditions of existence and their mutual relations, that is, their particular economic form of society." (Marx: *Capital,* vol. III, p. 952.) The process of *capitalist* distribution, which also proceeds in quite specific historical forms (purchase and sale of labour power, payment of their value by the capitalists, origin of surplus value), is merely an ingredient, a specific phase of this process of the capitalist mode of production as a whole. While the relation between capitalist and worker is the fundamental production relation of capitalist society, the forms of capitalist distribution—the categories of wages for labour and of profit—reproduce this fundamental relation. Unless, therefore, we confound the process of production and distribution "as such" with their economic-historical forms at the moment—which determine the "economic social structure", *i.e.,* the provisional type of human relations—we may attain a definite result, as follows: in order to explain any concrete social structure, we must conceive it merely as a specific historically developed type of relations, *i.e.,* as a type with historical limits and peculiarities of its own. The bourgeois political economy, by reason of its limitations, never transcends the bounds of *general* definitions. "Political economists have confused or confounded the *natural* process of production with the *social* process of production, which is very definitely conditioned by property in land and capital, arriving as a result at a conception of capital for which there is no parallel in the *real* world of political economy." (Karl Rodbertus: *Das Kapital,* p. 230.) Yet even Rodbertus left a little loophole for himself, when compared with the rigorous and consistent system of Karl Marx, by isolating the "logical" concept of capital as a category peculiar to all forms of economy; but this is entirely superfluous from the standpoint of terminology (since this concept is well covered by the words "means of production") and has dangerous possibilities, since it leads not infrequently to the habit of smuggling in a solution of *social* problems of entirely different type under the cloak of innocent discussions as to the means of production ("capital").

Once we have set ourselves the task, therefore, of investigating the nature of distribution in *modern* society, we can attain our object only by keeping sight of the peculiarities of capitalism. Marx has briefly and brilliantly formulated this view in the following sentence: "Wage labour and private land, like capital, are historically determined social forms; one a social form of labour, the other, a social form of the monopolized terrestrial globe, and both forms belong to the same economic formation of society corresponding to capital." (Marx: *Capital,* vol. III, p. 949.) In his theory of profit, Böhm-Bawerk, as might be expected after our investigation of his theory of value, proceeds entirely along the path of those economists who consider it appropriate to "derive" profit not from the historical conditions of social production, but from its *universal* conditions. This fact alone should be sufficient to condemn his "new paths";[118] for we might rightly say of all the economists who regard profit, land rent, and wages for labour, not as historical categories, but as "logical categories", that they have "gone astray".[119] We have already seen from the preceding treatment whither Böhm-Bawerk's unhistorical point of view in his theory of value has led him. But this same point of view leads him into still greater contradictions and conflicts with reality when he applies it in his theory of distribution, particularly in that of profit.

2. *The Concept of Capital; "Capital" and "Profit" in the "Socialist" State.*

Böhm-Bawerk begins his analysis of the concept of capital by having his old favourite, the "isolated man", work both "with his bare hands" as well as with means of production produced by himself. From this, Böhm-Bawerk infers that there are two modes of production in general: "Either . . . we evaluate our work immediately before its consummation . . . or we intentionally resort to a roundabout method" (Böhm-Bawerk: *Positive Theorie*, p. 15,) *i.e.*, we either proceed directly to the goal or engage in certain preliminary operations (the production of the means of production). Since man, in the latter case, obtains the aid of the forces of nature, "stronger than his bare hands", it is more efficacious to resort to the "roundabout way" than to work with one's "bare hands" alone.

These general statements are a sufficient foundation, in Böhm-Bawerk's eyes, for a definition of capital and of the capitalist mode of production.

"Production, when it resorts to wise detours, is nothing more or less than what political economy terms *capitalist* production, while production depending on its bare hands alone represents production without capital. *But capital is nothing more or less than a general term for all the intermediate products arising at the various stages of this extended detour.*" (*Op. cit.*, p. 21.) In another passage: *"Capital is the general term for products serving as a means for the acquisition of goods.* From this general concept of capital we may isolate that of *social* capital as a narrower concept. Social capital is our term for the group of products serving as a means of the social-economic acquisition of commodities; or . . . since a social-economic consumption of commodities can take place only in production . . . or, in brief, a general term for intermediate products." [120]

The definitions quoted above are sufficient to characterise the "foundations" of the Böhm-Bawerk theory of profit; this theory cloaks the social character of the modern mode of production and—what is worse in this case—conceals the nature of this mode of production as a capitalist production in the true sense of the word, a production based on wage labour, on a monopoly of the means of production by a specific social class; the theory thus completely eliminates the characteristic trait of modern society, its class structure, which is torn by internal contradictions, by a savage class struggle.

What are the logical foundations for such a construction? Böhm-Bawerk reasons as follows: at all the stages of social evolution, there are "paths of production"; in connection with these there are many phenomena connected with the final *results* of production. These phenomena may, depending on the concrete historical conditions (for instance, private property), assume different *forms*.

But we must here distinguish between the essence and the "form" of the manifestation. Precisely for this reason it is necessary, in a thorough scientific investigation, to undertake an analysis of "capital", of "profit", of the "capitalist mode of production", not in their present formulation, but in the abstract. Such is Böhm-Bawerk's point of view in general.[121] Furthermore this is all that may be said in favour of his point of view, or of other attempts to represent capital and profit as "eternal" economic categories. Even if a distinction between the "essence" and the "form of manifestation" is perfectly proper as such, it is not in place here. In fact, the concept of "capital", "capitalistic", etc., is not associated with the idea of social harmony, but with that of class struggle. Böhm-Bawerk himself is well aware of this. In his criticism of the economists who include the concept of labour power in the concept of capital, he says: "The learned as well as the laity have long been accustomed to dispose of social problems under the catchword of capital, in which practice they have had in view not a concept also embracing labour, but a *contradiction* to labour. Capital and labour, capitalism and socialism, interest on capital, and wage labour, may certainly not be considered as innocent synonyms. They are rather the slogans of the most powerful social and economic conflicts that may be conceived."[122] This is all very well, but a recognition of the fact should oblige one to proceed consistently and not content onself with the "habits of the laity" and the "learned", but to place the *class contrast* in a capitalist commodities economy consciously in the foreground of one's investigations. *This means that the trait of the class monopoly in the means of production, as practised under the conditions of the commodities economy, must be included in the concept of capital as its most essential constituent determining factor.*

Böhm-Bawerk's concept of capital retains the old notion of the means of production (*cf.* his "intermediate products") whose manifestation in present-day society is "capital". And, therefore, the means of production monopolised by the capitalists, according to Böhm-Bawerk, are not indeed the *manifestations of capital* peculiar to modern society, but are capital as such; but they are a "manifestation" of the means of production *as such,* having no relation whatever to any concrete historical structure.

The question may also be approached from another angle. If *all* the "intermediate" products are capital, how may the intermediate products in the *modern* order of economy be distinguished? Let us assume—ridiculous though this assumption may be at bottom—that profit will exist even in the "socialist state"; this "profit" would now fall into the hands of the entire society, while in the modern order of economy it accrues to a single *class.* This difference is more than to the point. But Böhm-Bawerk fails to furnish a word to represent "present-day" profit, although we have seen how vigorously he belabours his opponents, criticising them for being guilty of precisely his own omissions. In his criticism of the application of the concept of capital to the soil, in which he refers to the principle of the "terminological economy," he says: "If we apply the name *capital* to *all* physical means of acquisition, then the narrower of the competing concepts, and, together with it, the corresponding branch of income, will remain nameless in spite of its great importance." (*Ibid.,* p. 87.) Yet it is obvious that the difference between "profit" in the socialist state, which presupposes the absence of classes, and the "profit" of the present day, is far greater and more important than the difference between profit and rent. In the former case, we are dealing with the difference between a class society and a classless society; in the latter case, only with the difference between two classes in the same society, belonging, in the last analysis, to merely the same class category, namely, that of proprietors and owners.

The absurdity of the Böhm-Bawerk terminology is further increased by the fact that his concept of an "uncapitalistic" production in reality corresponds to no economic fact at all;

production with "one's bare hands" is one of Böhm-Bawerk's numerous make-believes. And, on the other hand, he transforms the savage poking his stick into the ground into a "capitalist" who conducts a "capitalist" economy and even secures "profits"! But if *any* production (there being no production without means of production) is to be considered as "capitalist", certain distinctions must really be drawn within the realm of these capitalist productions, for it will continue to be necessary to point out differences between the "capitalist" *capitalist* mode of production, the "capitalist" *socialist* mode of production, the "capitalist" *primitive communist* mode of production, etc. But Böhm-Bawerk offers us only one term for these three different varieties of "capitalist production."

An excellent illustration of the confusion which Böhm-Bawerk introduces into the science is the section entitled "Interest in the Socialist State". Even in this "State" the principle of profit is to retain full validity, although we recognise this principle as a consequence of exploitation. Böhm-Bawerk expounds this "socialist exploitation" as follows: "Let us assume the existence of two branches of production: the baking of bread and forestry." The yield of a day's labour on the part of the baker is the product in bread, estimated by Böhm-Bawerk at two florins (Böhm-Bawerk assumes that the florins will also be retained by the "Socialist State"). A day's labour on the part of the forestry worker will consist of the planting of 100 young oak trees, which after the lapse of a century will be transformed into great trees without further labour, with the result that the total value of the forestry worker's labour will amount to 1000 florins. This fact, namely, the difference in time in production (our general appreciation of Böhm-Bawerk's reasoning in this connection will be given below) is precisely the element Böhm-Bawerk makes responsible for the origin of profit. "But if we pay," he says, "no more to the forestry workers than to the bakers, namely, two florins per day, we are guilty of the same 'exploitation' toward them as is now practiced by capitalist employers." (*Ibid.*, p. 583.)

During the lapse of one hundred years there is an increment of value, and this "surplus" "is pocketed by society and thus taken away from the workers producing it; in other words, others enjoy the fruit of labour." "In distribution, it [the interest] accrues to persons in no way connected with those by whose labour and output it was earned . . . to *other persons* precisely as to-day [!], who draw their claim not by the right of labour but from the claims of property, or, *share in* property." (*Ibid.* p. 584.)

This thought is wrong from start to finish. Even in a socialist society there will be no increment of value from the soil.[123] It will be a matter of indifference to a socialist society whether labour is applied to the direct production of articles of consumption or to some "more remote purpose", since labour in such a society is performed according to an economic plan drawn up in advance, and the various categories of labour are considered as parts of a general social labour, all of which is necessary for an uninterrupted progress of production, reproduction and consumption. Just as the products of the units of various remoteness are being consumed uninterruptedly and *simultaneously,* so the processes of labour, however different their goals, also proceed with the same quality of continuousness and simultaneity. All the parts of the general social labour are fused in a unified indivisible whole, in which only one factor is of importance in determining the share of each member (after deductions going to the fund of means of production), namely, the *amount* of labour put in. Even Böhm-Bawerk's example will show this; in speaking of bakers, whose labour product is *bread,* he forgets completely that bread is by no means the labour product of the bakers only, but of all the workers, beginning with those employed in agriculture; the work of the baker is merely the final link in a long chain. When the forestry workers are repaid in products corresponding to their labour, they thus obtain social labour units of varying degrees of remoteness, *i.e.,* their situation with regard to the other members of society is the same as that of any other labour category, for, as we have said, where there is a fixed economic plan, the importance of labour does not depend on "the remoteness of its goal".[124]

But there is another more important phase of this question. Let us assume that the socialist society obtains a certain surplus in "value" in a given production cycle (it is of no importance to us in this case to know *why* it obtains it and on the basis of *which* "theory of value" the estimation of the product is to be made). Böhm-Bawerk agrees that this "surplus value" "serves for a general improvement of the wage quota [!] of the people's workers". But this obviously removes every foundation for an interpretation of the surplus obtained, as profit. Yet here Böhm-Bawerk raises the following objection: "Profit," he says, "does not cease to be profit because it is placed in a relation with the purpose of use, for no one will venture to claim that the capitalist and his profit cease to be capitalist and profit because some business man has accumulated a fortune of millions and then disposes of it in public benefaction." (*Ibid.*, p. 583.)

This "objection" at once reveals the basic fallacy of Böhm-Bawerk's position. Why will no one "venture to maintain" that profit ceases to exist merely because capitalists are addicted to charitable donations? The reason obviously is that such cases are isolated, have no influence at all on the general structure of the social-economic life. They do not destroy the class nature of profit, they do not destroy the category of income, appropriated by the *class* as a result of its monopoly of the means of production. No doubt the case would be different if the capitalists as a *class* should renounce their profits and expend them in works of public interest. In this—entirely impossible—case, the category of profits would disappear and the economic structure of society would assume a different aspect from that of capitalist society. The monopolisation of the means of production would entirely lose its meaning from the point of view of the private employer, and capitalists as such would cease to exist. This brings us face to face once more with the *class character* of capitalism and of its category—profit.[125] And it requires an incredible daltonism to prevent one from grasping this *class* character and to enable one to say such things as: "Even the lonely economy of Robinson Crusoe could not be completely lacking in the fundamental trait of interest." (Böhm-Bawerk: *Positive Theorie*, p. 507.) How shall we explain this daltonism? Böhm-Bawerk himself affords an excellent explanation. "Even in our circles" [*i.e.*, among bourgeois economists—*N.B.*], he says, "we are much addicted to covering up uncomfortable contradictions, to passing carelessly over thorny problems." This open confession best reveals the psychological basis on which it is possible to escape recognising the contradictory social economy and to seek refuge in artificially devised constructions dragged in by the hair, in order to *justify* present-day reality. "Even Böhm-Bawerk's theory of interest on capital," says Heinrich Dietzel, "which arose on the basis of the theory of marginal utility, is intended not only to explain the phenomenon of interest, but also to contribute material for refuting those who attack the institution of interest". (Heinrich Dietzel: *Theoretische Sozialökonomik*, p. 211.) This apologetic activity induces Böhm-Bawerk to behold cases of interest even where there are neither classes nor an exchange of commodities (Robinson Crusoe, the socialist state); it induces him to derive the social phenomenon of interest from the "universal qualities of the human mind". We shall now proceed to an analysis of this remarkable theory, the success of which can be explained only by assuming a complete demoralisation of bourgeois political economy.

3. General Description of the Capitalist Production Process; The Formation of Profits.

As we have already seen, Böhm-Bawerk defines as capitalist production a production achieved with the aid of means of production, or, to use his language, "proceeding along a roundabout path". This "capitalist" mode of production presents both an advantageous and a disadvantageous aspect; the former consists in its producing a greater number of products; the latter is due to the fact that this increase is connected with a greater loss of time. As a consequence of preceding operations (the production of means of production and of all intermediate products in general), we do not obtain articles of consumption at once, but after a comparatively long time: "The disadvantage associated with the capitalist mode of production lies in the *loss of time*. The capitalist détours are profitable but time-consuming; they furnish more or better consumption articles, but they furnish them later." This theorem is one "of the fundamental pillars of the entire theory of capital." (Böhm-Bawerk: *Positive Theorie,* p. 149.) [Italics mine.—*N.B.*] This embarrassing "difference of time" obliges us to wait: "In the overwhelming majority of cases, we must resort to roundabout paths in production under such technical conditions as oblige us to wait for a time, often a very long time, for the achievement of the final product capable of consumption." (*Ibid.,* p. 149.) This peculiarity of the "capitalist mode of production", according to Böhm-Bawerk, is the basis for the economic dependence of the workers on their employers; the workers cannot wait while the "roundabout path" is being taken, until the consumption products are delivered; [126] on the contrary, the capitalist can not only wait, but under certain circumstances may even advance the articles of consumption to the workers—directly or indirectly—in return for the commodity in the possession of the workers, which is *labour.* The entire process is as follows: the employers acquire commodities of the "more remote order" (raw materials, machines, the use of the soil and real estate, and particularly, *labour*), and transform them by means of the process of production into commodities of the first order, *i.e.,* into goods ready for consumption. In this process, the capitalists, after deducting payment for their own labour, etc., still retain a certain surplus in value, the magnitude of which usually corresponds to the amount of capital invested in the enterprise. This precisely is the "original interest on capital" or "profits". (*Ibid.,* p. 502.)

Now, how shall we explain the origin of profit? Here is Böhm-Bawerk's answer: "I must begin my explanation with a reference to an important fact. Goods of the more remote order are, though already present in their physical state, really *future goods* as to their economic nature." (*Ibid.,* p. 503.) Let us dwell for a moment on the concept of a "present" and "future" goods, which is one of Böhm-Bawerk's innovations and plays an extremely important rôle in his "system". The needs which determine the value of commodities may be divided into various epochs; they are either concerned with the present, in which case they are felt directly and with great acuteness ("feelings of the immediate moment") or with the future (for obvious reasons we omit a discussion of the past). Those goods which satisfy present demands Böhm-Bawerk calls "present goods", while those which satisfy demands in the future he calls "future goods". For instance, if I have a certain sum of money at present, with the aid of which I may duly satisfy my current requirements, this sum is accounted by Böhm-Bawerk as a "present possession". But if I cannot obtain an equivalent sum until a certain time has passed, I may not use it for satisfying my present requirements, since it can only serve to satisfy future requirements; therefore this sum of money is "future goods". Present and future needs, whether they be distributed over any period whatsoever, must be compared with each other; therefore the value of the present and future goods may also be compared. We arrive at the following law: "Present goods are as a general rule worth more than future goods of the same type and number." (*Ibid.*, p. 426.)

"This theorem," Böhm-Bawerk goes on to say, "is the nucleus and centre of the theory of interest which I have to expound." (*Ibid.*, p. 426.) Applying this doctrine to the relations between capitalists and workers, we obtain the following condition. Capitalists purchase, among other means of production, also labour. But labour, like any other means of production, is, "in its economic nature", future goods; its value is therefore less than the goods it—labour—will produce. Assuming that X units of labour produce Y units of commodity a, whose present value is A, the value of Ya, in the *future*, separated from the present by the entire length of the production process, will be less than A; it is this *future value* of the product which is equivalent to the present value of the labour.

If the labour, therefore, is purchased now, wherefor its value is expressed in *present* florins, we shall pay a smaller sum of florins for it than is obtained by the employer himself on the sale of his products, *i.e.*, after the conclusion of the production process. "This and no other is the reason for the 'cheap' purchase of the means of production and particularly of *labour*, which the socialists rightly designate as the source of profit for capital, but wrongly designate as a fruit of the exploitation of the workers by the capitalists." (*Ibid.*, p. 504.) In other words, it is the *exchange* of present goods for future goods that results in profit.[127] The transaction of exchange itself does not yet involve profit, for the employer has purchased the labour according to its full present value, *i.e.*, the value of the future product. "For his future commodity is gradually maturing during the progress of production into a present commodity and thus ultimately acquires the full value of a present commodity." (Böhm-Bawerk: *Positive Theorie*, p. 505.) Precisely this increment in value, achieved in the process of the transformation of future goods into present goods, of means of production into articles of consumption, is the profit of capital. The main cause for this profit is therefore to be found in the varying estimation of present and future goods, which in turn is a consequence of the "elemental facts of human nature and of the production technique" and not at all of the social relations peculiar to the modern structure of society.

So much for the fundamental outlines of Böhm-Bawerk's theory of profit. Its essential phase is the justification of the theory of future goods as compared with present goods, which phase has been exhaustively elaborated by Böhm-Bawerk and will be expounded and analysed by us later on. For the present, let us devote a few introductory remarks of a general nature to this subject.

We have already seen that the notion of the necessity of *waiting*, of postponing the act of consumption, is one of the theorems constituting the "fundamental pillars of the entire theory of capital", because the "capitalist mode of production" postpones the delivery of the finished product for a comparatively long time. According to Böhm-Bawerk, this conditions the economic dependence of the workers on the capitalists. *But in reality we need neither to "wait" nor postpone consumption*, for the simple reason that the social product, whatever may be the section of production we are considering, is present *simultaneously in all the stages* of its manufacture, if we are dealing merely with a social production process. Marx already pointed out that the division of labour replaces the "succession in time" by a "succession in place". Karl Rodbertus describes the process as follows: "In all the 'enterprises' of all the branches of all stages of production, simultaneous uninterrupted labour is going on. While in the production establishments of the branches of raw production, new raw materials are being won from the earth, the production establishments in the branches of intermediate products are simultaneously transforming the raw materials of the preceding epoch into intermediate products; while the tool-producing factors are replacing tools that have been used up, and while, finally, at the last stage of production, new products are being turned out for immediate consumption." (Karl Rodbertus: *Das Kapital*, p. 257. Berlin, 1884.) As the production process goes on without interruption, so does the process of consumption. In modern society we need not wait for our "consumption" of goods until the "roundabout path" has been travelled, since the production process *neither begins* with the winning of raw materials and the various "intermediate products" *nor concludes* with the manufacture of articles of consumption; on the other hand, this process is an aggregate of all the partial processes at work at the same time. An investigation of the modern economy will of course show that we are dealing with an already developed system of social production; this presupposes a social distribution of labour and the simultaneous availability of various phases of the production process.

The entire process as expounded by Karl Marx is as follows: Let us assume the constant capital (in simple reproduction) as equal to $3c$, of which one third, c, is annually transformed into articles of consumption. Let us designate the variable capital circulating within the year as v, and the annually accruing surplus value as s. The annual product will then have a value equivalent to $c + v + s$, while the new value annually produced will only be equal to $v + s$; c is not reproduced at all but merely added to the product; it is only the yield of an *earlier* production of the past year or of preceding years. A portion of c therefore "matures" annually into "consumption goods" but the number of hours of labour $(v + s)$ is decreased annually by c hours for the production of means of production. We thus find that any given production cycle *simultaneously* embraces both the production of means of production as well as of articles of consumption; that, furthermore, consumption need not be "postponed" to a later epoch; that the production of means of production has not the character of an introductory operation, but that the processes of production, consumption, and reproduction are constantly going on without interruption. Böhm-Bawerk's idea of a necessity of "waiting", which seems to have some relation with the old notions of abstinence, is therefore not tenable.[128]

We have still to consider the bearing of this idea in connection with Böhm-Bawerk's appreciation of the social nature of profit. We have already seen that Böhm-Bawerk considers this *necessity of waiting* as the cause of the economic dependence of workers on employers. "Only because the workers," he says, "cannot wait until the roundabout path, inaugurated by them in the winning of raw materials and the production of instruments, delivers its mature fruit for consumption, that they become economically dependent on those who already possess these intermediate products in the finished state, on the 'capitalists'." But we already know that the workers need not "wait", in fact, they may sell their intermediate products immediately, without waiting for the "mature fruit for consumption", and thus evade economic dependence. The essence of the matter is not at all in the fact that the workers must "wait" for their enjoyment of the goods, but in the fact that they have at present no opportunity at all to produce independently, for two reasons. In the first place, a "production without capital" is a technical absurdity in a capitalist economy. In order to produce so much as a single plough with the aid of one's bare hands alone, one would need a period of time far exceeding the age of man (for which reason a second Böhm-Bawerk might perhaps conclude that the cause of the economic dependence of the workers and of the origin of profit is the short duration of human life). In the second place, a "production for the moment, completely without capital", as, for example, the collecting of roots for food, or other such work, is likewise impossible, since the soil under the capitalist society is by no means a *res nullius*, but very definitely bound by the fetters of private property. It is, therefore, not the fact of "waiting", but rather the *monopoly in the means of production* (including the soil and real estate) by *the class of capitalist proprietors,* which is the basis for the "economic dependence" and the phenomenon of profit. But the theory of "waiting" cloaks the historical character of modern relations, the class structure of modern society, and the social class character of profit.

Let us now consider another point in this theory. "The essence and nucleus of the theory of interest," according to Böhm-Bawerk, is to be found in our lower evaluation of future goods as compared with present goods. Wilhelm Roscher's famous savage will return 180 fish at the end of the month for 90 lent him at its beginning, and has still a considerable surplus of 720 fish.[129] And he estimates the "present" 90 fish as of greater value than the "future" 180. Approximately the same occurs in modern society; only, the value difference, according to Böhm-Bawerk, is not so great. But what determines this difference? Böhm-Bawerk offers the following answer: "They [the value differences.—*N.B.*] are greatest with persons who live from hand to mouth. . . . The difference . . . is less . . . with persons who already possess a certain supply of goods." (Böhm-Bawerk: *Positive Theorie,* pp. 471, 472.) But since there is "an extraordinarily great number of wage labourers", since, by reason of their "numerical preponderance", the price is so constituted as to yield a certain commission as a result of the subjective evaluations, which amounts to profit,[130] the following circumstance becomes clear. Even if we assume that the higher evaluation of present goods as compared with future goods is one of the indirect causes for the origin of profit, the difference in economic situation of the various classes remains the nucleus of this "fact". The difference in the evaluations here also inevitably presupposes the "social difference".[131] Yet Böhm-Bawerk makes every effort to shut out the idea of the social basis of profit. "Of course," he says, "there may be causes, besides those causes of apparently cheap purchases [of labour, —*N.B.*] that have been developed in the text, of an isolated occurrence of other reasons for a *truly* abnormally cheap purchase: for example, skilful utilisation of a favourable business situation, usurious oppression of the seller, particularly the worker." (Böhm-Bawerk: *Positive Theorie,* p. 505, *footnote.*) But these cases, Böhm-Bawerk thinks, must be considered abnormal; the profit thus obtained is "an extra profit"—not to be confounded with the category under discussion—based on a different basis and possessing a different social-political significance. Yet, a closer view will show us that the differences involved are not differences of principle. In both cases, "profit" or "interest" is the result of the exchange of present goods for future goods, a result of the *sale of labour;* in both cases the *overestimate* of the present goods as compared with the future goods plays a part; in both cases this overestimate is conditioned by the *social situation* of the buyers and sellers; "the skilful utilisation of a favourable situaation" may in this case constitute a new factor as little as the usurious oppression of the seller. For the capitalists are *always* trying to utilise the situation, which is always "favourable" for them and "unfavourable" for the workers. On the other hand, it is quite unclear what must be considered as "usurious" and what "non-usurious" oppression; we completely lack any motives of *economic* type; we also cannot see why in one case the purchase of labour should be "apparently" cheap while in the other case it is "truly" cheap. In the case of "usurious oppression", Böhm-Bawerk's theory represents the facts precisely as in the case of the "normal" process of formation of profit; the difference is only that in the former case the worker overestimates the present goods by fifteen per cent as compared with the future goods, for example, while in the second case his overestimate extends only to ten or five per cent; Böhm-Bawerk offers no other difference, no difference of principle. If he maintains that the "social category" plays no part in his normal cases, he is exposing only his own inconsistency in dropping this assumption in his explanation of the "abnormal deviations". But he is constantly guided by a sure instinct: a denial of social oppression, even in the "abnormal cases", would obviously reduce the whole theory *ad absurdum.*

We have analysed the general thesis of Böhm-Bawerk's

theory of profit and found that he seeks to avoid any contact with the social side of the reality which he is interpreting. Our object has been merely to illuminate the *theoretical background* on which Böhm-Bawerk projects his outlines. It may be inferred either that the fundamental presuppositions of his theory are in direct contradiction with reality (the "waiting argument"), or that the social factor is being with difficulty concealed and smuggled in (the evaluation of future goods as dependent on the economic position of the evaluator). For this reason, as Charasoff says, "labour always has lower value . . . than the present wages. This by no means denies the fact of surplus labour, it is merely equivalent to furnishing the latter with a logically untenable explanation, or rather with the pretence of justification." (G. Charasoff: *Das System des Marxismus,* p. XXII.) Parvus also,[132] indulges in this delicate irony: "Present value and future value: what could not be proved with their aid! If a man takes money from another with the threat of violence, what shall we term this act? Robbery? No, would be Böhm-Bawerk's reply. It is a legitimate exchange: the robber prefers the present value of the money to the future value of eternal bliss; the robbed prefers the future value of his life retained to the present value of his money!"

But alas! Even with the aid of the most neatly constructed reasoning concerning present and future values, Böhm-Bawerk has not succeeded in clarifying the problem. If even the fundamental ideas of his structure present elements that are absolutely incompatible with a scientific theory of profit and of distribution, these defects will necessarily recur again and again in the questions taken up by him and here analyzed by us; they cannot possibly fail to present themselves.

Let us therefore now devote our attention to the internal (as it were) constitution of Böhm-Bawerk's theory, particularly to a criticism of his proofs of the predominant weight attached to present goods.

CHAPTER V.

The Theory of Profit (Continued)

1. Two causes for an overestimation of present goods; (*a*) the difference in the relation between needs and the means for their fulfilment at various times; (*b*) the systematic underestimation of future goods.

2. Third cause for the overestimation of present goods; their technical superiority.

3. The subsistence fund; the demand for present goods and the supply; the origin of profit.

1. Two Causes for the Overestimation of Present Goods.

In the preceding section we found that the *realisation* of profit is made when the capitalist sells goods; potentially, however, the profit arises when labour is purchased. As a rule, the subjective evaluations of present goods exceed those of future goods. But since the subjective evaluations determine the objective exchange value of the price, present goods as a rule surpass future goods of the same type not only in their *subjective value,* but also in *price.*[133] The difference between the prices paid by the capitalist when purchasing future goods, particularly labour,[134] and those obtained in the sale of the commodity resulting from the production process (the "maturing of future goods into present goods"), constitutes capital's profit. We must therefore trace the formation of this profit and begin with an analysis of the subjective evaluations from which the objective value—in each concrete case, the price—takes its origin.

Böhm-Bawerk points out *three* causes for a higher evaluation of present goods as compared with future goods: (1) the difference in the relation between requirements and the means for their fulfilment at various times; (2) the systematic underestimation of future goods; (3) the technical superiority of present goods. Let us consider each of Böhm-Bawerk's arguments in order. As to the first "cause": "The *first* chief cause calculated to produce a difference in the value of present and future goods is to be found in the difference between the relations of demand and 'covering' at various periods." (Böhm-Bawerk: *Positive Theorie,* p. 440.) This "cause" for the higher evaluation of present goods is represented as occurring in two typical cases: first, in all the cases in which persons find themselves in a difficult situation; second, in the evaluations of all persons who count on a secure position in the future (young physicians, lawyers, etc.). For both these categories the "present" one hundred florins are far more important than the "future" florins, as the future "relation of demand and covering" may involve far more favourable opportunities for both categories. But there are a number of persons for whom precisely the reverse relation exists between demand and "covering", namely, a comparatively favourable situation at present and a poorer one in the future. In this case, Böhm-Bawerk says, the following must be considered: The present goods, a florin for instance, may be consumed either in the present or in the future. This is true particularly of money, which is capable of easy preservation. The relation between present and future goods may cover *only* future needs, while the present goods may cover *these future needs and also* such present needs as are situated in a more proximate epoch. Again, two cases may be distinguished: (1) *the present and more proximate future needs are less important* than future needs; in this case, the present goods are set aside to cover the future needs; the value of these goods is determined by the importance of the latter; the present goods will be equivalent to the future goods in value; [135] (2) *the present goods are more important;* in this case the value of the present goods surpasses that of the future goods, since the latter obtain their value only from the future needs, not at all from the present. It follows that the *present goods may be equal to the value of the future goods, but may in no case have less than that value.* But this equality is further weakened by Böhm-Bawerk with the assertion that the possibility of a relative worsening of the material situation in the *near* future is always present; this possibility adds to present goods further opportunities of more advantageous use, which cannot apply to future goods: "Present goods are therefore in the most unfavourable case equal to future goods in value, but as a rule superior by reason of their usefulness as a reserve stock." (*Ibid.*, p. 443.) According to Böhm-Bawerk, only those cases constitute an exception in which the preservation of present goods is connected with difficulties or rendered impossible. We thus obtain three categories of persons: (1) a very great number of persons is situated in poorer circumstances at present than in the future; these will value present goods higher than future goods; (2) a second, likewise very numerous group, who are holding present goods as a reserve stock in order to make use of them in the future, will estimate present goods as either equal to future goods in value, or at a somewhat higher value; (3) there is a small number of persons with whom "the communication between present and future is obstructed or menaced by special circumstances"; these will estimate present goods as lower than future goods. But in general, subjective evaluations have a tendency to be higher for present goods and lower for future goods.

This is Böhm-Bawerk's "first cause" for the overestimation of present goods.

We shall now analyse this "cause", pointing out above all that such a formulation of the question has very definite *historical* limits, being valid only for an exchange economy, and entirely impossible in all types of economy in kind. Furthermore, this statement applies not only to goods that are difficult to keep, but, as Karl Pearson and Ladislaus von Bortkievitz have pointed out, to other goods also: "A man who should be offered as much coal, wine, etc., as would be needed to supply him throughout the presumable course of his life, would show but little gratitude for such an offer," is Pearson's remark in his discussion of Böhm-Bawerk's theory, although Pearson on the whole accepts this theory, "while the case is of course different with money." (Ladislaus von Bortkievitz: "Der Kardinalfehler der Böhm-Bawerkschen Zinstheorie," *Schmoller's Jahrbücher*, vol. XXX, p. 947.) We have further seen that the overestimation of present goods as compared with future goods depends in great measure, according to Böhm-Bawerk, on the fact that present goods may also satisfy the more important future requirements, from which their value is furthermore derived. Let us assume we are dealing with a person whose present is comparatively secure, but whose future offers less security. The ten florins at present in the possession of this person will *now* satisfy a need of 100 units; as this person would in the future be likely to have a smaller sum at his disposal, the value of the ten florins would rise, let us say, to 150 such units. We must infer that the future ten florins would be esteemed more highly by the given person than the present ten florins. But Böhm-Bawerk draws a different conclusion; he declares that since the present ten florins may be saved and thus applied even in the *future,* they have even now (*at present*) the value of the future florins. In this manner the future value is projected into the present; but this presupposition—that of a possibility of a transfer of the value of the future possession of the present goods—contradicts Böhm-Bawerk's fundamental notion as to the origin of profit. What would be the result, for instance, if we should apply Böhm-Bawerk's assumption to instruments of production?

Every means of production—machinery or labour—may be viewed in two ways: as present goods and as future goods (the former only to the extent that it is possible to realize on its value in the present, and that a physical form of the possession is available, such as machines, etc.). We may realize on the value of a given means of production at present; we may sell it and get for it, let us say, 100 value units; we may apply it in the production process and get 150 value units after the expiration of a certain time; therefore the future value of the given means of production is equal to 150 value units, while its present value is 100 such units. If we now assume, with Böhm-Bawerk, the possibility of an evaluation of present goods according to their future value, we shall find that this is quite inadmissible, particularly with regard to means of production, for in this case all difference between what the capitalist himself pays and what he later receives would disappear; the commission (the *agio*) which Böhm-Bawerk considers the basis of profit would be absent. Böhm-Bawerk's fallacy is in his excluding for *future* value the possibility of a *present* application.[136] To be sure, the imaginary future goods cannot realise their value at present. Yet precisely the means of production which are already physically available in the present time cannot be accommodated at all to the category of "imaginary florins". Either present goods *cannot* borrow their value from future utility (of course within the limits of the first cause to which we have already devoted our attention), in which case there is no occasion for an overestimation of present goods, for the equality in the estimation of present and future goods disappears; or, the present goods *can* derive their value from the future utility, in which case it remains to be explained whence Böhm-Bawerk will derive his profit (of course, again only within the limits of the first cause). In both cases the outcome is not exactly flattering to Böhm-Bawerk.

Let us consider the subject now from the point of view of the present capitalist reality, *i.e.*, the point of view of capitalists and workers, taking the latter first. The workers sell their commodity, labour, which is purchased by capitalists as a means of production, *i.e.*, a future goods, in exchange for "present" florins. The worker "voluntarily" sells his labour (future goods) at an evaluation lower than that placed upon the product of his labour. *But this is done not at all for the reason that the worker may count on a better relation between demand and covering*, but rather as a result of the *comparatively* weak social position of the worker. (Stolzmann, *op. cit.*, pp. 306, 307.) He has no hope, furthermore, of "rising in life", and this constitutes the peculiarity of the proletarian position in all countries. The "first cause" for the overestimation of present goods as compared with future goods is therefore not at all present in the *worker's* evaluation motives. Nor is this explanation at all applicable as a reason for the evaluations of the *capitalist employers*. Böhm-Bawerk himself has the following to say on this point: "If the capitalists would evaluate their entire possessions as present goods, *i.e.*, consume them in present enjoyment, the needs of the present would obviously be superabundantly supplied, while the needs of the future would remain entirely unprovided for. . . . Insofar as we are concerned only with the relations of demand and covering in present and future, the opposition of an aggregate holding of present goods exceeding the demands of the present is of less value to its possessors (as present goods) than future goods." (*Positive Theorie,* p. 510.)

For the capitalist such goods, insofar as they exceed his own needs, are useful in that he consumes them *productively, i.e.,* in that he transforms them into future goods. This circumstance causes the *future* goods, in this case labour, to be evaluated higher than the *present* goods. We thus see that the "first cause" is completely untenable both from the point of view of demand and that of supply.

Turning now to the "second cause", we find that Böhm-Bawerk conceives it as follows: "We systematically underestimate our future needs and the means serving for their satisfaction." (*Ibid.,* p. 445.) Böhm-Bawerk has no doubts as to the fact itself but finds that it manifests itself in various degrees, depending on the race, the age, the individual; its crudest manifestation is in children and savages, for which there are three reasons: (1) the incompleteness of the conceptions of future needs; (2) the defective nature of the will, causing one to prefer present satisfaction even though the harmfulness of such preference may be apparent; (3) "the consideration of the brevity and uncertainty of our life."

In our opinion, this "second cause" is as incorrect as the first. If we are dealing with an economic establishment, there must exist a definite *economic plan,* which will consider not only the needs of the present but also those of the future. Böhm-Bawerk's reference to savages and children can hardly be taken as evidence. What can be the influence of a defective quality of our will, of our imperfect "conceptions of the future" or even of "considerations as to the brevity and uncertainty of our life", on the calculated plans of a modern industrial magnate? Economy has its own logic, and the motives of economic activity, the economic considerations, are as far apart from the motives of children and savages as earth from sky. The accumulation of money, where such is advantageous, the waiting for a favourable business situation, intricate plans for the future—such are the characteristic traits of a capitalist economy; though the capitalist may at times be a "child", his childishness is operative only in the case of his "pocket money"; in his essential valuations, however, in his purely economic operations, all proceeds in accordance with definite calculation. Friedrich von Wieser rightly observes in this connection: "It appears to me . . . that in civilised conditions every good economist and, for the most part, even every mediocre economist has learned to govern in a certain connection this weakness of human nature [the underestimation of future goods.—*N.B.*]. . . . The need of care and foresight in this connection is particularly great, and it should not surprise us to find it effective here above all."[137] Aside from the above, it is undesirable, even from Böhm-Bawerk's point of view, to resort to the risk connected with the "future" in one's explanation of the origin of the profit of capital, for, as Ladislaus von Bortkievitz observes, "the Böhm-Bawerk theory is concerned with an explanation of the interest on capital in the proper sense, *i.e.*, with net interest and not with gross interest, which contains, among its other components, the premium on risk, representing a discounting of the factor of uncertainty, and may be disregarded in considering net interest." (Bortkievitz, *op. cit.*, p. 950.)

Let us now take up the question of workers and capitalists. It appears to Böhm-Bawerk that the worker himself might appear in the rôle of a capitalist and obtain the product of his labour in the future; yet he prefers to receive at least a part of it at present, since he systematically "underestimates" future goods. As a matter of fact, the process is quite different from Böhm-Bawerk's understanding of it. The worker does not sell his labour power because he "underestimates future goods", but because he lacks completely the means of obtaining any goods at all except by the sale of his labour power. In his case there is no choice between producing himself and producing in the employer's factory; he has no opportunity at all to transform the future goods—labour—into present goods; he therefore does not evaluate his labour as future goods at all. Such an attitude is quite foreign to him, in fact, the situation is so clear that even bourgeois economists grasp it unless they are engaged in a systematic apology for capitalism, even though it would be difficult for them to develop such an apology with the zeal displayed by Böhm-Bawerk. "The industrial worker," writes Professor Wilhelm Lexis, "was now unable to realise on his labour power with his own resources; he needed for this the immense new means of production that were owned by capital, under the conditions dictated by capital. *The worker does not conduct his own production establishment; the product of his labour does not belong to him and is a matter of indifference to him; economic husbandry for him means the acquisition and expenditure of his wages.*" [The italics are the author's.] [138]

Such is the situation from the point of view of the worker; let us now examine the same situation from the point of view of the capitalist. Böhm-Bawerk himself here admits that *capitalists,* when acting as such and not as spendthrifts, are never guilty of any overestimation of present goods. (*Positive Theorie,* pp. 520, 521.) We thus find that the "second cause" also is not at all valid, either for demand or supply.

"Of the three factors, therefore . . . for the capitalists as a mass [we have seen that this is true for the workers also. —*N.B.*], the former two are *not* operative. On the other hand, the third factor, with which we are already acquainted, may become effective: *the technical superiority of present goods* [the italics are the author's] or what is otherwise termed the 'productivity' of capital." (*Op. cit.,* p. 521.) We have therefore still to examine only the third "cause"—the technical superiority of present goods.

2. *The Third Cause for the Overestimation of Present Goods; Their Technical Superiority.*

This third cause, which Böhm-Bawerk considers as having a decisive significance, consists in the fact that "*as a general rule present goods constitute a more perfect means for the satisfaction of our requirements, for technical reasons, and therefore assure us a higher marginal utility than future goods.*" (*Op. cit.,* p. 454; italics mine.—*N.B.*) We shall first make a preliminary remark. Böhm-Bawerk has thus far always assumed present goods to mean "consumption commodities", goods of the first order, or, in the worst case, "present" florins, which may easily be transmuted into articles of consumption, which in turn represent an immediate satisfaction of human needs. It was florins which the capitalist exchanged for the "future possession", labour, as a true commodity. But here the case is quite different; Böhm-Bawerk is no longer contrasting means of production with means of consumption, but comparing the means of production, the various categories of means of production, *among themselves*. A number of consequences result from this, which we shall discuss below. To return to our theme: we know from the preceding section that the production process, according to Böhm-Bawerk, is the more successful as it occupies more time. If we assume any unit means of production, for instance, a month's labour, applied in technically unequal production processes, the result will be quite different, depending on the duration of the production process. Böhm-Bawerk adduces the following table in elucidation of this theorem:

TABLE I

One Month's Labour in the Year

will yield for the economic period, *i.e.*, up to the end of the year.

	1909	1910	1911	1912
1909	100	...	...	...
1910	200	100	...	...
1911	280	200	100	...
→ 1912	350	280	200	100 ←
1913	400	350	280	200
1914	440	400	350	280
1915	470	440	400	350
1916	500	470	440	400

units of product

In order to satisfy needs in the year 1909, says Böhm-Bawerk, a month's labour performed in 1910 or 1911 is of no effect at all. The month's labour in 1909 will produce 100 production units; in order to satisfy needs in the year 1914, a month's labour in 1911 will yield 350 units; in 1910, 400; in 1909, 440 units of product.

"Whatever be the epoch taken as a basis in the comparison, the older (present) average of means of production is always technically superior to a younger (future) means of equal magnitude." This superiority, Böhm-Bawerk further intimates, is not only technical but *economic* in character: the product turned out in a "more capitalistic" branch, *i.e.*, by means of a longer course of production, is superior to that of the "less capitalistic" branch not only in the number, but also in the general *value* of the units produced.

"But is it [the older aggregate of means of production. —*N.B.*] also superior in the magnitude of its marginal utility and of its *value?* Indeed it is. For if it places at our disposal, in any conceivable sphere of requirements in whose satisfaction we might or would apply it, more means of satisfaction, it must surely be of greater importance for our welfare." (*Ibid.*, p. 457.)

For one and the same person, at one and the same epoch, says Böhm-Bawerk, a greater mass of products will also have greater value. Such is the case with the value of the product; but how is it with the value of the means of production? As we have seen from the corresponding section on value, the value of the means of production is determined in various types of consumption by the maximum of the value of the product, *i.e.*, by the value of the product turned out under the most advantageous conditions.

"In the case of commodities permitting of an alternate and different application with varying magnitudes of marginal utility, the *highest* marginal utility is the determining one—in our concrete case, therefore, *that* product which represents the *highest* value sum." (*Ibid.*, p. 458.)

But, obviously, the inference should have been drawn that the value of the means of production depends on the *maximum mass of products, i.e.*, on the maximum prolongation of the production process. But the Böhm-Bawerk theory actually —and let the reader mark this particularly—furnishes *an entirely different answer*. The highest value sum, says our author, "must not coincide with that product which contains the greatest number of individual units. On the contrary, it rarely or never coincides with this product. For the greatest number of units would be secured by means of an immoderate duration, perhaps 100 or 200 years, of the production process. But commodities which will not be rendered available until the days of our great-grandsons and great-great-grandsons have practically no value in our present-day estimation." (*Ibid.*, p. 460.) Therefore the greatest value sum will belong to that product whose number of units, multiplied by the value per unit, yields a maximum sum, in which connection we must also consider "the relation between demand and covering in the given economic period and . . . the reduction in perspective that becomes operative in the case of future goods"[139] [*i.e.*, the reduction in value.—*N.B.*].

Let us assume the "first reason", *i.e.*, "progressively improving means of providing", to be given; let us further assume that the corresponding (decreasing) value of a unit of product, termed the "true value" by Böhm-Bawerk, amounts for the annual product of 1909 to 5; of 1910, to 4; of 1911, to 3.3; of 1912, to 2.5; of 1913, to 2.2; of 1914, to 2.1; of 1915, to 2; and of 1916, to 1.5. The corresponding figures, when the *second* reason is operative, *i.e.*, the *reduction in perspective*, will be equal respectively to 5; 3.8; 3; 2.3; 1.8; 1.5; 1. We are therefore assuming, together with Böhm-Bawerk, a reduction in the value of "future goods" as compared with "present goods", by virtue of the two reasons we have previously investigated. On the basis of this material, Böhm-Bawerk constructs the following tables:

TABLE II

One Month's Labour in the Year 1909 Yields

For the economic period	*The following number of units product*	*The true marginal utility per unit product*	*Reduction in perspective of value per unit*	*The value sum of the total product*
1909	100	5.0	5.0	500
1910	200	4.0	3.8	760
1911	280	3.3	3.0	840
1912	350	2.5	2.2	770
1913	400	2.2	2.0	800
1914	440	2.1	1.8	792
1915	470	2.0	1.5	705
1916	500	1.5	1.0	500

TABLE III

One Month's Labour in the Year 1912 Yields

For the economic period	*The following number of units product*	*The true marginal utility per unit product*	*Reduction in perspective of value per unit*	*The value sum of the total product*
1909	...	5.0	5.0	...
1910	...	4.0	3.8	...
1911	...	3.3	3.0	...
1912	100	2.5	2.2	220
1913	200	2.2	2.0	400
1914	280	2.1	1.8	504
1915	350	2.0	1.5	525
1916	400	1.5	1.0	400

These tables show that the maximum of value for the work expended in the year of 1909 (840 value units) is higher than that of the value which resulted as a consequence of the later labour of the year 1912 (525). If we make these calculations also for the years 1910 and 1911, recapitulating the results in a table similar to Table I, the following figures will be obtained:[140]

TABLE IV

One Month's Labour in the Year

will yield for the economic period.	1909	1910	1911	1912	units of value
1909	500	...	...	...	
1910	760	380	...	...	
1911	*840*	600	300	...	
→ 1912	770	616	440	220 ←	
1913	800	700	560	400	
1914	792	*720*	*630*	504	
1915	705	660	600	*525*	
1916	500	470	440	400	

"The present labour month is therefore actually superior to all future months not only in its technical productivity, but also in its marginal utility and value."[141]

Böhm-Bawerk therefore considers it proved that the present

productive *commodities* are not only technically but also *economically* superior to *future productive commodities*. Böhm-Bawerk now passes over to a consideration of present goods proper, *i.e.*, to present consumption commodities, by way of the following considerations: The possession of a certain supply of present consumption commodities permits one to consume means of production in the most productive processes; if one possesses but scant means of existence, one cannot wait very long for the product to be completed. Furthermore, a certain duration of production is connected with a certain quantity of means of existence, and the earlier the means of production are obtained, the better can they be utilised. If we have a stock of present consumption commodities sufficient for ten years, the present productive commodities may continue to be consumed for the whole period of ten years; but our future goods can stay only a shorter time in the production process, on the other hand, if we are not to obtain the means of production until three years have elapsed; in this case the maximum age of the production process will be ten minus three, *i.e.*, seven years, etc.[143] "The state of the case," says Böhm-Bawerk, "is as follows: Our control over an aggregate of present means of consumption covers our subsistence in the current economic period and thus releases our available means of production during this period (labour, utilisation of the soil, premiums on capital) for the technically more profitable service of the future." (Böhm-Bawerk: *Positive Theorie*, p. 469.) In other words, since the present productive goods have a higher value than the future goods, and since the availability of present consumption commodities favours this factor, the latter acquire a certain premium. The increased value of present productive commodities involves an increase in the value of the present consumption commodities.

So much for the "third" cause. Before proceeding to a criticism of this most important and in our opinion most scholastic argument of Böhm-Bawerk, let us once more recapitulate the course of his reasoning:

1. Present productive goods yield a higher mass of products than future productive goods.

2. The value of this product at any given moment, as well as the *maximum value*, is greater in present productive goods.

3. Therefore the value of present means of production is greater than that of the future means.

4. Since present articles of consumption make possible the utilisation of means of production in the most productive operations, *i.e.*, their immediate pre-emption for a long period of time, present articles of consumption have a higher value than future articles of consumption.

Now for our critical examination of this reasoning. On Point 1 above: Present productive commodities, we read in Böhm-Bawerk, yield a greater mass of products, in support of which Table I is offered. If Böhm-Bawerk's reasoning is to have any meaning at all, we must exclude everything connected with the above-discussed first two "causes" of the overestimation of present goods. The number of products obtained must be taken as independent of *when* they were obtained. Yet the production series in Böhm-Bawerk's table terminate at the end of the given year in each case. But if we assume that the period at which the product is completed is of no importance for us, we shall arrive at entirely different results, as does Ladislaus von Bortkievitz.

TABLE I

One Month's Labour in the Year

will yield for the economic period.	1909	1910	1911	1912	units of product
1909	100	...	...	...	
1910	200	100	...	...	
1911	280	200	100	...	
→1912	350	280	200	100←	
1913	400	350	280	200	
1914	440	400	350	280	
1915	470	440	400	350	
1916	500	470	440	400	

TABLE Ia

One Month's Labor in the Year

will yield for the economic period.

	1909	1910	1911	1912
1909	100	...	...	...
1910	200	100	...	...
1911	280	200	100	...
1912	350	280	200	100
→1913	400	350	280	200
1914	440	400	350	280←
1915	470	440	400	350
1916	500	470	440	400
1917	...	500	470	440
1918	...	...	500	470
1919	...	...	...	500

units of product

If we assume that the production series of the years 1909, 1910, 1911, and 1912 are of equal duration, the *number of products* will also be the same as in 1909; there is no difference in the *quantity* of product. The only difference now will be that this equally great quantity of product is not obtained at the same time, but rather, as a means of production is more remote from the "present" means of production, an equally great result would be attained all the later, depending on its absolute magnitude. While a month's labour in the year 1909 will yield 500 units of product as early as 1916, a month's labour in 1910 would not yield these 500 units of product in 1916, but only in 1917, and a month's labour in 1911 would not yield this quantity until 1918. It follows that if we ignore the varying evaluation of earlier and later products, the total quantity of the product will remain the same.

On Point 2: We now come to the question of the value of the product and the maximum value. We have seen above that a consistent application of the Böhm-Bawerk position would necessarily result in a maximum value if the production process should be materially prolonged, and consequently also if the mass of products should rise to a maximum. But Böhm-Bawerk denies this, appealing to the fact that *products to be turned out in the epoch of our great-grandsons will have practically no value for us.* This presupposition, which is the basis of his calculations, is methodologically inadmissible: if we already discount in advance the effect of the underestimation of the future possessions ("which is conditioned either by the first or the second cause"), we are thus rendering impossible the analysis of the "third cause", *i.e.*, of precisely the question which now interests us. As a matter of fact, Böhm-Bawerk surreptitiously introduces the effect of the first and second factor and it is only this circumstance that enables him to arrive at results which he—on the contrary—assigns to the effect of the third factor. Indeed, where does Böhm-Bawerk obtain his different maximum value for the product of the means of production of various lengths of production periods? Surely only from the fact that he has *twice* diminished the value of the product as dependent on time:

1909—5	1913—2.2	1909—5	1913—2.0
1910—4	1914—2.1	1910—3.8	1914—1.8
1911—3.3	1915—2	1911—3.2	1915—1.5
1912—2.5	1916—1.5	1912—2.2	1916—1

The first two columns show the diminution of the value of the goods under the influence of the "progressively improving conditions of providing", the other two show the diminution of value under the influence of reflections on the insufficiency of human life, etc., *i.e.*, the influence of the second cause. If this were not the case, we should have the same figure for all the years, namely, 5. If we now set up a table analogous to Table IV, assuming a diminution of value in all the vertical columns as the mass of products increases, we shall have the following results:[143]

TABLE IV

One Month's Labour in the Year

will yield for the economic period.	1909	1910	1911	1912	units of value
1909	500	...	...	...	
1910	760	380	...	...	
1911	*840*	600	300	...	
→1912	770	616	440	220←	
1913	800	700	560	400	
1914	792	*720*	*630*	504	
1915	705	660	600	*525*	
1916	500	470	400	400	

TABLE IVa

One Month's Labour in the Year

will yield for the economic period.	1909	1910	1911	1912
1909	500	...	...	...
1910	760	500	...	...
1911	*840*	760	500	...
1912	770	*840*	760	500
→1913	800	770	*840*	760
1914	792	800	770	*840*←
1915	705	792	800	770
1916	500	705	792	800
1917	...	500	705	792
		...	500	705
		...	...	500

units of value

A comparison of Tables IV and IVa will show that the "maximum of value" in Table IV is different (840, 720, 630, 525), while it is equally great in Table IVa (840). This difference is due *only* to the fact that the diminution in Table IV is assumed as dependent *on time,* with the result that the second vertical column begins with a different number (380 instead of 500). The diminution in value in Table IVa, on the other hand, is made dependent only on the quantity of product; the initial figures of all four columns are equal, since the quantities of product also are equal.[144] It thus becomes clear that the higher results for the economic productivity for the present means of production are obtained only by reason of the fact that both factors alluded to have been included in the calculations. It goes without saying that we shall obtain the same result (but quantitatively somewhat lower) if we permit only one of the two factors to operate, it matters not whether we choose the first or the second. It is clear, at any rate, that the notorious "third cause" simply is non-existent as an independent factor, and this disposes completely of the question as to the value of present and future means of production also (Point 3).

On Point 4: If we assume that the first three "causes" of the "third cause" are valid, we are by no means able to grant Böhm-Bawerk his transition from productive commodities to consumption commodities. Here Böhm-Bawerk indulges in the following considerations: since present production commodities are more valuable than future production commodities, present consumption commodities are also more valuable than future consumption commodities. The consumption commodities are therefore regarded here as a means of production for means of production, in which connection the productive commodities are taken as the determining factor, and the consumption commodities as the factor to be determined. But this theorem contradicts the fundamental view of the entire School, which considers articles of consumption as of primary character and articles of production as goods of a more remote order, as derived quantities, at least as to their value. We therefore find that Böhm-Bawerk's explanation here again moves in a circle.[146] The value of the product determines the value of the means of production; the value of the means of production determines the value of the product. This alone would constitute a contradiction. But aside from this, the relation between the determination of the value of present goods, as influenced by their marginal utility and by their destination as resulting from the operation of the greater technical and economic productivity of the present means of production, remains unexplained still. Let us assume the marginal utility of a certain supply of present goods to be 500; if the first two causes should not be operative at all, while the effect of the third cause remains in abeyance for the time, the future supply of the given commodities will also have a marginal utility of 500. Let us assume, further, that the result of the most advantageous production period, whose appearance is due to the availability of our assumed supply, yields us 800 units of value, while a postponement of one year (*i.e.*, assuming a shorter production process) will yield us only 700 units of value. According to Böhm-Bawerk, there would result in this case a superiority in favour of the value of the present goods over the future goods. This would be the case (we take the two *principal* cases) if either the value of the present goods should rise above 500, or that of the future goods should fall below 500. The first case is out of the question, for this would be an obvious violation of the law of marginal utility. Nor is the second case possible, for how on earth could commodities lose in value merely because something *cannot* be made of them which is not embraced in the "scale of requirements" at all? This is obvious drivel and the explanation is very simple. The artificial construction of Böhm-Bawerk here assumes that the articles of consumption are dependent for their value on the articles of production; the articles of consumption are considered up to a certain limit as means of production for the manufacture of means of production. Böhm-Bawerk thus sacrifices completely the seriousness of his *fundamental* constructions. The basis of the theory depended on the marginal utility of the articles of consumption which constituted the primary foundation of all value. But if the articles of consumption themselves are now to be regarded as means of production, the theory of marginal utility will lose its meaning altogether.

Aside from this, Böhm-Bawerk's entire reasoning as to the "third cause" is based on the assumption that there are production processes of varying duration; in fact, in this case it is precisely the advantage of a longer production process which results in the deriving of profit. But since Böhm-Bawerk, as we have already seen, admits the insufficiency of the two former causes, the "technical superiority of present goods" appears in reality as the *only* foundation for an explanation of profit. Yet there is no doubt at all that if we assume production processes equal also in duration, profit does not yet cease to exist. If (to use the Marxian terminology) the organic composition of capital is equal in all the branches of production, or, to put the matter in different terms, if the organic composition of capital in each specific branch of production is equal to the average social composition of capital, profit will none the less not yet have disappeared. A deviation from "concrete reality" is to be found only in the fact that the average norm of profit is realised directly, without any flowing of capitals from one branch of industry to another. On the other hand, however, the "differential profit"; or surplus profit, arising in a specific enterprise by reason of improved technique, but not yet having become a common possession of all, cannot be taken as an example of *profit in general;* for the latter arises even in a completely similar technique, namely, as a specific income not of a single *entrepreneur,* but of the entire capitalist *class.* "If all capitalists," says Stolzmann, "are capable of obtaining equal advantage from the increase in productivity, there will remain no means of surplus profit; 'surplus value' can no longer be derived between the divergence of the quantity of product produced without resorting to the capitalist detour and the quantity of product obtained by its utilisation." (Stolzmann: *Op. cit.,* p. 320. See also Bortkievitz, *op. cit.,* p. 943.)

Turning now to a consideration of the motives of capitalists and workers, we find the following condition of the facts. The worker has no choice at all between this path of production or that, for the very simple reason that, being a worker, it is impossible for him to produce unaided. Merely to formulate the problem in this way is, as far as the worker is concerned, completely ridiculous. But, in the case of the capitalists, we may turn Böhm-Bawerk's own weapons upon him, in the following manner: labour as a means of production permits the capitalist to resort to any roundabout way he likes; the present florins would remain dead capital if they were not fructified by labour; in other words, the "present goods" are of significance to the capitalist only insofar as he can transmute them into labour (we here ignore the other means of production). Insofar, therefore, as we are here concerned with contrasting *money* and *labour* (disregarding articles of consumption, which as such are completely superfluous for the capitalist), *labour has a higher subjective value from the point of view of the capitalist.* This might be inferred even from the exchange transaction: if it were not advantageous for the capitalist to purchase labour, *i.e.,* if he had not estimated it as higher in value than his florins, he would not purchase it at all. For the capitalist considers in advance the profit which he may derive, a circumstance which influences him in all his evaluations.

Let us now formulate the question in a more general way. Let us assume that we are dealing with 1000 florins of present money or of future money. Will the capitalist estimate the present 1000 florins higher than the future 1000 florins?

He will, for the simple reason that "money breeds money". His higher evaluation of cash money is based on the possibility of credit operations, in other words, therefore, on the basis of profit. Such a case, which is, furthermore, *typical* for capitalist society, cannot be adduced in explanation of "income without labour", since the case presupposes the existence of such income. On the other hand, we may prove in another manner also that the superiority of the value of present goods does not explain the creation of profit. We have seen that Böhm-Bawerk, in his investigation of the "third cause", offers as his chief argument in favour of the overestimation of present goods, *and of the explanation of the phenomenon of profit,* the fact that present goods make possible the application of productive methods. Let us assume for a moment that this advantage of present goods really exists; let us assume, furthermore, that the capitalist has no cash at his disposal but must, on the other hand, obtain money on interest in order to be able to resort to the long-term production processes. It is obvious that his profits cannot be explained by the superiority of the present sum as opposed to the future sum. Even the "third cause" is thus shown to be invalid.

We have examined Böhm-Bawerk's principal argument in its various aspects, and all our paths have led to the same result. The argument is based on perfectly scholastic presumptions, which are dragged in by the hair, and which either contradict reality (such as the assumption of evaluations by both the worker and the capitalist) or are contradictory within themselves (such as the "third cause", which is dependent as it were, on the former two causes, defining the value of consumption commodities by the value of the production commodities, and vice versa, etc.). In his effort to trace profit back to the different character of the technique in various production branches (longer or shorter duration of production), Böhm-Bawerk evidently conceals the wish to cloak the *general causes* of profit, which arise from the *class position* of the bourgeoisie, and the origin of profit cannot be explained but only obscured by applying a peculiar terminology and a scholastic hair-splitting type of argument.

3. *The Subsistence Fund; The Demand for Present Goods and the Supply of such Goods; The Origin of Profit.*

We must now investigate the question of the nature of the "present goods" whose exchange for future goods (labour) is declared to be the cause of the formation of profit. This question is answered by Böhm-Bawerk in his theory of the "subsistence fund":

" . . . The supply of subsistence advances [*Vorschüsse*] in any national economy is represented, with an insignificant exception, by the totality of all the resources existing in it, with the exception of the soil. The function of this totality of resources consists in maintaining the population during the interval obtaining between the application of its [the population's] original productive forces and the attaining of their fruits mature for consumption, in other words, during the average social period of production; and the social period of production may be extended over any desired epoch, depending on the magnitude of the accumulated totality of resources." (*Positive Theorie*, p. 525.)

"In truth, therefore, the entire accumulated totality of the resources of society, with the extremely insignificant exception of those aggregates of resources that are consumed by their possessors themselves, are brought to market as an offer of subsistence advances." (*Ibid.* p. 527.)

"The totality of resources in a national economy serves as a subsistence fund or advance fund from which society draws its subsistence during the socially customary production period." (*Ibid.*, p. 528.)

Regardless of the fact that the entire "totality of resources" of society also includes means of production, *i.e.*, material elements of constant capital, which are not suitable for immediate consumption, Böhm-Bawerk nevertheless counts this "totality of resources" as a part of the subsistence fund, since a constant "maturing" of future possessions into present possessions takes place in society.

We have still to clarify the position of the parties, *i.e.*, the buyers and sellers, who engage in trade with the various present and future goods. Böhm-Bawerk points out the following with regard to the *supply of present goods.*

The *volume* of the supply of means of subsistence is represented by the entire accumulated stock of resources, with the exception of the soil and those portions of the resources which "are consumed, definitively or by way of an installment, on the one hand, by the impoverishing possessors of resources, and on the other hand, by those possessors of resources who are producing independently." (*Ibid.*, p. 538.)

"The 'intensity' of the supply"[146] is of such nature that "the subjective utility value of present goods for the capitalists is not *greater* than that of future goods. They would therefore be willing, in an extreme case, to pay, for ten florins to be available at the end of two years, or, what amounts to the same thing, for one week of labour which will net them ten florins in two years, practically the entire sum of ten present florins."[147]

The *demand for present goods* is made by:

1. Numerous wage workers; some of these estimate their labour at 5, others at as low as 2½ florins [!!].
2. A small number of persons who seek consumption credits and are ready to pay a certain commission for present goods.
3. A number of independent petty producers, who seek production credits required by them for prolonging the production period.

Since all sellers, in Böhm-Bawerk's opinion, estimate present and future goods at approximately the same value, while purchasers have a higher estimate of present goods, the resultant depends on which side has the numerical superiority.

It must therefore be proved "that the supply of present goods must be numerically exhausted by the demand" (*Ibid.*, p. 541), which Böhm-Bawerk seeks to prove in the following manner:

"The supply," he says, "is limited even in the richest nation by the present status of the national wealth. The demand, however, is practically a limitless quantity; it extends at least as far as the yield of production may be expanded by a prolongation of the process of production, and even in the case of the richest nations this limit lies far beyond the present condition of resources." [148] The superiority is therefore on the side of demand. And since the market price must be higher than the price offered by those prospective purchasers who are excluded from the competitive struggle, and since this price, furthermore, already includes a certain commission for present goods (the overestimation of present goods by the purchasers), the market price must also include a certain commission for present goods. (*Ibid.*, p. 540.)" Interest and commission," says Böhm-Bawerk, "must now put in their appearance." (*Ibid.*, p. 541.)

Having presented the final conclusion of the Böhm-Bawerk theory of profit, we shall now proceed to an analysis of it.

In the first place, the artificial and contradictory nature of the "subsistence fund" is glaringly apparent. The "subsistence fund", which is now made to embrace only present goods, includes—with the exception of the soil and the articles of consumption of the capitalist—everything, *i.e.*, it embraces all the means of production. Böhm-Bawerk believes he has a right to make this assumption for the reason that the future goods "mature" into present goods, that the means of production are transformed into articles of consumption. But this assumption is only partially correct, since the means of production are transformed not only into means of consumption, but also into means of production. In the process of social reproduction, not only the articles of consumption, but also the means of production *must* be manufactured. Furthermore, with an expanding reproduction, the share which is charged to the expenditures for labour—devoted to the means of production—will constantly increase. It is thus entirely inadmissible to eliminate constant capital from the analysis. At bottom, Böhm-Bawerk is here repeating the old fallacy of Adam Smith, exposed by Karl Marx in the second volume of *Capital;* Smith divides the value of commodities into v (available capital) and s (surplus value) and completely ignores c (constant capital). "But so much more," says Marx, "Adam Smith [or Böhm-Bawerk.—*N.B.*] should have seen that this excludes the value of the means of production serving within the sphere of production,—the means of production which produce means of production—a portion of value equal to the value of the constant capital employed in this sphere and excluded from the portions of value forming a revenue, not only by the natural form in which it exists, but also by its function as capital." [149]

Such a conception of the "subsistence fund" becomes even more ridiculous when we deal with an *opposition* between present and future goods, for does not Böhm-Bawerk's task consist in elucidating the exchange relation between present goods on the one hand and future goods (labour) on the other? Present and future goods must here be revealed as opposite poles; from this point of view the subsistence fund can be nothing else than *the total mass of present goods offered on the market.* (Böhm-Bawerk himself calls his section dealing with this subject: "The General Market for the Means of Subsistence.") Under these circumstances, Böhm-Bawerk quite consistently excludes those articles of consumption—the "present goods"—which enter into the consumption of individual capitalists, for these goods do not come upon the market as objects of demand on the part of the workers. On the other hand, Böhm-Bawerk includes in this fund the means of production, *i.e.*, obviously future goods, whereupon he contrasts them with labour, which is likewise future goods, in spite of the fact that these two categories of commodities have no relation whatever with each other. Furthermore, Böhm-Bawerk includes, in his classification of demands, persons seeking production credit, *i.e.*, persons interested in means of production rather than articles of consumption (while the worker desires to eat, the capitalist desires to "prolong the production processes"). The entire system thus acquires the appearance of an incredible hodge-podge of heterogeneous elements. On the other hand, persons who seek production credits may be placed on the same level with workers only inasmuch as both categories obtain their commodity equivalent in the form of *money.* It is only from this point of view that we may say: "The loan market and the labour market are two markets on which . . . the same commodity is supplied and demanded, namely, present goods. . . . Wage workers and credit seekers thus constitute two branches of one and the same demand, mutually supporting their effects and together forming the price resultant." (*Positive Theorie*, p. 524.) We cannot consider these two categories under the same head, except by fixing our eyes on the money element. As soon as the demand for "articles of consumption", in other words, the "market for means of subsistence", receives the chief attention, all similarity between the worker and the person seeking production credits at once disappears.

Let us now turn our attention to an analysis of the relation between the demand for present goods and the supply of such goods. We may distinguish two principal attitudes on Böhm-Bawerk's part in this question. On the one hand, his entire theoretical structure is apparently based on the fact of the purchase of labour, in which profit results from the fact that the *workers* underestimate the value of future goods; on the other hand, it is the demand for present goods on the part of persons seeking production credits which is made the explanation for profit in the last analysis.

In the former case, the decisive part is played by the competition between the *workers;* in the latter case by that between *capitalists*. The second point of view[150] will not bear criticism if only for the reason that it cannot explain the origin of the profit of the capitalist *class*. The loan market, the payment of interest on loans—all this is merely a redistribution of values between two groups of the same capitalist class; but even this *redistribution* cannot explain the *origin* of surplus value. A society is conceivable in which there will be no loan market at all, yet profit will continue to exist in such a society. There remains only the competition between the *workers* as a basis for the formation of profit. Böhm-Bawerk, as we have already mentioned, presents the facts in the following way: The capitalists advance the means of subsistence to the workers (purchase of labour), the workers meanwhile estimating their labour as less valuable than the future value of its products; there results the commission (the *agio*) on present goods. The numerical superiority of the workers also moulds *prices* in such manner as to cause the commission on present goods to be shaped in the *market*. It might be inferred from this that it is precisely the socially weak position of the working class which constitutes the cause of profit. But since the slightest suggestion of such a thought completely disconcerts Professor Böhm-Bawerk, he is untiring in his efforts—regardless of all the resulting contradictions with the most important forms of his own theory—to assure us again and again that *all* workers are constantly finding work to do, that the demand for labour is by no means smaller than the supply of labour, and that profit may therefore not be explained by the competition between the workers. Here is an example of such reasoning: "No doubt the circumstances unfavourable to the purchasers may be counterbalanced *by an active competition between the sellers*. Even though there be few sellers, they have all the greater present goods to fructify. . . . Fortunately these cases are the regular rule in life." (*Ibid.*, p. 575; italics mine.—*N.B.*)

But let us ignore these blunders, important though they are in their consequences for Böhm-Bawerk's theory. Let us assume for the sake of argument that profit arises from the purchase of future goods (labour) and let us consider the transaction between capitalists and workers both as it actually transpires and also in the form in which Böhm-Bawerk conceives it. We here encounter a thought which completely overthrows all of Böhm-Bawerk's discussion; for his theory is based on the assumption that the capitalist grants an *advance* to the worker; in fact, all his principal notions are based on the gradual maturing of labour which affords profit only after it has attained its mature state; the difference in value between the costs and the yield results precisely from the fact that the compensating of labour takes place *before the beginning of the* labour process, *i.e.*, in accordance with the value inherent in labour as a "future goods". *But this assumption is precisely* the unproved condition, which contradicts reality. In fact, the very opposite is the case; it *is not the capitalist* who makes an advance of *wages to the worker*, but the worker who makes an *advance of labour power* to the capitalist. The payment of wages is made *not before* the labour process but *after* it, which is particularly clear in the case of piece work, where wages are paid for the actual number of *completed* products. "But the money which the labourer receives from the capitalist is not given to him until after he has given the capitalist the use of his labour-power, after it has already been realised in the value of the product of labour. The capitalist holds this value in his hands, before he pays for it. . . . Labour power first supplies, in the form of commodities, the equivalent which is to be paid to the labourer, and then only is it paid to the labourer in money. In other words, the labourer himself creates the fund out of which the capitalist pays him." (Karl Marx: *Capital,* vol. II, p. 439.) To be sure, cases also exist in which payment is made in advance; but, in the first place, this phenomenon is *not* at all *typical* for modern economic life, and in the second place, it would prove nothing against our assertion. For if profit may even result in cases in which wages for labour are paid after the labour process, it is clear that some other phenomenon than the difference between present and future goods must be responsible for the origin of profit.

The phenomenon in question is the social power of capital, based on the fact that the capitalists as a class have monopolised the means of production, thus compelling the worker to surrender a portion of his product. Social inequality—the existence of antagonistic social formations—this is the fundamental fact of modern economic life; precisely these relations between the classes, in the field of economy, the production relations, constitute the "economic structure" characteristic of capital society; any theory which neglects to analyse these conditions is doomed to impotence in advance. Yet the effort to obscure the antagonism between classes is so great that modern bourgeois science prefers to hatch a thousand empty "explanations", to accumulate one foolish argument after the other, to create entire "systems", to resuscitate long forgotten theories, and produce mountains of printed matter—all for the simple purpose of proving to us that "there is nothing in the nature of interest . . . nothing that might be considered unreasonable or unjust as such".

CHAPTER VI

Conclusion

If we consider Böhm-Bawerk's "system" as a whole and then seek to determine the specific weight of its various parts, it becomes apparent that his *theory of value* constitutes the basis for his *theory of profits.* His theory of value is therefore a mere subterfuge; and this is not true only of Böhm-Bawerk. The theory of "assignment" (imputation) in Friedrich von Wieser serves the latter in deriving the share of capital, of labour, and of the soil, from which he thereupon, by a confusion of conceptions, derives the shares of the capitalists, the workers, and the landed proprietors, as if the latter were "natural" quantities, independent of the condition of the *social* exploitation of the proletariat. We find the same situation again in John Bates Clark, the most prominent representative of the American School. Everywhere we encounter the same motive: the theory of value is used as a theoretical starting point in order to justify the modern order of society; in this lies the "social value" of the theory of marginal utility for those classes which have an interest in maintaining this social order. The weaker the logical foundations of this theory, the stronger is one's psychological attachment to it, since one does not wish to desert the narrow mental sphere defined by the static conception of capitalism. But Marxism is characterised particularly by the broad view constituting the basis of its entire structure, namely, the *dynamic* point of view which considers capitalism as merely a phase of the social evolution. The Marxian political economy makes use even of the law of value as an epistemological aid in the revelation of the laws of motion of the entire capitalist mechanism. The fact that the category of price, for the explanation of which we need particularly a theory of value, constitutes a general category of the commodities universe, is by no means sufficient to make political economy as such a mere science of "chrematistics";

on the contrary, the analysis of the exchange relations leads us far beyond the limits of exchange, if the problem is rightly formulated. From the point of view of Marxism, exchange itself is merely one of the historically temporary forms of the distribution of commodities. But since any form of distribution occupies a definite place in the process of reproduction of the production conditions which this form of distribution involves, it is obvious that only the narrow-minded attitude characteristic of all the trends of bourgeois theoretical thought could limit the discussion to the market relations or to the available "supply of commodities" as a basis for study. The functional rôle of exchange, as a necessary natural law phenomenon, immanent in any society of producers of commodities, cannot be understood either by those who limit their attention to an analysis of the *"richesses vénales"* with which the market deals, or by those whose eyes are fixed on the relation between the consumption object given in advance, the "goods", and the economic individual. Yet it is perfectly clear how the problem may be correctly formulated.

"In the operation of all the exchange transactions possible in this [*i.e.*, a commodities-producing.—*N.B.*] society, there must ultimately emerge an element which, in the case of a communist society, consciously regulated, is consciously determined by the social central organ, namely, what is to be produced and how much, where and by whom. In short, the exchange must give to the producers of commodities the same thing which is given to the members of the socialist society by their authorities, consciously regulating production, determining the order of labour, etc. It is the task of theoretical economy to determine the law of the exchange transactions thus determined. From this law, we must likewise derive the regulation of production in the commodities-producing societies; just as we must derive the undisturbed progress of the socialist economy from the laws, ordinances and regulations of socialist authorities. But this law does not directly and consciously prescribe human conduct in production, but rather operates after the fashion of a natural law, with 'social inevitability'." (R. Hilferding: *Das Finanzkapital*, pp. 2, 3.)

In other words, we are faced wth the problem of analysing

an inorganically constructed society of commodities producers in course of evolution and growth, *i.e.*, a definite subjective system operating under the conditions of dynamic equilibrium. The question is *how is this equilibrium possible under these conditions?* The labour value theory has an answer to this question. The evolution of human society is possible only when its productive forces are expanding, *i.e.*, when social labour is productive.[151] In a commodities economy, this fundamental fact must find expression on the surface of phenomena, *i.e.*, on the *commodities market.* It is an empirical observation constituting the basis of the labour value theory, that prices fall as the productivity of labour increases. On the other hand, it is precisely the fluctuations of prices in a social commodities economy which produces the *redistribution of the productive forces.* Thus the phenomena of the market are connected with those of reproduction, *i.e.*, with the dynamics of the entire capitalist mechanism in its social bearings.

Again, assuming that there is a connection between the fundamental phenomenon, namely, the evolution of the productive forces, and the objectively realised prices, the problem is to find the characteristic traits of this connection. A careful analysis will show that this connection is quite complicated; the entire third volume of Karl Marx's *Capital* is devoted to the treatment of this connection. The theory of value here appears as an objective law expressing the connection between various series of social phenomena. There is nothing more ridiculous, therefore, than the attempt to make Marx's theory an "ethical" theory. Marx's theory knows no other natural law than that of cause and effect, and can admit no other such law. The value theory discloses these causal relations, which express not only the logical sequence of the market, but of the entire mechanism of the system.

The case with distribution is similar. The process of distribution proceeds by means of formulations of value, the "social" relation between the capitalist and the worker is expressed in an "economic" formula, for labour power becomes a commodity. But having once become a commodity, and having been drawn into the cycle of the circulation of commodities, it becomes at once subject, if for no other reason, to the elemental law of price and value. As little as the capitalist system could continue to exist at all in the field of commodities circulation without the regulative effect of the theory of value, so little also could capital reproduce its own domination were it not for the existence of laws immanent in the reproduction of labour power as such. But since the expended labour power develops more social labour energy than is necessary for its social reproduction, the conditions are realised for a possible surplus value which accrues constantly to the purchasers of labour power by virtue of the laws of the circulation of commodities, *i.e.*, to the owners of the means of production. The evolution of the productive forces, which is accomplished in capitalist society by the mechanism of competition, here assumes the form of the accumulation of capitals, on which depends also the movement of labour power; the evolution of the productive forces, furthermore, is constantly accompanied by a displacement and a dying out of whole production groups, in which the individual labour value of the commodities exceeds their social labour value.

Thus the theory of value is the fundamental law of the entire working of the capitalist system. It is obvious that this law manifests itself to the accompaniment of constant "disturbances", since it constitutes an expression of the contradictory nature of capitalist society. It is self-evident that the contradictory nature of capitalist society, which is leading the latter to an inevitable débâcle, will ultimately cause the collapse of the "normal" capitalist law, the law of value also.[152] In the new society, however, value will lose its fetish character; it will no longer be the blind law of a planless society, *i.e.*, it will cease to be value.

Such are the general outlines of the Marxian theory, the political economy of the proletariat, which derives the "laws of motion" of the specific social structure in a truly scientific manner.

But precisely because Marxism goes beyond the limited outlines of the bourgeois mentality, it is becoming more and more hateful to the bourgeoisie. The social collaboration in the field of the social sciences—particularly in the field of economics—has by no means improved; on the contrary, more and more difficulties are making themselves felt. Bourgeois economics can at present advance only by keeping within the outlines of a purely descriptive science. Within these limits, it may and does discharge a socially useful work. To be sure, not everything that is done in this field must be accepted without question, for even the "merest" description has a certain point of view behind it: the choice of material, the emphasis of one factor and insufficient attention paid to another, etc.—all these are determined by the so called "general views" of the authors in question. Yet, with a sufficiently critical attitude, it is possible to obtain from such performances abundant material for making one's own conclusions. As for the actual theoretical work of the bourgeoisie, the example of Böhm-Bawerk has revealed it to be a barren desert. But it does not follow that Marxists must entirely ignore this field, for the process of evolution of the proletarian ideology is a process of struggle. Just as the proletariat advances on the economic and political field by means of countless struggles against hostile elements, so it must be also on the higher levels of ideology. Ideology does not descend from the sky, a system perfect in all its parts, but is gradually and painfully built up in a hard and toilsome process of evolution. By means of our criticism of hostile views, we not only ward off the enemy's attacks, but also sharpen our own weapons; a criticism of the systems of our opponents is equivalent to a clarification of our own system.

We have another reason also for devoting attentive study to bourgeois economics. The ideological struggle, like any other direct practical struggle, must make use of the rule: utilise all the oppositions within the ranks of the enemy, all their disagreements between themselves. The fact is that, in spite of the uniformity of their goal—an apology for capitalism—there still exists a considerable difference of views among bourgeois scholars. While a certain unity has been attained in the field of the value theory on the foundations created by the Austrian School, when it comes to distribution almost every theoretician will set up his own theory and justify himself by a "generally valid" theory of value. But this again proves only how difficult—from a purely logical standpoint—is the problem, and how great the "mental labour" it requires of the modern scholastic. This circumstance, however, simultaneously renders much easier the task of criticism and affords an opportunity to disclose the general logical blunders and the other weak points of the opponent. Thus a criticism of bourgeois economics aids the development of the proletariat's own economic science. Bourgeois science has now ceased to see its goal in an understanding of the social relations, being occupied now only with an apology for them. The scientific field of battle is left to Marxism alone, for the latter does not hesitate to analyse the social laws of evolution, even though they may lead to an inevitable destruction of present-day society. In this sense, Marxism remains, as ever, the red thread of theory, the emblem about which gather all those with courage enough boldly to face the impending storm.

APPENDIX

The Policy of Theoretical Conciliation [153]

TUGAN-BARANOVSKY'S THEORY OF VALUE

The swift evolution which the former "legal Marxists" were obliged to pass through during the nineties includes a very specific tendency, namely, the rise of a liberal-bourgeois ideology, as opposed not only to the ideology of the *Narodniki* (Populists), who were hostile to capitalism, but also to that of the revolutionary proletariat, *i.e.*, to Marxism. This tendency, a unit at the time, was accordingly of complicated character, like any social phenomenon. Not all the bearers of the bourgeois ideology were equally adroit in accomplishing the transformation "from Marxism to idealism".

In the heat of the race, some have already attained the goal and now look back in pride on those who have not yet reached it; others have nearly attained the goal; still others have been left far behind. It is worth while to pay some attention to the individual participants in this noble emulation.

For instance, there is Sergey Bulgakov, the "former Marxist" and a professor of political economy. Give him a cassock, and you have your full-fledged learned dominie. Also, there is another "former Marxist", Mr. Berdyayiev, likewise a pious Christian, who reasons with great predilection (for who has not his hobby?) concerning both the "earthly and heavenly Aphrodite". Somewhat apart from them stands the incomparable Peter Struve, the heavy artillery of the Cadet-Octobrist [Liberal-Conservative—*Translator*] erudition. All these honourable gentlemen have broken definitely with their past, which they now include among their "youthful indiscretions". They are advancing unswervingly, these knights-errant of Russian capitalism. Lagging far behind them, but obviously inspired with the ambition to overtake his colleagues, moves Professor Tugan-Baranovsky, the former Marxist and present counsellor of the industrial magnates. Tugan-Baranovsky's Christian mumblings began much later than those of the others. He is still flirting with Marxism, wherefore many naïve persons still count him among the almost "reds". In a word, he is an "apostle of conciliation". He cannot make up his mind to join the camp of the enemies of the proletariat and accept their theory wholeheartedly; he merely prefers, as he says, to "cleanse Marxism from its unscientific elements". For this reason, he is more misleading than the others; his theoretical activity is the more harmful. He will not "deny" the labour value theory outright, but seeks to reconcile it with the theory of Böhm-Bawerk, this classical representative of bourgeois aspirations. The reader may judge for himself what are the results of these efforts of Tugan-Baranovsky in the field of the principal problem of political economy, namely, the theory of value.

1. Tugan-Baranovsky's formula.

Tugan-Baranovsky begins with a pæan on Böhm-Bawerk.

"The great merit of the new theory," he says, "is in the fact that it offers a promise of definitely terminating the dispute as to value, for, proceeding from a *single* uniform fundamental principle, it affords a complete [!] and exhaustive [!!] explanation for *all* the phenomena of the process of evaluation." (Tugan-Baranovsky: *Foundations of Political Economy*, p. 40, 1911, in Russian.)

In another passage: "The theory of marginal utility will have remained the fundamental theory of value; it may in its various parts suffer change and amplification in the future, but in its fundamental ideas it remains an eternal achievement of economic science." (*Ibid.*, p. 55.)

"An eternal achievement of economic science"—these are proud words. Unfortunately this "achievement" looks less brave on closer inspection; but for the present let us postpone our objections and examine Tugan-Baranovsky's "platform of conciliation".

According to the doctrine of the adherents of the Austrian School, the value of a possession is determined by its marginal utility. This in turn depends on the *volume of possessions* of the same type. The greater the volume, the more "saturated" the demand, the lower will be the urgency of the requirement, and the lower the marginal value of the possession in question. In other words, the Austrian School concludes its analysis by assuming as given a specific volume, a specific quantity of the possessions to be evaluated. Tugan-Baranovsky quite consistently asks a further question: what determines this quantity of goods? In his opinion, this quantity depends on the "economic plan"; the factor of *labour value* plays the decisive part.

"Marginal utility is the utility of the last units of any type of goods," says Tugan-Baranovsky, "it varies together with the compass of production. By expanding or diminishing production, we may produce corresponding expansions or diminutions of marginal utility. On the other hand. the labour value of a unit affords us something given objectively, something independent of our will. It follows that in the elaboration of the economic plan, labour value is the determining element, while marginal utility is the element to be determined. Expressed mathematically, marginal utility must be a function of labour value." (*Ibid.*, p. 47.)

As to the nature of the relation between the marginal utility of goods and their labour value, Tugan-Baranovsky reasons as follows: Let us assume we are dealing with two branches of production, *A* and *B*. A rational economic plan would require that the distribution of labour in both these branches of production be so organised as to make the resulting utility equal in both cases during the last unit of time.[154] Without such an equilibrium, a rational plan, *i.e.*, the attainment of the highest utility, is inconceivable. For, assuming that the last hour in production branch *A* yield a utility of ten units, while that in production branch *B* yield only five units, it is obvious that it would be more profitable to stop producing commodity *B* and devote the time thus gained to the production of commodity *A*. But if the labour value of the commodities, the utility produced during the last unit of time, is equal, it will follow that the "*utility of the last units of every type of freely reproducible goods—their marginal utility—is inversely proportional to the relative quantity of these goods producible within a unit of time; in other words, it must be in direct proportion with the labour value of these goods.*" (*Ibid.*, p. 47.)

So much for Tugan-Baranovsky's remarks on the relation between the marginal utility and the absolute labour value of commodities. We here find no contradiction at all, only harmony: "In spite of the prevalent opinion," says Tugan-Baranovsky, "to the effect that the two theories mutually exclude each other, perfect harmony prevails between them. The difference is only that they investigate two different phases of the same process of economic valuation. The theory of marginal utility explains the subjective factors in economic evaluation, while the labour value theory explains its objective factors." (*Ibid.*, p. 49.)

He goes on to say that the two theories cannot be spoken of as diametrically opposed, with the result that the adherents of the theory of marginal utility may extend a friendly hand to the adherents of the labour value theory. We believe we can show nevertheless that the assumption of neighbourly relations is based on a very naïve conception of both theories. But before we proceed to an unmasking of the fundamental fallacy of Mr. Tugan-Baranovsky, let us make a critical study of the manner in which our peace apostle views the labour value theory. This will reveal a few interesting peculiarities of his mental processes, and thus throw some light on the reasons for his conciliation policy.

2. *Mr. Tugan-Baranovsky's "Logic".*

The above presentation would lead any sensible person to the following conclusion: [155] since value (the subjective value determined by the marginal utility of goods) is proportional to labour value, and since this value, furthermore, constitutes the basis of price, it follows that labour value is the true basis for price. As a matter of fact, if labour value and marginal utility are connected by any such firm, definite, relation as direct proportion, it is obvious that these magnitudes must in analysis be mutually replaceable. If we assume with Tugan-Baranovsky that "the determining factor is labour value while marginal utility is the factor to be determined" (*Ibid.*, p. 47), the above point of view assumes compulsory cogency. The succession of phenomena then becomes: price, marginal utility, labour value. The labour costs are here connected with the subjective *value* and consequently also with the price. This circumstance even makes Tugan-Baranovsky declare that "the labour value theory . . . from a certain point of view is . . . an economic theory of *value par excellence,* while the theory of marginal utility is a more universal psychological theory of value, and not a specifically economic theory of value." [*Ibid.,* p. 50; italics mine.—*N.B.*]

Labour value, therefore, determines marginal utility, which in turn determines price; in other words, labour value is the ultimate basis of price. So far, so good; but only eight pages further on we encounter the following "criticism" of Karl Marx:

"In spite of offering a criticism of *labour costs,* Marx gives us a theory of absolute labour *value. . . .*"

"In his well-known criticism of the third volume of *Capital,* Sombart attempts [156] to defend Marx's labour value theory by interpreting it as a theory of labour costs. By labour value he understands 'the degree of the social power of production of labour'. *If this is the case, why should it be necessary to designate the expenditure in labour as 'value' and thus give rise to the notion that the expenditure of labour is the basis of the price, of the exchange relations between commodities (which is obviously not the case), instead of recognising the independent right to existence of both these categories: value and costs.*" (*Grundzüge der Theorie des wirtschaftlichen Güterwerts,* p. 58.)

Mr. Tugan-Baranovsky asks whether it is proper to interpret labour *value* as social labour *costs.*[157] This is quite right, but everything that Tugan-Baranovsky adds is wrong. He is so enamoured of his own criticism, that he cannot grasp that he is criticising not only Marx, but also himself. We have already seen that Tugan-Baranovsky's principles result in the inference that labour value is the basis of price. We now suddenly find that this is "obviously not the case". Which of the statements is true? the former or the latter? It is a most peculiar form of mental clarity which Tugan-Baranovsky here offers us, one might almost term it "cast-iron logic". But perhaps the reader has doubts as to the permanence of Tugan-Baranovsky's last "thought". Let Tugan-Baranovsky give himself strength:

"In Karl Marx, labour is in its essence nothing more or less than labour costs. But this must not be taken as a terminological fallacy on the part of Marx. Marx did not only term the socially necessary labour of production simply the *value* of the commodity, but he was constantly at effort to trace back to labour the exchange relations between commodities themselves. . . . *It is only by absolutely distinguishing between the conceptions of value and of costs* that a correct logical theory of value and costs in accordance with the facts, can be built up." [*Ibid.*, p. 69; italics mine.—*N.B.*] We quote another passage:

"Marx's fallacy was . . . that of failing to understand the independent significance of this category [*i.e.*, the category of costs.—*N.B.*] and of attempting to relate it with the theory of price; for this reason he called labour costs, not costs, but value." [158]

No doubt; and Tugan-Baranovsky has already forgotten that he himself had connected labour costs with value and price, and that he now finds himself engaged in the process of dissolving this criminal alliance. His logic is indeed astonishing! We shall now permit ourselves a question. If the category of costs is so independent of the question that Tugan-Baranovsky has a right to consider it a mortal sin to drag it into this above-mentioned connection, what is left of the *economic* importance of these categories? To be sure, he assures us that they are of "very great" importance, yet we find nothing here but "ethical rhetoric", which we need not take seriously.

We may pass on to Tugan-Baranovsky's "fundamental fallacy". In spite of his pronounced ability to construct a system consisting of the most contradictory principles, it will here be shown that his "formula" is an even more outrageous achievement.

3. Tugan-Baranovsky's Fundamental Fallacy.

Thus far we have been assuming Tugan-Baranovsky's formula as to the proportional relation between labour value and marginal utility without offering any criticism. We shall now reveal the theoretical emptiness of this famous formula, for which perhaps we must first state Tugan-Baranovsky's view on political economy, and therefore on any "formula", a view shared by us also. But we have too much respect for Professor Tugan-Baranovsky to deprive him of the opportunity of presenting this absolutely correct position in his own words:

"What distinguishes the science of economics from the other social sciences, namely, the construction of a system of causal laws for economic phenomena, is precisely the result of the characteristic peculiarities of their present subject of investigation: the condition of a free exchange commodity. . . . We have every reason to recognize political economy as an original science dealing with the causal interrelations of economic phenomena, closely connected with modern economic life. This science arose and grew up together with this economic life; it will disappear from the scene together with it." (*Grundzüge der Theorie des wirtschaftlichen Güterwerts*, p. 17.)

This is a clear statement to the effect that political economy makes the exchange system the object of its investigation, particularly the *capitalist* exchange system. And it is from this point of view that we shall proceed to an analysis of Tugan-Baranovsky's formula. As we have already stated, he assumes that a proportional relation exists between marginal utility and labour value. Let us begin our analysis with the latter half of the formula, namely, with labour value. Tugan-Baranovsky assumes that labour value determines the economic plan. Yet the "economic plan" he has in mind is a category of the *individual* economy and, moreover, of an *economy in kind*, producing the most "varied goods" for its own use. But a glance at the *modern* individualistic economy, *i.e.*, the capitalist system, will present no "economic plan" at all in Tugan-Baranovsky's sense, for the simple reason that factory production has become *specialised;* there is no room here for a distribution of time over various "branches". For each industry produces a single product. Aside from this, the category of labour value does not concern the economic individual working in the capitalist enterprise, for this individual "works" with the aid of hired hands and of means of production purchased on the market. If there is no reason at all for mentioning labour value here, the latter can be considered only as a *social* category, as far as the modern mode of production is concerned (which constitutes the real object of the study of political economy), *i.e.*, a conception that is applied not to individual establishments, but to their totality, to their social aggregate. This is Marx's conception of labour value. Its correctness or error is not a question that concerns us at this moment; we consider it to be correct; Tugan-Baranovsky assumes the opposite. At any rate, however, Karl Marx fully appreciated the absurdity of a category of labour value as a category of an individual economy, since this category may acquire meaning only when understood in its *social* character.

The second half of the formula is concerned with marginal utility. According to the understanding of all the adherents of the theory of marginal utility, marginal utility signifies a possession serving the will of an "economic subject"; this is a certain evaluation, presupposing a conscious calculation. It is obvious that the category of marginal utility can have meaning only if used of an *individual* economy; it is completely worthless (even from the point of view of its advocates) as soon as the entire social economy is concerned. Certainly the latter does not "evaluate" as an individual entrepreneur may do. For, the social economy is a system which unfolds by the operation of natural law, and with a peculiar and characteristic logical sequence. If, therefore, marginal utility is to have any significance at all, it can be only that of a category of individual economy.

We already know that Tugan-Baranovsky states that there is a proportional relation between marginal utility and labour value. Labour value may be understood in two ways: either as a social category (this view is the only correct one when dealing with a *capitalist* economy) or as an individualistic category. Obviously, labour value in the former sense cannot be brought into any direct relation with marginal utility; they are two quantities having nothing in common, in *principle,* since they lie in entirely different planes. To maintain that a quantity that is applicable only in the field of an individualistic economy is proportional to another quantity applicable only in the field of *social* economy, is equivalent to "grafting telegraph poles on pockmarks".

We thus find that a *correct* understanding of the labour value theory will lead precisely to the conclusion that it constitutes a diametrical opposite to the theory of marginal utility. There is still to be considered the connection of the *nonsensical* notion of labour value as the category of an individualistic economy, with the conception of marginal utility. Tugan-Baranovsky succeeds in accomplishing even this, which of course does not improve his theory, which collapses completely as soon as an attempt is made to compare it with the capitalist reality. The result is about the same as with the advocates of the Austrian School, whose doctrines work very well as long as we limit ourselves to the sphere of interests of the economic Robinson Crusoe, and—consciously or unconsciously—keep aloof from capitalist relations. But as soon as we study these relations, which constitute the proper subject of political economy (as Tugan-Baranovsky himself maintains), the theory is revealed as the wretched and empty thing it is.

We shall make one more remark before concluding. Tugan-Baranovsky's entire theory is concerned with enterprises *producing* commodities. This is an honourable distinction between him and the pure marginal utilitarians who seem to forget that commodities do not descend from the skies but must be produced. And it is precisely in the case of productive economies that Tugan-Baranovsky sets up his "proportional law". We shall take another passage from the second section of his book:

"We must stick to the real economic relations," he says, "under which price is formed in modern capitalist economy. We must not assume, as does Böhm-Bawerk, for instance, that the seller of a commodity needs the latter for himself and will even be willing, if the price should be too low, to keep it for himself." (*Ibid.*, pp. 212, 213.)

This is true. Furthermore, it is a great advance over the theoreticians of marginal utility of the purest water. Yet how will Mr. Tugan-Baranovsky's own theory hold water if his producing establishments should not estimate commodities according to their utility (*i.e.*, their marginal utility)? In order that the above-mentioned proportional relation should be applicable, it is surely necessary that the required quantities should be in existence. We have seen above that the principle does not work as far as labour value is concerned. Now Tugan-Baranovsky himself tells us that an evaluation according to the marginal utility is completely nonsensical, as far as sellers are concerned, under the conditions of capitalism (or even of a simple commodities economy).

We have investigated Tugan-Baranovsky's theory without dwelling on one of its ingredients, the theory of marginal utility. And our theoretician has failed to substantiate that portion of his theory also. This is a noteworthy fact. In their quest for new weapons, the Russian bourgeois philosophers are very "critically" disposed toward Karl Marx only; but when dealing with the capitalist scientific ideology of Western Europe, they are inspired with an almost religious awe. It is this fact which again reveals the true nature of the "new ideas in political economy" so zealously preached by Messrs. Tugan-Baranovsky, Bulgakov, Struve, *e tutti quanti.*

NOTES

NOTES

1. The success of the "new" theories is therefore based on the altered condition of the social psychology and not at all on their logical perfection. One of the reasons for hostility to the theory of labour value on the part of the bourgeoisie is surely to be found in the latter's opposition to socialism. In part, Böhm-Bawerk admits this when he says: "To be sure, I feel that the labour value theory for a number of years has rather gained in general acceptance, as a result of the dissemination of socialist ideas, but in the most recent epoch it has decidedly lost ground among the theoretical circles of all countries, and this is particularly due to the increasing importance now attached to the theory of 'marginal utility'." Böhm-Bawerk: *Kapital und Kapitalzins*, second edition, vol. I, p. 444, *note*. (A translation of this work, *Capital and Interest*, by W. Smart, appeared in London in 1890. The quotations, however, are from the German original.)

2. By cosmopolitanism, Karl Knies understands the view of the classical economists, who held that the economic laws remain the same for each country and nation; on the subject of perpetualism—which is the corresponding view of the classical school with regard to the various historical epochs, see Knies: *Die politische Ökonomie vom geschichtlichen Standpunkte*, new edition of 1883, p. 24.

3. Friedrich List may be considered the chief theoretician of the Historical School; List's platform was that of a protectionist policy. See his *Das nationale System der politischen Okonomie*, 1841.

4. Thus, A. Miklashevsky enumerates Professor Gustav Schmoller's "accomplishments": "It was his aim to postpone the introduction of state insurance of workers; he was opposed to an extension of protective legislation to agricultural workers and artisans. . . . He considered it appropriate to apply penal law in the case of violations of labour contracts by agricultural workers; he resisted the legal competence of trade unions and workers' associations; he was in favour of the anti-socialist laws. . . ." *History of Political Economy.—The Philosophical, Historical and Theoretical Bases of the Nineteenth Century*, Yuryiev (Dorpat), 1909, p. 578 (in Russian).

5. One of the most moderate advocates of the historical school, F. Neumann, imagines, for instance, that "there is no possibility of *exact* laws in the economic field" (*Naturgesetz und Wirtschaftge-*

setz, in *Zeitschrift für die gesamte Sozialwissenschaft,* edited by Arthur Schäffle, 1892, vol. XLVIII, p. 435). The same author, discussing the concept of the "typical", has the following to say: "We there *find* [*i.e.,* in the natural sciences.—*N.B.*] typical conditions, from which in turn typical conditions may emanate and which may be studied as typical conditions. Here [in the social sciences.—*N.B.*] the word *typical* is to be assumed, *i.e., pretended* (*ibid.,* p. 442).

6. Schmoller emphasises three "fundamental thoughts" of the Historical School: "1. Recognition of the principle of evolution. . . . 2. A psychological-moral view. . . . 3. A critical attitude toward an individualistic interpretation of nature, as well as toward socialism." (*Op. cit.,* p. 123.)

7. Very appropriate is Heinrich Dietzel's observation on this point: "It would be just as easy to speak of an 'ethical' anthropology, physiology, etc., as of an 'ethical' *theory* of economy or an 'ethical' *history of economy.*" (*Theoretische Sozialökonomie. Cf.* also Emil Sax: *Das Wesen und die Aufgaben der Nationalökonomie,* Vienna, 1884, p. 53.) Léon Walras similarly pokes fun at "morality" in a general theory and compares this process with an attempt to "*spiritualiser la géométrie*". (Léon Walras: *Etude d'Economie sociale. Théorie de la répartition de la richesse sociale.* Lausanne-Paris, 1896, p. 40.)

8. The terminology is taken from A. A. Chuprov, Junior; *cf.* Chuprov's *Foundations of a Theory of Statistics* (St. Petersburg, 1909, in Russian). The same terms are used with somewhat different connotation in Rickert and Windelband.

9. Particular attention was paid to handicrafts. The basis of this study is found in an explanation by Gustav Schmoller: "Only the maintenance of a . . . middle class can . . . guard us from ultimately heading toward a political evolution which will consist of alternating dominations by the moneyed interests and by the fourth estate. . . . Only it [social reform.—*N.B.*] will maintain the aristocracy of mind and education at the head of the state." (*Über einige Grundfragen der Sozialpolitik und der Volkswirtschaftslehre,* Leipzig, 1898, pp. 5 and 6.)

10. Heinrich Dietzel, who has no connection with socialism whatever, makes the following observation on this point: "Hohoff's statement that the polemic opposition to the labour value theory owes its origin not to the intellect, but to the will, is entirely correct. . . ." (*Theoretische Sozialökonomik,* p. 211.) On the same page, some attention is also paid to the "apologetic exercises" of Kamorschinsky and the pillar of the Austrian School, Böhm-Bawerk himself.

11. A characterization of these classes may be found in Sombart's *Luxus und Kapitalismus* (published by Duncker & Humblot, 1903), particularly on pp. 103, 105, *et seq.* All of which does not prevent Charles Gide from maintaining that "idleness is merely a well regulated division of labour", for "even the ancients already recognized the necessity that citizens should have their entire leisure time free for occupation with concerns of the state." (*Foundations of Political Economy,* quoted from the Russian translation by Scheinis, St. Petersburg, 1898, p. 288.) But the ancients considered even *slavery* to be an absolutely "necessary institution" and a "well regulated division of labour". And it may be said that these gentlemen-economists of the bourgeoisie are therefore not to be outdistanced in any way, in their glorification of slavery, by the "ancients".

12. These examples are actually taken from the illustrations Böhm-Bawerk offers in his discussion of his theory of value.

13. Karl Marx: *Capital,* vol. II, p. 133. The example of the mercantilists illustrates with particular force the connection between theory and practice; its most prominent ideologists were at the same time men prominent in practical life: Sir Thomas Gresham, for example, was an adviser of Queen Elizabeth and had direct charge of the struggle against the Hanseatic League; Thomas Mun was a member of the Board of Directors of the East India Company; Dudley North was one of the greatest princes of commerce, men who were carrying on an extraordinary international trade for that period, etc. (*cf.,* August Oncken: *Geschichte der Nationalökonomie*). On the subject of exchange as a point of departure for our science, *cf.,* Karl Pribram: "Die Idee des Gleichgewichts in der älteren Nationalökonomischen Theorie", *Zeitschrift für Volkswirtschaft, Sozialpolitik und Verwaltung,* vol. XVII, p. 1, where a bibliography will also be found.

14. The outline given above may be considered merely as an *outline,* merely as a diagram presenting the types in bold relief and ignoring all subsidiary factors. T. R. Kaulla, who, in his book, *Die geschichtliche Entwicklung der modernen Werttheorien* (Tübingen, 1906) attempts to present among other things an analysis of the Austrian School, has completely failed to grasp the significance of the phenomenon pointed out above.

15. We are applying the terminology of Rudolf Hilferding (*cf.,* Hilferding's *Finanzkapital,* particularly pp. 282-284).

16. The reader should consult the analysis of the American economists, from the point of view of the Austrian School, in Schumpeter: "Die neuere Wirtschaftstheorie in den Vereinigten Staaten", in *Jahrbuch für Gesetzgebung, Verwaltung und Volkswirtschaft im*

Deutschen Reiche, edited by Gustav Schmoller, 34th year, No. 3, particularly pp. 10, 13, 15.

17. Werner Sombart: *Der Bourgeois,* p. 193. It must not be overlooked that even very many of the American multi-millionaires are self-made men who have not yet had time to become old and decrepit in spirit.

18. L'Abbé de Condillac: *Le Commerce et le gouvernement considerés relativement l'un à l'dutre,* Paris An III (1795), pp. 6-8.

19. Consult the French translation of Comte de Verri: *Economic politique ou considération sur la valeur de l'argent et les moyens d'en faire baisser les intérêts, sur les Banques, la balance de Commerce, l'Agriculture, la population, les Impôts,* etc., Paris, An III (particularly pp. 14, 15).

20. Jevons' book appeared in 1871 (W. Stanley Jevons: *Theory of Political Economy,* London and New York); Karl Menger; *Grundsätze der Volkswirtschaftslehre,* in Vienna, in 1871; while that of Walras: *Principe d'une théorie mathématique de l'échange,* appeared in the *Journal des Economistes* in 1874. On the matter of priority, consult the correspondence between Walras and Jevons: *Correspondence entre M. Jevons et M. Walras,* which the latter quotes in his *Théorie mathématique de la richesse sociale* (Lausanne, 1883, pp. 26-30).

21. In his preface to the first volume of *Capital,* Karl Marx designates his method as the deductive method of the Classical School. It would be absurd, furthermore, to assume, as is done by the representatives of the Historical School, that every abstract law is entirely out of all relation with concrete reality. "An exact scientific law", says Emil Sax, one of the representatives of the Austrian School, "is an inductive conclusion of the highest and most general type; as such, and not as an *a priori* axiom, it becomes the point of departure for deduction." (Conrad's *Jahrbücher für Nationalökonomie und Statistik,* 1894, third series, vol. VIII, p. 116.) A precise analysis of this question is given by Alfred Ammon in his *Objekt und Grundbegriffe der theoretischen Nationalökonomie,* Vienna and Leipzig, 1911.

22. *Cf.,* for instance, Karl Menger: *Untersuchungen über die Methoden der Sozialwissenschaften und der politischen Ökonomie insbesondere* (1883, p. 259), where fairly correct definitions are presented for a true theoretical point of departure. The theory of marginal utility reached its highest culmination of self-criticism in Robert Liefmann: *Über Objekt, Wesen und Aufgabe der Wirtschaftswissenschaft,* Conrad's *Jahrbücher,* vol. XIII, p. 106.

23. Werner Sombart: "Zur Kritik des ökonomischen Systems

von Karl Marx", in Braun's *Archiv für soziale Gesetzgebung und Statistik,* vol. VII, pp. 591, 592. *Cf.* also Robert Liefmann, *op cit.,* p. 5: "The principal methodological problem in the future appears to me to be the contrast between individualistic and social modes of regarding questions, or, in other words, between the profit and the general economic point of view." We recommend Liefmann's work to the reader as that in which the individualistic method is most consistently and clearly carried out.

24. *Cf.* for example, Adam Smith: *An Inquiry into the Nature and Causes of the Wealth of Nations,* London, 1895, vol. I, p. 129: "Equal quantities of labour, at all times, and places, may be said to be of equal value *to the labourer.* In his ordinary state of health, strength and spirits; in the ordinary degree of his skill and dexterity, he must always lay down the same portion of *his ease, his liberty and his happiness* (italics mine.—*N.B.*). A number of similar quotations might also be included here. For this reason it is entirely wrong for Georg Charasoff to state, as he does in his polemic against Karl Kautsky: "There can be no serious doubt in our mind of the fact that the Classical School by no means advocated in its doctrine of the laws of value an individualistic point of view, but rather a consistent social point of view, precisely as did Marx himself." (*Cf.* Charasoff: *Das System des Marxismus,* Berlin, 1910, p. 253.) On the other hand, Charasoff's assertion that even certain Marxian studies contain a subjective interpretation of the Marxian theory, is entirely correct; but this is not the place to discuss this question.

25. Karl Marx: *Capital,* vol. I, p. 23. The quotation is taken from a criticism by Kaufmann, which is quoted by Marx himself and with which Marx expresses himself as fully in agreement.

26. Böhm-Bawerk: "Grundzüge der Theorie des wirtschaftlichen Güterwerts", in Hildebrandt's *Jahrbücher für Nationalökonomie und Statistik,* vol. XIII, New Series, p. 78; also Karl Menger: *Untersuchungen über die Methoden der Sozialwissenschaften und der politischen Ökonomie insbesondere* 1883; also Robert Liefmann, *op. cit.,* p. 40.

27. This circumstance alone is sufficient to destroy completely the teleological view of society as a "purposeful structure" which is found in particularly definite formulation in Stolzmann: "Just as we find completely lacking in the life of nature all definite tendency of purpose, all systematic intention, economy, husbanding of resources . . . so is the case also with the relations between humans." (Professor Wipper: *Foundations of the Theory of Historical Science,* Moscow, 1911, p. 162, in Russian.) *Cf.* also the brilliant presentation of the "independence" of the result of individual actions in

Friedrich Engels: *Ludwig Feuerbach.* R. Liefmann, in his criticism of the "social", *i.e.,* the objective method, attaches himself precisely to the criticism of the teleological view, in which he claims that the latter must be accepted by everyone who consistently advocates this method. He accused even the Marxians (Hilferding, for example) of practicing teleology, and his victory over the latter is therefore comparatively easy. As a matter of fact, the Marxist theory treats society as a completely non-subjective system.

28. "In economic relations," says Peter Struve, "the economic man is considered in his relations with other men, who are also economic men, and the intermediate economic categories [*i.e.,* the categories of a commodities economy.—*N.B.*] express the objective resultants (or those that are becoming objective) of such relations: they contain nothing "that is subjective" although their origin is "in the subjective". On the other hand, they include no direct expression for the relations between economic men and nature, the external world; in this sense they include no "objective" or "natural" element. (Peter Struve: *Economics and Price,* Moscow, 1913, pp. 25, 26, Russian.) Struve, however, points out the naturalistic element in the value theory ("coagulated labour") and thus builds up a contradition between this element and the "sociological" element. With this we must compare Karl Marx's *Theorien über den Mehrwert,* vol. I, p. 277: "But the materialisation of labour is not to be taken in so Scottish a sense as Adam Smith takes it. When we speak of a commodity as the material exponent of labour—in the sense of its exchange value—this is of course merely an imaginary, *i.e.,* a merely social mode of existence of the commodity, which has nothing to do with its corporeal reality." "The fallacy in this connection is traceable to the fact that a social relation has expressed itself in the form of an object." (P. 278.)

29. Peter Struve creates a connection between a "universalistic" method of this type and a logical realism (as opposed to the "singularistic" method which is associated in logic with the so-called nominalism). "In social science," says Struve, "the realistic trend of thought evidences itself particularly in the fact that the system of the psychical relations between men, *i.e.,* society, is regarded not only as a real unit, as a sum, or (!) system, but also as a living unit, a living creature. Such concepts as society, class, power, either appear as, or they may easily be regarded (!!!) as 'universalities' of sociological thought. They are easily hypostasized" (*op. cit.,* p. XI). Struve does not adduce this opinion—as one might think—in order to prove the incompetence of the Marxian mode of investigation, which he identifies with the "logical-ontological realism of

Hegel . . . and the scholastic philosophers" (*op cit.*, p. XXVI). Yet it is quite clear that Marx offers not even the slightest indication of any tendency to regard society and social groupings as a living creature (the expression "living unit" is something different and even more vague). It will suffice, in this connection, to compare Marx's method with—let us say—the method of the "social-organic" movement which finds its latest formulation in the work of Stolzmann. Marx himself was quite conscious of the fallacies of the Hegelian logical realism. "Hegel fell into the error . . . of considering the real as the result of self-coördinating, self-absorbed, and spontaneously operating thought, while the method of advancing from the abstract to the concrete is but a way of thinking by which the concrete is grasped and is reproduced in our mind as a concrete. It is by no means, however, the process which itself generates the concrete." (Karl Marx: *Introduction to a Critique of Political Economy,* in *Contribution to a Critique of Political Economy,* Chicago, 1913, p. 293.)

30. It may be pointed out that Bastiat is speaking of isolated human beings, an abstraction which he considered useful from the methodological point of view, while historically he considers this abstraction to be merely "one of Rousseau's deceptive delusions" (see also pp. 93, 94).

31. W. Stanley Jevons: *The Theory of Political Economy,* London and New York, 1871, p. 21. The "mathematical economists" and the "Americans" for the most part abandon this position. *Cf.* Léon Walras: *Etudes a' économie sociale* (*Théorie de la répartition de la richesse sociale*), Lausanne, Paris, 1896: "It should not be said that the individual is the basis and the goal of all society without adding, simultaneously, that the social condition is also the centre of all individuality" (p. 90). In John Bates Clark, objectivism is dominant. But the extent to which all this thinking is unclear and undigested may be gathered, for instance, from the following definition presented by the American economist, Thomas Nixon Carver: "The method pursued is that of an analytical study of the motives which govern men in business and industrial life." (*The Distribution of Wealth,* New York, 1904, p. XV.) Yet Carver himself attempts to "objectivise" the theory of value.

32. "To such totalities, constructed by ourselves, as do not exist at all outside of our consciousness, we may oppose the real totalities, constructed by life itself. Among all the infants existing in the entire territory of European Russia, there is no other relation than that set up in our statistical tables: the trees in the forests are engaged in a process of permanent mutual interaction and

constitute a certain unit, regardless of whether they have been associated under a generalising concept or not." (A. Chuprov: *Foundations of a Theory of Statistics,* St. Petersburg, 1909, p. 76, in Russian.)

33. "Proceeding inductively from the facts, a consideration of the economic reality will bring us face to face . . . with veritable mountains of facts proving to us that the individual engaged in economic practices, in spite of all his thoughts and actions, is dependent on the given state of an objective framework of the existing economic order." (R. Stolzmann, *op. cit.,* p. 35.)

34. "The point of departure of every social phenomenon is always the individual; but not the isolated individual who is investigated by the critics of Marx as well as by the students of the eighteenth century. . . . But the individual in his connections with other individuals, the *totality of individuals* . . . in which the single individual himself develops a different mental life than he would in a condition of isolation." (Louis B. Boudin: *The Theoretical System of Karl Marx,* German translation, Stuttgart, 1909, Karl Kautsky's Preface, p. XIII.) Marx himself has often depicted in very realistic form the necessity of a social point of view. "Material production by individuals as determined by society, naturally constitutes the starting point. The individual and isolated hunter or fisher who forms the starting point with Smith and Ricardo belongs to the insipid illusions of the eighteenth century.". (Karl Marx: *Introduction to a Critique of Political Economy,* printed with *A Contribution to a Critique of Political Economy,* Chicago, 1913, pp. 265-266.) "The production of the isolated individuals outside of society . . . is as much a monstrosity and an impossibility as the evolution of a language occurring without individuals living *together* and speaking to each other" (*op. cit.*). Rudolf Hilferding very appropriately remarks on this point: "From the motives of the operating economic individuals, which are themselves, however, determined by the nature of the economic relations, we may never derive more than a tendency toward the setting up of an equality in economic conditions: uniform prices for uniform commodities, equal profit for equal capital, equal pay and equal rate of exploitation for equal labour. But I shall never arrive at the quantitative relations themselves in this manner, proceeding thus from the subjective motives." (*Das Finanzkapital,* p. 325, *footnote.*)

35. Böhm-Bawerk: *Zum Abschluss des Marxschen Systems.* (*Staatswissenschaftliche Arbeiten. Festgaben für Karl Knies.*) Berlin, 1896. This work was translated into English by Miss Alice Macdonald, with a Preface by James Bonar, London, 1898.

36. Of course, even the Austrians admit that they are here dealing only with an abstraction: "Man does not carry on his husbandry of resources as an isolated creature; an individual establishment in the strict sense of the word is an abstraction." (Emil Sax: *Das Wesen und die Aufgaben der Nationalökonomie,* Vienna, 1884, p. 12.) But not every abstraction is an admissible abstraction; Böhm-Bawerk himself states on this point that "in science even the thoughts and the 'logic' may not be permitted to wander away from the facts in too unbridled a manner. . . . Only those peculiarities may be abstracted which are irrelevant to the phenomenon to be subjected to investigation, and they must be *truly, actually,* irrelevant to be so abstracted." (Böhm-Bawerk: *Zum Abschluss des Marxschen Systems,* p. 194.)

37. Böhm-Bawerk, *ibid.,* p. 201. Struve, who calls this mode of study scholastic (see the notes on pp. XXV and XXXII of the Russian edition) speaks in another passage of the empirically correct application of the universalist method. But this does not prevent the same author from stating that the sociological point of view which is necessary in political economy must proceed in the last analysis from the human being, from his psyche [*i.e.,* from the "individual".—*N.B.*] p. 26. At the same time, Struve will assign "no particular importance to the subtleties of psychological subjectivism", as if these "subtleties" were not necessarily and logically related with their "bases". The reader will discern that Struve has selected a very convenient position for himself. A negative answer to Böhm-Bawerk's question is afforded by R. Liefmann, *op. cit.*

38. Even John Keynes, an adherent of the theory of marginal utility, assumes that the "phenomena of industrial life in all their compass may be explained by the deductive method alone, beginning with a few elementary laws of nature." (*The Object and the Method of Political Economy,* quoted from the Russian translation edited by Manuilov, Moscow, 1899, p. 70.)

39. See Tugan-Baranovsky: *Grundlagen der Nationalökonomie.* It must be noted in this connection, however, that while the Physiocrats really had a correct understanding of capitalism, of which they were quite unconscious, Tugan-Baranovsky makes every effort to understand it but sets up only the most meaningless formulas. (*Cf.,* N. Bukharin: "Eine Ökonomie ohne Wert", *Die Neue Zeit,* 1914, pp. 22, 23.)

40. The quotation is taken from a review by Kaufmann, cited by Marx in the preface to the second edition of *Capital* (vol. I, pp. 22, 23).

41. Even the "benevolent" critics fail to understand this; *cf.* George Charasoff, *op. cit.*, pp. 260, 261.

42. In his *Geschichte der Nationalökonomie,* Professor August Oncken distinguishes three methods: the exact or philosophical method; the historical or rather the historical-statistical method; the historical-philosophical method, which is synthetic in character (p. 9). Furthermore: "In the field of socialism, the historical-philosophical method has been advocated on the one hand by Saint-Simon and, later, in the extremely materialistic sense, by Karl Marx and Friedrich Engels. . . . It [historical materialism.—*N.B.*] can be effectively combated only on the same, *i.e.*, historical-philosophical ground" (*op. cit.*). This amounts precisely to a recognition of the fruitfulness of the Marxian method, which must, to be sure, according to Oncken, be united with the idealism of Kant in order that the disastrous effect of the materialistic theory may be better combated.

43. It is natural that Bulgakov should entirely fail to grasp this. See Bulgakov's criticism of the Marxist prognosis in his *Philosophy of Economy,* in Russian.

44. "Natural law phenomena of the present-day type . . . not met with until all forms of isolation, including that of local inaccessibility, had become matters of the past." (Neumann: "Naturgesetz und Wirtschaftsgesetz," in *Zeitschrift für die gesamte Staatswissenschaft,* edited by Artur Schäffle, 1892, 48th year, No. 3, p. 446.) Mr. Struve praises Marx highly for his analysis of the fetishism of commodities, yet he believes that Marx as well as the entire school of scientific socialism was guilty of an error in ascribing an historical character to this phenomenon. But this circumstance does not prevent the same writer from associating this fetishism closely with the commodities economy, which represents, in his view, an historical category (see Struve: "Wirtschaftssystem", in *op. cit.*).

45. Karl Marx: *Introduction to a Critique of Political Economy,* Chicago, 1913, p. 269. Although written in the year 1859 these words are perfectly applicable now.

46. A complete statement of Marx's methodological views will be found in his *Introduction to a Critique of Political Economy,* frequently quoted by us. With regard to the historical and unhistorical "conditions of production", Marx summarises his ideas as follows: "To sum up: All the stages of production have certain destinations in common, which we generalize in thought; but the so called general conditions of all production are nothing but abstract

conceptions which do not go to make up any real stage in the history to production." (*Ibid.*, p. 274.)

47. Böhm-Bawerk: *Kapital und Kapitalzins*, 1909, vol. II, part I, pp. 54, 55. Peter Struve, who served his apprenticeship in the Marxian school, likewise advocates this extremely superficial point of view: "Pure economic activity," he writes, "also recognises such categories, as production costs, capital, profits, rents" (*op. cit.*, p. 17); by pure economic activity he means "the economic relation of the economic man to the external world" (*op. cit.*). A more delicate variant of the same thought may be traced back to Karl Rodbertus, who distinguishes between the logical and the historical conception of capital. In reality this terminology serves as a cloak for the apologetic tones of the bourgeois economists, for in its essence it is completely superfluous, since there exists a term for the "logical categories", for instance, means of production. Further details under this head will be found below, in the analysis of the theory of profits.

48. "In the first stone which he (the savage) flings at the wild animal he pursues, in the stick that he seizes to strike down the fruit which hangs beyond his reach, we see the appropriation of one article for the purpose of aiding in the acquisition of another, and thus discover the origin of capital." (Sir Robert Richard Torrens: *An Essay on the Production of Wealth*, pp. 70, 71; *cf.* Karl Marx: *Capital*, vol. I, p. 205, *footnote*.) The Böhm-Bawerk definition of capital as a "collective concept of intermediate products" therefore coincides perfectly with the view of Torrens, which Marx ridiculed in the first volume of *Capital*. (*Cf.* Böhm-Bawerk: *Kapital und Kapitalzins*, vol. II, part I, p. 587.)

49. Marx's critics often ignore this point; see for example, Franz Oppenheimer: *Die Soziale Frage und der Sozialismus*, particularly the section, "Robinson—Kapitalist".

50. *Cf.* R. Stolzmann, *op. cit.*, p. 26, and John Keynes, *op. cit.*, p. 66: "Even the law of diminishing returns of the soil considered as a natural phenomenon, cannot be regarded as an economic law strictly speaking."

51. "The point of departure, the basis of the 'system', is the analysis of the elementary phenomena of the entire field of man's economic activity *in abstracto*, disregarding, therefore, the idiosyncrasies of the social relations." (Emil Sax: *Das Wesen und die Aufgaben der Nationalökonomie*, p. 68.)

52. Friedrich Engels: *Herrn Eugen Dührings Umwälzung der Wissenschaft*, Third Edition, Stuttgart, 1894, p. 150. The unhistorical character of the objectivism of the "mathematicians" and

the "Anglo-Americans" causes them to accept a purely mechanical view which in reality does not recognize society at all, but only a congeries of moving objects.

53. R. Stolzmann, *op. cit.*, preface, p. 2; *cf.* R. Liefmann, *op. cit.*, p. 5: "The so called social method of observation . . . which was applied . . . fully half a century ago by Karl Marx." In this passage, Liefmann emphasizes quite correctly the peculiarities of the Marxian method.

54. Stolzmann considers it necessary to regard social phenomena as social-ethical phenomena. In this connection, he confuses ethics considered as a totality of standards serving as a point of view for a study of the economic reality, with ethics as a fact closely related with the fact of the economic phenomena. To speak of political economy as an ethical science in the former case would mean nothing more nor less than changing this science into precepts; if we should follow Stolzmann's example in the second case, we might speak with equal right of political economy as a philological science, and the "sufficient reason" for this assumption would be that the phenomena of language likewise bear a relation to the economic life. How great is at times the insipidity of the "ethics" of these "critics" may be shown by the following passage: "Wages constitutes a *moral* quantity" (*Der Lohn bedeutet eine moralische Grösse,* p. 198; italics mine.—*N.B.*). Wages are not determined by custom and law only, "but also by the voice of conscience and an inner compulsion, *i.e.,* by the peculiar imperative of the heart." (*Sondern auch durch die Stimme des Gewissens und den Zwang von innen, d.h., durch den eigenen Imperativ des Herzens,* p, 198.) Similar sweet sentimentality may be encountered in other passages also (*cf.* pp. 199, 201, etc.). The "practical understanding" of Mr. Stolzmann induces him to protect men from the embraces of socialism (see p. 17). With this goal in view, he is not indisposed even to resort to demagogy: "Of course," is Stolzmann's utterance against the Marxists, "it is by far simpler and less responsible to content oneself with a discrediting of the existing order and, by offering to the starving stones instead of bread, to console them with the prospect of the impending upheaval. . . . Yet the worker will not enjoy waiting so long," etc. This sad stuff has evidently also been inspired in Privy-Councillor Stolzmann by the "imperative of the heart". Wherever Stolzmann is interesting, it is because of his understanding of the Marxian theory and method; but his much inflated ethics can entice only such persons as Bulgakov, Frank, and Tugan-Baranovsky.

55. Jevons also says: "Political economy must be founded upon

a full and accurate investigation of the conditions of utility: and, to understand this element, we must necessarily examine the character of the wants and desires of men. We, first of all, need a *theory of the consumption of wealth*." (*The Theory of Political Economy*, 1871, p. 46 [italics mine.—*N.B.*].) Léon Walras: *Etudes d'économie sociale*, p. 51, assigns only the consideration "de la richesse" to *pure* economics, while he considers the analysis of production to belong to the field of applied economics (*économie politique appliquée*). In Thomas Nixon Carver, we find a further approach to the point of view of production, in which Carver agrees with Marshall: "In other words, economic activities, rather than economic goods, form the subject matter of the science" (xi). In another passage, Carver arranges these "activities" in the following order: production, consumption and valuation. (*The Distribution of Wealth*, New York, 1904.) In all these authors, we find various shades of eclecticism, sometimes with regard to Marx, sometimes with regard to Böhm-Bawerk.

56. Kautsky is right in his observation that the Austrian School even improves on the Robinsonades of the eighteenth century in having Robinson not construct his articles of consumption by his own labour, but receive them as a gift from heaven. (Louis B. Boudin, *The Theoretical System of Karl Marx*, Karl Kautsky's preface to the German edition: *Das Theoretische System von Karl Marx*, p. X.) The well known exchange equations of Léon Walras are completely in agreement with the Austrian standpoint (Léon Walras: *Principes d'une théorie mathématique de l'échange*, p. 9): "Given the quantities of merchandise, to formulate the system of equations of which the prices of the merchandise are the roots," such is his formulation of his task. The reader will note that here again there is no thought of production.

57. "Production thus produces consumption: first, by furnishing the latter with material; second, by determining the manner of consumption; third, by creating in consumers a want for its products as objects of consumption." Karl Marx: *An Introduction to a Critique of Political Economy*, *ibid*, p. 280.

58. According to Karl Marx, production is "the actual starting point and is, therefore, the predominating factor." (*An Introduction to a Critique of Political Economy*, *ibid.*, p. 282. The connection between the economic theory of Karl Marx and his sociological theory is here clearly expressed and should be noted by those who consider it possible to declare their "agreement" with one phase of the Marxian doctrine while they reject the other phase.

59. Herr Frank does not understand why labour should be

singled out from among the remaining "conditions of production"; for is not the possession of real estate not only a specific form of the distribution of products, but also an "eternal necessity for mankind"? It remains undemonstrated why precisely labour should serve as a constituent stigmatum of the economic phenomena. (G. Frank: *Die Werttheorie von Marx und ihre Bedeutung,* pp. 147, 148.) The forms of distribution are the quantity derived from the "mode of production"; as for real estate ownership, the merely static element "of the possession of the soil" cannot explain any changes, any dynamics.

60. George Charasoff: *Das System des Marxismus,* Berlin, 1910, p. 19. Léon Walras' "exchange equations", already mentioned, are static. Similar is the fallacy of Vilfredo Pareto, *Cours d'économie politique,* tome premier, Lausanne, 1896, p. 10.

61. This holds true also for Tugan-Baranovsky, who is considered an "authority" in the field of the theory of crises.

62. "In a state of society, however, in which the industrial system is founded entirely on purchase and sale . . . the question of value is fundamental. Almost every speculation reflecting the economical interests of a society thus constituted implies some theory of value: the smallest error on that subject infects with corresponding error all our other conclusions." (John Stuart Mill: *Principles of Political Economy,* one-volume edition, London, 1923, p. 436.) To be sure, voices have recently been heard, inspired by Mr. Peter Struve, to the effect that the problem of value has no relation with the problem of distribution, while David Ricardo, for instance, considers the problem of value as the fundamental problem of political economy. (David Ricardo: *Political Economy.*)

The same position is taken by Tugan-Baranovsky, even though the latter's "theory of distribution" is in every way the most serious argument against this "innovation." Struve imparts a clearer logical form to the question, which makes the formulation of a theory of distribution an impossibility. The same remark applies also to Shaposhnikov (see his *Theory of Production and Distribution,* Moscow, 1912, p. 11, in Russian).

63. The only exception is Peter Struve's theory of value, which explains value as due to an average price determined by statistical method. Yet this in reality is equivalent to the annihilation of *all theory.* Bulgakov, in his *Philosophy of Economy* (in Russian) reproaches Marx for having transferred the problem of labour and its function "from the exalted position of a principle to the mercantile practice of the market" (p. 106); Bulgakov considers this to be a point of view informed only with a specious principle: the

obverse of vulgarity, so to speak. The same "critic" writes: "Is a general theory of capitalist economics of any use? I believe it is. . . . Yet can we grant the same utility to the individual theories, those on value, profit, capital? . . . I believe not. . . ." (P. 289.) Our erudite professor obviously considers it possible to present a general theory of capitalism *without* a theory of "value, profit, capital".

64. We here refer to the fact that prices do not coincide with value, do not even fluctuate around value, but rather approximate the so called "production prices".

65. Böhm-Bawerk: *Grundzüge,* etc., p. 4. Similarly Karl Menger says: "Value is not . . . a peculiarity inherent in goods, a quality of goods, but rather merely the significance which we immediately assign to the satisfaction of our needs, or attach to our lives and our well being, and, more remotely, to the economic goods as their exclusive causes." (*Grundsätze der Volkswirtschaftslehre,* Vienna, 1871, p. 81, footnote.) "Value is a judgment" (*der Wert ist ein Urteil, op. cit.,* p. 86); *cf.* Friedrich von Wieser, who considers value as a human interest conceived as a condition in the object. (*Ursprung des Wertes,* p. 79.)

66. Böhm-Bawerk: *Grundzüge,* etc., p. 4. *Cf.* also Böhm-Bawerk: *Kapital und Kapitalzins,* vol. II, second edition, Innsbruck, 1909, p. 214.

67. Böhm-Bawerk, *ibid.,* p. 5. Menger's terminology is different (*cf.* his *Grundsätze,* etc., pp. 214, 215).

68. Neumann remarks in this connection: "It is subject to dispute whether, following the analogy of purchase and yield value, we may also speak of *heating* value, *nutrition* value, *fertilisation* value, etc., in our science." ("Wirtschaftliche Grundbegriffe", in *Handbuch der politischen ökonomie,* edited by Schönberg, fourth edition, vol. I, p. 169.) J. Lehr expresses himself more specifically; Lehr objects to confusing concepts in this manner and thinks that political economy "must not lose sight of the fact that value exists always for and through man." (Conrad's *Jahrbücher für Nationalökonomie und Statistik,* New Series, vol. XIX, 1889, p. 22.) *Cf.* also H. Dietzel: *Theoretische Sozialökonomik,* pp. 213, 214. It is considered fashionable among bourgeois scholars and their adherents to point out that Karl Marx in his theory of value rather crudely concocted a mechanistic-materialistic brew. Yet there is materialism and materialism. In so far as the Marxian materialism is expressed in Karl Marx's economic system, it not only fails to lead to a fetishism of commodities, but on the contrary it makes possible for the first time a surmounting of this fetishism. Particularly, in

Karl Marx, value is one of the "forms of thought expressing with social validity the conditions and relations of a definite, historically determined mode of production, viz., the production of commodities." (*Capital,* vol. I, p. 87.) But "objectively" here does not mean "physically". . It would be just as reasonable to regard language as a physical thing. *Cf. Capital,* vol. I, p. 85, also R. Stolzmann: *Der Zweck in der Volkswirtschaftslehre,* 1909, p. 58.

69. Many eclecticists found in this statement a pretext for assuming that the theory of the classical economists as well as that of Karl Marx were not in "contradiction" with the Austrian School, but merely "complemented" the latter. For example, *cf.* Heinrich Dietzel: *Theoretische Sozialökonomik,* Leipzig, 1895, p. 23. These persons do not even understand that there is not a single thought to be found in Karl Marx that has any analogy whatever with the subjective concept of value of the Austrian School. On this point, consult the excellent pamphlet of R. Hilferding: *Böhm-Bawerks Marx-Kritik,* Vienna, 1904, pp. 52, 53, *et seq.* Particularly amusing in this connection is Tugan-Baranovsky, who, in his *Foundations of Political Economy* (in Russian) finds it possible to apply a law of proportionality between labour value—which after all has no significance except in relation to the entire society, and which cannot possibly be applied to an isolated science—and the marginal utility, which is "suited", on the contrary, only to the evaluations of the individual and lacks all meaning with regard to "political science", even from the point of view of Böhm-Bawerk.

70. Böhm-Bawerk: *Grundzüge,* etc., p. 9. This is particularly important for the Austrians. "Its [*i.e.,* the marginal utility theory's. —*N.B.*] cornerstone is the distinction between usefulness in general and the very specific concrete utility which depends in a given economic situation, on the control exercised over the goods to be evaluated. Böhm-Bawerk: "Der letzte Masstab des Güterwertes", *Zeitschrift für Volkswirtschaft, Sozialpolitik und Verwaltung,* vol. III, p. 187.

71. Böhm-Bawerk: *Ibid.,* p. 13. "All goods have usefulness, but not all goods have value. In order that value may exist, rarity (*Seltenheit*) must be associated with usefulness, not absolute rarity, as compared with the requirements for goods of the kind in question." (Böhm-Bawerk: *Kapital und Kapitalzins,* vol. II, "Positive Theorie des Kapitals", third edition, Innsbruck, 1912, p. 224.) Similarly, Karl Menger: "For instance, if the demand for a goods is greater than the available supply of it, it is simultaneously apparent that even though a portion of the indicated requirement be left unsatisfied, the available quantity of the goods in question may

not be reduced by any perceptible fraction without causing a condition in which some need or other, previously provided for, may now be satisfied either not at all, or at least less adequately than would have been the case had the above-mentioned condition not been met with." (Karl Menger: *Grundsätze der Volkswirtschaftslehre,* Vienna, 1884, p. 77.)

But the originators of the theory of marginal utility have no right at all to maintain that this thesis is original with them. We find it already in the Comte de Verri (*Economie politique,* etc., Paris, An VIII) in objectivised form, to be sure: "What are, therefore, the elements which form the price? Surely the latter is not based on utility alone. To be convinced, one has only to reflect that water, air, and sunlight have no price—yet, is there anything more useful and more necessary than these things; . . . *mere utility, therefore, cannot impart price to an object. Yet, it is its rarity only that gives it its price*" (p. 14). "Two principles, in their combination, determine the prices of objects: need and rarity" (p. 15). Similarly also Condillac (*Le Commerce et le gouvernement, considérés relativement l'un à l'autre,* Paris, An III, 1795, vol. I), while Condillac formulates the question subjectively ("nous estimons", "nous jugeons"; "cette *estime* est ce que nous appelons valeur", etc.).

In the elder Walras (M. Auguste Walras: *De la nature de la richesse et de l'origine de la valeur,* Paris, 1831), the factor of rarity is closely related with that of property, which is again connected with the capacity for exchange and the (objective) value of the article of consumption. (They "sont naturellement bornés dans leur quantité".) Leon Walras, in his "Principes d'une théorie mathématique de l'échange", gives a clear formulation: "Ce n'est donc pas l'utilité d'une chose qui en fait la valeur, c'est la rareté" (see pp. 44, 199, *et seq.*). Vilfredo Pareto (*Cours d'économie politique,* tome I, Lausanne, 1896) makes use of the term *ophelimité* (from the Greek ὠφέλιμος, useful, affording assistance) instead of the term *utilité,* for "utility" is an antonym of "injury", while political economy also recognizes "noxious utilities" (tobacco, alcohol, etc.).

72. Even Böhm-Bawerk was obliged to recognize this; in his *Grundzüge der Theorie des wirtschaftlichen Güterwerts,* he formulates the question at issue in a rather peculiar manner, maintaining that in the division of labour the evaluation of the sellers "*is usually very low*", p. 521. [Italics mine.—*N.B.*] *Cf.* also Böhm-Bawerk: *Positive Theorie:* "At the present time . . . most sales take place through the agency of professional producers and traders, who

possess a surplus of their goods which is far too great for their own consumption. In their case, therefore, the subjective use-value of their own goods is, in most cases, very close to zero: it follows that their 'evaluation figure' . . . will continue to decline almost to zero." (*Kapital und Kapitalzins*, vol. II, part I, pp. 405, 406.) Yet even this formulation is wrong, for the evaluation by the purchasers is not based on usefulness *at all* (the latter being not "approximately" but *actually* zero).

73. "But the exchange of commodities is evidently an act characterized by a total abstraction from use-value." (Karl Marx: *Capital*, vol. I, p. 44.)

74. Karl Marx: *Capital*, vol. I, p. 177. Ferdinand Lassalle also brilliantly ridiculed this theory: "Herr Borsig," says Lasalle, "first proceeds to produce machines for his *family use;* the surplus machines he then proceeds to sell. The establishments that sell widow's weeds are in the first place operating judiciously in anticipation of deaths in their own families, and then, since the latter are too infrequent, have a large surplus of mourning styles to exchange with other persons. Herr Wolff, the proprietor of the great telegraph agency in our country (Germany) first has telegrams forwarded to him for his own instruction and amusement; whatever remains after he has sufficiently sated himself in this occupation, he proceeds to exchange with the wolves of the stock exchange and the editorial offices of newspapers, who compensate him with their surplus news items and shares of stock." (Ferdinand Lassalle: *Reden und Schriften*, published by *Vorwärts*, Berlin, 1893, vol. III, p. 73.) In the precursors of the Mathematicians (Léon Walras), the exchange of surpluses is also taken as the point of departure. ("Principes d'une théorie mathématique de l'échange", *Journal des Economistes*, 1874.)

75. In his *Kapital und Kapitalzins*, Böhm-Bawerk says that the whole Marxian argumentation on this point is "fallacious". He considers that Marx has confused an "independence of a *circumstance in general,* with an independence *of the specific modalities* in which this circumstance is manifested" (first edition, 1894, p. 435). Hilferding appropriately answers as follows: "If I make an abstraction of the specific modality in which the use-value may appear, in other words, of the use-value in its concreteness, I have, *as far as I am concerned,* made an abstraction of use-value altogether. . . . It will be of no avail to declare that use-value consists in the capacity of this commodity to be exchanged against other commodities. For this would mean that the magnitude of the 'use-value' was now given by the magnitude of the exchange-

value, not the magnitude of the exchange-value given by the magnitude of the use-value" (*op. cit.*, p. 5). Further details will be found below in our analysis of "substitution value".

76. This is the so-called "Gossen Law". Gossen's formulation is as follows: "I. The magnitude of one and the same enjoyment—if indulged in uninterruptedly—will progressively decrease until satiety is attained.—II. A similar decrease in the magnitude of the enjoyment will ensue if we repeat an enjoyment previously experienced, not only in the sense that the enjoyment is smaller to the extent above noted, with each repetition, but that the magnitude of the enjoyment, at its inception, will also be less, and the duration of time during which it is experienced as an enjoyment will decrease with repetition; satiety will ensue at an earlier stage, and both the initial magnitude and the duration of the enjoyment will decrease the more, the more rapidly the repetitions are undertaken." (Hermann Gossen: *Entwicklung der Gesetze des menschlichen Verkehrs und der daraus fliessenden Regeln für menschliches Handeln*, Braunschweig, 1854, p. 5.) Friedrich von Wieser declares, in connection with this law, that "it holds good for all impulses, from hunger to love." (*Der natürliche Wert*, Vienna, 1889, p. 9.)

77. The interruptions in the vertical series are concerned with needs in which a successive partial satisfaction is not altogether, or not at all, possible (Böhm-Bawerk). It is quite admissible, in the nature of the case, to assume an uninterrupted course of the functions of utility, since "that which is correct only with regard to the uninterrupted functions may also be correct as an approximation in the case of the functions of uninterrupted type." (N. Shaposhnikov: *The Theory of Value and of Distribution*, Moscow, 1912, p. 9; in Russian.)

In Léon Walras we find a mathematical expression of the same thought, but in objectivised form ("uneven prices", depending on the relation between demand and supply). A still more elaborate objectivised formulation of the "diminution of urgency" of a given requirement as it achieves satisfaction may be found in the Americans. Thomas Nixon Carver designates utilities as the capacity to satisfy demands, etc. ("Utility is the power to satisfy a want or gratify a desire, but value is always and only the power to command other desirable things in peaceful and voluntary exchanges," p. 3).

According to Carver, price is the expression of value in money. Price varies with "utility" and relative "scarcity". Yet, Carver speaks of the wants not of the evaluating individual but of society ("wants of the community", p. 13). Carver calls the law of satiation the "*principle of diminishing utility*" (p. 15), and moves the social "standpoint" into the foreground (p. 17). The diminishing utility is considered as a social category (p. 18). The economic theory of the leisure class is here obviously transformed into an economic theory of the trust promoter.

78. "The magnitude of the want value . . . depends on the type of the want, but, within a specific type, always depends in turn on the degree of satiation achieved in each case." (Friedrich von Wieser, *op cit.*, p. 6.)

79. The designation "marginal utility" was first introduced by Friedrich von Wieser, in his work *Der Ursprung des Wertes*. The same concept is found in Gossen as the "value of the last atom"; in Jevons as the "final degree of utility", "the terminal utility"; in Walras, as the *"intensite du dernier besoin satisfait"* (*raretè*). *Cf.* Friedrich von Wieser, *Der natürliche Wert*. Von Wieser proposes to make use not of the method of deterioration but of the method of growth, which does not involve any essential difference. (*Der natürliche Wert* appeared in English translation by C. A. Malloch in London in 1893; the quotations are from the German original.)

80. *Ibid.*, p. 52. Von Wieser does not agree with Böhm-Bawerk on this point: "Any stock of goods at all has a value equivalent to the product of the number of items (or the number of partial quantities) and the specific marginal utility" (*Der natürliche Wert*, p. 24). Von Wieser's reasoning is this: Let us assume the maximum marginal utility of a goods to be equal to ten; by increasing the number of units to eleven we obtain the value of the supply, and indeed, for a possession of

	1	2	3	4	5	goods
equal to	1 x 10	2 x 9	3 x 8	4 x 7	5 x 6	
or	10	18	24	28	30	value units

and for	6	7	8	9	10	11	goods
equal to	6 x 5	7 x 4	8 x 3	9 x 2	10 x 1	11 x 0	
or	30	28	24	18	10	0	value units

(*ibid.*, p. 27)

From this point of view, the stock has no value after it attains a specific number of specimens. But this contradicts the theory and the definition of subjective value. Indeed, if we consider the entire totality of goods as a unit, we are no longer in a position to satisfy the needs connected with this type of goods. *Cf.* Böhm-Bawerk: *Grundzüge*, etc., p. 16; also, *Kapital und Kapitalzins*, vol. II, pp. 257, 258, *footnote*.

81. As to the indefiniteness of the unit of measure, *cf.* Gustav

Cassel: "Die Produktionskosten-Theorie Ricardos und die ersten Aufgaben der theoretischen Volkswirtschaftslehre," *Zeitschrift für die gesamte Staatswissenschaft*, vol. LVI, pp. 577, 578.

82. See Wilhelm Scharling: *Grenznutzentheorie und Grenznutzenlehre*, Conrad's *Jahrbücher*, Third Series, vol. XXVII (1904), p. 27. We are here not speaking of the "discounts" given on great purchases; these are based on entirely different psychological presuppositions, and should not be treated here.

83. Böhm-Bawerk: *Op. cit.*, p. 39. "The purchasers," says Scharling, "determine the price which they wish to give for the commodity, not according to their own evaluation of its utility, but according to the *conjectured* price which it is expected the consumer shall pay" (*op. cit.*, p. 20).

84. Böhm-Bawerk has the following to say concerning another theoretician of the theory of marginal utility, Friedrich von Wieser, who does not analyze the conditions of the exchange economy: "Von Wieser's theorem (Friedrich von Wieser: *Ursprung und Hauptgesetze des wirtschaftlichen Wertes*, p. 128), to the effect that the marginal utility always belongs 'to the utility sphere of the *same* class of goods' may therefore be maintained only with the modifying clause added by von Wieser himself, to the effect that no attention is being paid to the existence of an exchange traffic" (Böhm-Bawerk: *Grundzüge*, etc., p. 39). We therefore find in von Wieser no explanation of the exchange process; Böhm-Bawerk attempts to give such an explanation but at once strikes a snag. Verily, we are here dealing with an apt application of the Russian proverb: "The snout is saved, but the tail goes down; the tail is saved, but the snout goes down." *Cf.* also Léon Walras: *Principes d'une théorie mathématique de l'échange*, chapter III, paragraph *Courbes de demande effective*, pp. 12, 13, 14. Walras' formulas are in their essence nothing more than plain tautologies. *Cf.* p. 16, *op. cit.*

85. Böhm-Bawerk: *Grundzüge*, etc., p. 516; *cf.* also *Kapital und Kapitalzins*, vol. II, part I, p. 497.

86. Böhm-Bawerk: *Grundzüge*, etc., p. 519. We shall again encounter the concept of subjective exchange value in the later course of our discussion, which will provide an exhaustive criticism of this notion.

87. The difference is merely this: Roscher considers pre-social man as a proletarian, while Böhm-Bawerk considers the proletarian a pre-social man

88. "The attempts of the critics of this theory" [*i.e.*, the theory of marginal utility.—*N.B.*], says Tugan-Baranovsky, "are in most cases so weak that they require no serious refutation. The principal

objection raised against this theory, namely, to the effect that the magnitude of satisfaction we obtain from economic goods permits of no quantitative comparison, was already refuted by Immanuel Kant." (M. J. Tugan-Baranovsky: *Foundations of Political Economy*, second edition, St. Petersburg, 1911, p. 56, in Russian.) But we by no means consider this objection as one of the "chief objections", on the contrary it may be considered as one of the least important. It is quite noteworthy, however, that Tugan-Baranovsky entirely ignores the *other* objections, for instance, those raised by R. Stolzmann, both of whose works must be accessible to Tugan-Baranovsky.

89. "In order to carry out the investigation of the problem of value to its conclusion, it is necessary to attain clarity on . . . how it comes about that certain articles of utility are produced in small quantities while others are produced in large quantities." (Tugan-Baranovsky, *op. cit.*, p. 46.) Yet the reader would seek in vain for an answer to this question from the theoreticians of marginal utility.

90. "We may already state that, in the illustrations chosen by Böhm-Bawerk, we miss that earmark of economic life which is indispensable to any economy, namely, *the activity of the economic subject*. . . . A supply of goods is possible, both in the case of man as well as in the case of any other living creature, only as the result of a certain application of activity." (Alexander Schor: *Kritik der Grenznutzentheorie*, Conrad's Jahrbücher, vol. XXIII, p. 248.) *Cf.* also R. Stolzmann: *Der Zweck in der Volkswirtschaft*, p. 701: "Only as a result of the magnitude or the paucity of the given stocks, *i.e.*, in the long run, of the productiveness of the rudimentary prime factors, soil and labour, . . . do we obtain the volume of the possible supply, do we obtain the number of specimens of each goods to be brought to the spot in question, and only then do we attain an effective expansion of the possible consumption."

91. As is rightly observed by Zheleznov, the Austrians forget "that men in their economic activity seek to overcome quantitative defects in nature's gifts by exceptional exertions, thanks to which man's degree of dependence on the material world becomes more elastic and is being expanded more and more" (Zheleznov: *Foundations of Political Economy*, Moscow, 1912, p. 380, in Russian.)

92. "Its relative scarcity makes it [the commodity.—*N.B.*] subjectively an object of evaluation, while objectively—from the point of view of society—its scarcity is a function of the expenditure of labour and finds its objective measure in the magnitude of this expenditure" (Rudolf Hilferding: *Böhm-Bawerk's Marx-kritik*, p. 13).

93. In another section of his work, Böhm-Bawerk recognises the significance of this factor, but this merely illustrates his inconsistency, since the costs of production are, according to him, dependent only on the marginal utility. This is the origin of his *circulus vitiosus*; but we shall say more on this below, in another connection. Thomas Nixon Carver by no means contents himself with viewing meteors that have fallen from the skies, but analyses, above all, goods that have been produced (*cf.* Carver: *op. cit.*, pp. 27-31).

94. Let us point out also the following circumstance. Böhm-Bawerk previously maintained (in his effort to free himself from the contradictions of the theory of substitution utility) that price could not constitute a controlling principle, since the price paid by the specific individual has already been shaped with the active participation of this individual in the market; but he seems to have forgotten all this now.

95. With regard to the "direct" and "indirect" satisfaction of wants, it should be noted that Böhm-Bawerk here deviates from Karl Menger's terminology: "The value in the former [*i.e.*, in an economy in kind.—*N.B.*] and the value in the second case [subjective evaluation of exchange value.—*N.B.*] are . . . merely two different forms of the same phenomenon of economic life. But what bestows its specific character on the phenomenon of value in each of the two cases is the circumstance that the goods attain the significance which we call their goods value in the eyes of the economic man who has control of them, in the former case by reason of their direct use, and in the second case by reason of their *indirect* use. We therefore call the value in the former case use-value, but in the latter case exchange value" (Karl Menger: *Grundsätze der Volkswirtschaftslehre,* Vienna, 1871, pp. 53, 54).

96. "Rightly viewed," says Wilhelm Scharling, "the subjective evaluation of the condition of the goods appears then [in indirect evaluations.—*N.B.*] by reason of this 'subjective exchange value', to be the subordinate element" (Professor Wilhelm Scharling, *op. cit.*, p. 29).

97. Interestingly enough, Karl Menger, in a lengthy article dealing particularly with money (see *"Geld"* in the *Handwörterbuch der Staatswissenschaften,* vol. IV) presents practically no *theoretical* analysis of money.

98. "The use-value of the money commodity becomes twofold. In addition to its special use-value as a commodity (gold, for instance, serving to stop teeth, to form the raw material of articles of luxury, etc.), it acquires a formal use-value originating in its specific social function" (Karl Marx: *Capital,* vol. I, p. 102).

99. Gustav Eckstein: "Die vierfache Wurzel des Satzes vom unzureichenden Grunde der Grenznutzentheorie. Eine Robinsonade." *Die Neue Zeit*, vol. XXII, Second Half, p. 812. The Russian literature has also made reference to this fact: *cf.*, for instance, A. Manuilov: *The Concept of Value according to the Theory of the Economists of the Classical School*, p. 26, in Russian.

100. One of the latest advocates of the Austrian School, a specialist in the theory of money, Ludwig von Mises, admits, in his book, *Theorie des Geldes und der Umlaufsmittel,* that the Austrian money theory is not satisfactory. His words are as follows: "A study of the subjective value of money is impossible without dwelling on its objective exchange value; as opposed to commodities, we are dealing, in the case of money, with the existence of an objective exchange value, a purchasing power, the indispensable condition for utility. The subjective money value is always to be traced back to the subjective value of the other economic goods obtained in exchange for money; it is a derived concept. He who wishes to estimate the significance attaching to a specific sum of money by reason of its power to satisfy a certain requirement, can approach the task in no other way than by resorting to the aid of an objective exchange value of money. Every estimation of money is, therefore, based on a specific view of its purchasing power" (cited from a review by Hilferding in *Die Neue Zeit*, vol. XXX, Second Half, pp. 1025 *et seq.*). Mises attempts to eliminate this *circulus vitiosus* historically, somewhat after the same fashion as Böhm-Bawerk does in the section on substitution value, and of course with the same success. On this point *cf.* Rudolf Hilferding, *op cit.*, pp. 1025, 1026.

101. *Cf. Grundzüge*, etc., p. 62; *Kapital und Kapitalzins*, vol. II, part I, p. 28, *footnote:* "The physical share could hardly be calculated for the most part . . . and is, furthermore, of no interest at all. On the other hand, it could in most cases be easily determined what quantity of utility or value would have to be dispensed with if one should not have been in possession of a specific single factor—and this quota, determined by the possession or the existence of a single factor, I term its economic share in the total product."

102. "If one may judge from the economic practice, there exists a rule for distribution. No one, in practice, will stop with the fact that the yield is to be credited to all the productive factors together. Every one understands and applies—with greater or less accuracy—the art of distributing the yield. A good business man must and does know what a good worker is worth to him, how well a machine pays for itself, how much he must charge to raw ma-

terials, what is the yield of this parcel of land or that. If he were ignorant of these facts, if he could only make general and inclusive comparisons of investment and yield of production, he would be left entirely without information if ever the outcome should be found wanting as compared with the outlay" (Friedrich von Wieser, *Der natürliche Wert*, pp. 70, 71).

103. With the modification that this is true only insofar as we are concerned with the individual psychology of the producer of commodities. The question becomes quite different as soon as we assume a *social* point of view. Then the entire "economic assignment" (imputation) must refer to social labour alone. These two points of view are sharply distinguished by Karl Marx (*cf.* for instance, the calculation of profit on the entire invested capital, not only on its variable section). It appears to us that J. H. (Parvus) neglects this fact in his acute criticism of Böhm-Bawerk's theory of interest. See Parvus: "Ökonomische Taschenspielerei", *Die Neue Zeit,* vol. X.

104. "Yet there is nothing in the economics of traffic which could correspond to such a social marginal utility." Josef Schumpeter: "Bemerkungen über das Zurechnungs-problem," *Zeitschrift für Volkswirtschaft, Sozialpolitik und Verwaltung,* vol. XVIII, p. 102.

105. The differences of opinion between Friedrich von Wieser and Eugen von Böhm-Bawerk as to this question of imputation are based for the most part on their differing attitudes on the question of the *totality value* of goods, of which we have already spoken. *Cf.*, on this point, Böhm-Bawerk: *Kapital und Kapitalzins,* vol. II, part II, Exkurs VII. A similar criticism of von Wieser, in connection with a criticism of the concept of "totality value" is also given by Joseph Schumpeter in his already cited *Bemerkungen,* etc. (*Zeitschrift für Volkswirtschaft, Sozialpolitik und Verwaltung, vol.* XVIII.)

106. By "commodities related in production", Böhm-Bawerk means such commodities as are produced by the same means of production (*op. cit.,* p. 70).

107. We are here concerned with the reproducible "goods". The theory of non-reproducible goods (and their price, not their value, to make use of the Marxian terminology), would require separate study. In our opinion, precisely the value theory of freely reproducible goods is of great importance, since it is here that the course of the entire social evolution is reflected, and since the ascertaining of the laws inherent in this evolution is precisely the principal task of political economy. As an example of a price theory for non-repro-

ducible goods we may mention the Marxian theory of rent as connected with the question of the cost of real estate.

108. The complete text of this interesting passage is as follows: "Yet I have intentionally spoken above of 'causes' 'which become operative on the side of the productive goods', and not of 'causes' which become operative on the side of the *value* of the productive goods. For it appears to me that even though the causal impetus may have proceeded from circumstances accomplishing themselves on the side of the productive goods, the further causal chain is of such nature as to place the value of the productive goods in the chain not *before,* but *behind* the value of products. The greater number of a productive tool is (indirectly) the cause for the lesser value of the product; but the lower value of the productive tool, which is likewise an indirect result of this condition, is nevertheless not a cause, but a consequence of the lesser value of the products. The causal chain is as follows: the increased quantity of (copper ores and) copper results in a greater quantity of copper products. This produces a more pronounced satiation of the requirements to be satisfied with products of this kind; in this manner, a less important need advances to the position of the 'dependent wants', thereby the marginal utility and the value of the copper products, and, in the sequel, the marginal utility and the value of the productive goods, copper, as affected by the formal value, become depressed" (Böhm-Bawerk: *Kapital and Kapitalzins,* vol. II, part II, Exkurs VIII, p. 257).

109. To be precise, it is not a cause, but a *condition.* Failure to understand this results in the same kind of confusion as is produced in sociology by the theory of mutual interaction. *Cf.,* for example, Heinrich Dietzel: "This alternative [namely, as to which is to be considered as the cause: the value of the production costs or the value of the product.—*N.B.*] does not exist, however. On the other hand, the value of the productive goods and the value of the marginal goods mutually condition each other. No productive goods has economic value whose *products* (articles of consumption) are merely worthless—useless and superfluously abundant objects. Thus the value of the product appears as a cause of the value of the productive goods" (Heinrich Dietzel: *Zur Klassischen Wert- und Preistheorie* in *Conrad's Jahrbücher,* Third Series, vol. I, p. 694.)

110. "Böhm-Bawerk . . . imagines it is not its value, but the plentifulness of a means of production which, in such cases ('indirectly') decreases the value of the product. This is a very neat thought. But it can hardly be considered more correct than the theorem: It is not the value of the product, but the demand for

the product, which reacts on the value of the means of production. Surely the opposition between value and plentifulness does not appear very cogent. The plentifulness of production goods will have an influence on the presumable prospective value of the product—and, indeed, on its presumable quantity—only if it has already exerted an influence on the value of the means of production, or, at least, if this influence may be adjudged in advance. It will not have such an effect, if this effect on the value of the means of production has been frustrated by a cartel or by an increased demand in some other field in which this means of production may be utilized." (Dr. Karl Adler: *Kapitalzins und Preisbewegung*, published by Duncker & Humblot, München and Leipzig, 1913, pp. 13, 14, *footnote.*)

111. Exkurs XIII ("Wert und Kosten") p. 258, *footnote.*

112. Wilhelm Scharling: *Grenznutzentheorie und Grenzwertlehre*, *Conrad's Jahrbücher*, Third Series, vol. XXVII, p. 25: "The entire chain will be too long to enable one to carry out the calculation."

113. Böhm-Bawerk: *Grundzüge*, etc., p. 538: "Die Höhe des Marktpreises, den jeder Produzent für sein Produkt erlangen kann, ist massgebend für die Höhe des subjektiven (*Tausch-*) *Wertes,* den er auf dasselbe legt . . .", which, translated into English, is: "The magnitude of the market price capable of attainment for his product by each producer, is decisive in fixing the magnitude of the subjective (*exchange-*) value assigned by him to it. . . ."

114. *Cf.* Shaposhnikov: *The Theory of Value and Distribution,* in Russian, pp. 37, 38; the references to Stolzmann and Manuilov will also be found in this passage.

115. *Cf.* Gustav Eckstein, in *Die Neue Zeit,* vol. XXVIII, part I, p. 37. Böhm-Bawerk himself says: "A lumber dealer who wishes to buy lumber for manufacturing staves for barrels will quickly conclude his calculation as to the value the lumber has for him: he will estimate how many staves he can make of the lumber and he *knows* what the staves are worth according to the present market conditions; he needs to consider no other factor." *Grundzüge,* etc., p. 65. No doubt the lumber merchant will soon have finished his calculations and "needs to consider no other factor"; unfortunately, Böhm-Bawerk feels obliged to consider the other factors also.

116. *Ibid.*, p. 500. By "accepted for exchange" Böhm-Bawerk means the relation between the goods to be acquired and the goods in one's own possession. "Es ist also, allgemein gesagt, derjenige Tauschbewerber der tauschfähigste, der sein eigenes Gut im Vergleich zum einzutauschenden fremden am niedrigsten, oder was dasselbe ist, der das fremde Gut im Vergleich zu dem dafür hinzugebenden eigenen Gut am höchsten schätzt." (*Ibid.* p. 491.) Merely in order

to give an idea of the confused and stilted language employed at times by Böhm-Bawerk, we are here appending an English translation of the above quotation: "Generally speaking, therefore, that applicant for exchange will be most capable of effecting the exchange who estimates his own goods, as compared with the goods in another's possession to be obtained in the exchange, at the lowest value, or, what amounts to the same thing, who estimates the other man's goods, as compared with the goods to be given in exchange, at the highest value."

117. Peter Struve makes the difficulty of the task an excuse for not attempting it. See his article "A Contribution to the Criticism of the Fundamental Concepts . . . of Political Economy" in the Russian periodical *Zhizn;* see also N. Shaposhnikov, *op. cit.,* Preface. A similar scientific scepticism with regard to the theory of distribution may also be found in Eduard Bernstein: "The distribution of social property has at all times been a question of might and organization"; [is it possible?] or: "the problem of wages is a sociological problem which can never be explained by economics alone"; Eduard Bernstein: *Theorie und Geschichte des Sozialismus,* 4th edition, pp. 75, 76; cited by Lewin, *op. cit.,* p. 92.

118. Böhm-Bawerk says concerning his theory: "While in the remaining sections of this work [*i.e., Kapital und Kapitalzins.—N.B.*] I have on the whole been able to follow the lines of previous theory, I am in a position to expound a theory explaining the phenomenon of capital interest which is an entirely new one." *Positive Theorie,* first half-volume, p. 18.

119. Shaposhnikov, *op. cit.,* p. 81. Although Shaposhnikov formulates the problem correctly, he loses his way in the mazes of eclecticism. "Although we," he says, "do not hold their [*i.e.,* the aforementioned economists.—*N.B.*] fundamental point of view, we yet [!] recognize that they have offered such arguments in their principles of self-denial, ascription, and marginal utility as must be given serious consideration." Shaposhnikov entirely fails to see that these "principles" are indissolubly connected with the unhistorical standpoint, which is the point of the whole business.

120. *Op. cit.,* p. 54. Böhm-Bawerk also calls capital "earning capital" or "private capital"; social capital, on the other hand, might very aptly be termed "productive capital" (*op. cit.,* p. 55). It results that the concept of social capital is narrower than that of individual capital (earning capital equals private capital); furthermore, the concept of the "acquisition of goods" is of entirely different nature in the two cases. On this point see R. Stolzmann: *Der Zweck in der Volkswirtschaftslehre.* We are pointing out this

confusion though it is of no importance in our present discussion.

121. *Cf.*, for example, Böhm-Bawerk: *Positive Theorie*, p. 587, *footnote;* here Böhm-Bawerk reproaches R. Stolzmann for not distinguishing between the essence and the manifestation, between a "profit as such" and *present* profit.

122. Böhm-Bawerk: *Positive Theorie*, p. 82. A similar formulation of the question is also to be found in the Americans; *cf.*, J. B. Clark: *The Distribution of Wealth*, New York, 1908; also Thomas Nixon Carver, *op. cit.* It seems the Americans have reached a different solution of the question of profit.

123. In order to avoid misunderstanding, let us explain: Though we are here speaking of value in a socialist society, we must understand a specific category by this word, which is different from the concept of value in the commodities economy. In both cases, labour is the determining factor. But while in the socialist society the estimation of labour constitutes a *conscious social process*, it constitutes in present-day society an elemental basic law of prices, in which the genuine element of (labour) valuation is lacking.

124. Not to mention the fact that the socialist society presupposes the elimination of narrow specialisation.

125. It is interesting to note that even economists who distinguish between "purely economic" and "historic-legal" conceptions of capital, have eyes only for *private* capital and ignore entirely the fact of the class monopolization of capital. To a certain extent this is true even of Rodbertus. Adolf Wagner gives the following definition of capital: "Capital, as a pure economic category, considered independently of the existing legal conditions for the possession of capital, is a stock of such economic goods as may serve as technical means for the manufacture of new goods in an establishment: it is a stock of means of production or a 'national capital', or respectively, a section of the latter. Capital, in the historical-legal sense, or possession of capital, is that section of the total fortune of a *single person* (the italics are the author's own) which serves this person as a means of acquisition in the gaining of an income from the capital (rent, interest), in other words, is owned by this person for this purpose, a 'rent fund', 'private capital'" (Adolf Wagner, *Grundlegung*, second edition, p. 39, cited from Böhm-Bawerk's quotation, pp. 124, 125). In general, Böhm-Bawerk's frivolous attitude toward the historical phase of the question is very striking: on page 125, for instance, he remarks that of course everything is historical in character; machines did not arise before the eighteenth century; books have only begun to appear since the invention of printing, etc. He never suspects for a moment that he is dealing with entirely

different *types of economic* structure. Böhm-Bawerk can see in the Marxian point of view only the fact that Marx regards capital as "exploitation capital" (see p. 90).

126. "Merely for the reason that the workers cannot afford to wait until the roundabout course begun by them, in the winning of raw materials and the manufacture of implements, has achieved its final fruition, they become dependent economically on those who possess the above-mentioned intermediate products in the finished state, in other words, on the 'capitalists'" (*Ibid.*, p. 150).

127. It is for this reason that Macfarlane designated the Böhm-Bawerk theory of profits as an "exchange theory"; Böhm-Bawerk himself considers it more appropriate to call it an "Agio theory"; *cf.*, Böhm-Bawerk: *Kapital und Kapitalzins.*

128. An American advocate of this theory, S. N. Macvane, even supposed that the word "abstinence" might be replaced by the word "waiting"; *cf.* Böhm-Bawerk: *Kapital und Kapitalzins,* appendix: Macvane himself attempts to distinguish carefully between his theory and that of abstinence.

129. With his stock of ninety fish, he can make nets and thus increase the productivity of his fishery operations; furthermore, Böhm-Bawerk, as is quite natural for a leisured professor, terms this category of profits "interest".

130. See Böhm-Bawerk: *Positive Theorie,* pp. 539 *et seq.* Further details will be found below.

131. R. Stolzmann: *Der Zweck in der Volkswirtschaftslehre,* p. 288. ". . . For, what else is the 'detaxation', the 'agio' of the profit on capital, than the utilisation of an advantage accruing to the capitalist by reason of his happening to be the 'happy possessor', who occupies a peculiar status which he enjoys by reason of the property and distribution functions of the present order of society, a status to which the designation of 'surplus value', if we may use Böhm-Bawerk's own words, 'applies even more appropriately than could even have been dreamed of by the socialists who invented this terminology'."

132. J. H. (Parvus): "Ökonomische Taschenspielerei: Eine Böhm-Bawerkiade," *Die Neue Zeit,* Jahrg. 10, vol. I, p. 556.

133. "As a general rule, present goods have a higher subjective value than future goods of the same type and quantity. And since the resultant of the subjective evaluations determines the objective exchange value, as a general rule the present goods will also have a higher exchange value and a higher price than future goods of the same type and quantity" (*Positive Theorie,* p. 439).

134. In the last analysis, Böhm-Bawerk traces back expenditures

in the purchase of means of production to expenditures for the acquisition and the use of the soil and of labour. "For the sake of simplicity," he pays no attention to the former.

135. "Then the present goods will also be reserved for the latter [the future goods.—*N.B.*] and will derive its value from it, it then happens to be equal in value to a future goods that might serve the same use" (*Positive Theorie*, p. 442).

136. "The future goods which can derive its own [value.—*N.B.*] only from . . . a *future* (the italics are the author's own) use" (Böhm-Bawerk: *Positive Theorie*, p. 442).

137. Friedrich von Wieser: *Der natürliche Wert*, p. 17, *cf.* also Ladislaus von Bortkievitz: *Der Kardinalfehler der Böhm-Bawerkschen Zinstheorie*, p. 949. "The fact that cases of the opposite type are by no means rare militates against Böhm-Bawerk's assertion that a predisposition to underestimate the value of future goods is of very general occurrence." The same point is raised by Stolzmann: *op. cit.*, pp. 308, 309.

138. Wilhelm Lexis: *Allgemeine Volkswirtschaftslehre*, p. 72. *Cf.* also Parvus, *op. cit.*, p. 550: "The present value of labour for the worker is a fiction: it can at most be spoken of mathematically as a quantity equal to zero."

139. *Cf.* also p. 461 of the same work. Here Böhm-Bawerk determines, among other things, the value of the aggregate as the individual value multiplied by the number of individuals, which is in contradiction with his own theory. He attempts in vain to extricate himself from his contradiction on pp. 461, 462. Furthermore, this question really is of a different order and was already discussed by us in the appropriate portion of Chapter I.

140. The difference between Table IV and Table I is merely that Table I gives its figures in products, while Table IV gives its figures in values.

141. *Positive Theorie*, p. 462. In order to elucidate Böhm-Bawerk's position, we must point out that his concept of the "production period" is essentially different from the usual understanding of the term. According to him, this period is not the entire duration of time embracing all operations, including preparatory operations, for, in our epoch, in which "production without capital has almost entirely disappeared . . . such a strict calculation would be obliged to start the production period of almost every article of consumption in some long-past century" (p. 156). "It is more important and more correct, however, to consider the epoch that elapses, *on an average* between the expenditure of the successively applied productive forces, the labour, the utilisation of the soil, on

a certain task, and the completion of the ultimate articles of use. That production method is more pronouncedly capitalistic which as an average rewards more tardily the expenditure of original production forces upon it" (p. 157). If the production of a unit of goods on an average requires an expenditure of one hundred days of labour, and if, furthermore, the completion of the process would require one day of labour to be performed ten years before such completion, and one day each in the ninth, eighth, seventh, sixth, fifth, fourth, third, second, and in the last year preceding completion, while the remaining (ninety) days must be put in just before the completion of the entire process, the first day of labour would be rewarded in ten years, the second day in nine years, etc. The average reward for all ten days would be:

$$\frac{10+9+8+7+6+5+4+3+2+1}{100}=\frac{55}{100}$$

i.e., approximately in one-half year. This is the production period, *i.e.*, a unit of the means of production of one hundred days would be expended in the production process, whose production period is one-half year. The longer the production period, the greater the yield of production, the greater therefore "the productivity of capital". Lewin excellently characterises the complete confusion and folly of this notion: "First and foremost, we cannot understand how and why Böhm-Bawerk arrives at this average in the calculation of the production period. The tool produced in the above example, ten years ago, and which was necessary for the production of the now completed article of use, belongs entirely and not only one-tenth to the production of this commodity; the other intermediate products may also not be credited only as applications. In calculating costs, only a certain appropriate portion of the means of production may be considered; in determining the duration of production, on the other hand, each means of production must be considered as a *whole*" (*op. cit.*, p. 201). The concept of the production period, on which Böhm-Bawerk's calculations are based, is therefore completely nonsensical; even Böhm-Bawerk does not attempt to apply this definition at all places.

142. A similar interpretation of this point is given by Shaposhnikov, *op. cit.*, p. 120. As a matter of fact, the relation between the duration of the production process and the supply in stock is more complicated in Böhm-Bawerk (*cf. Positive Theorie*, pp. 532-536); yet this is of no import to us at this moment.

143. For the sake of simplicity, we are assuming the same degree of diminution as is taken by Böhm-Bawerk to be the result of the first two causes, *i.e.*, the series: 5, 3.8, 3.2, 2.2, etc.

144. Among other things, Böhm-Bawerk fails to consider in his tables the diminution of the value of the product, as its quantity increases, *i.e.*, he ignores the ***most important*** postulate of the theory of marginal utility.

145. Bortkievitz, *op. cit.*, pp. 957, 958: "Yea, the technical superiority of present production goods is supposed, indirectly, to result in a value agio in favour of present articles of consumption, since the availability of the latter is said to 'liberate' certain means of production in favour of 'a technically more profitable service of the future'. Here the argumentation is moving in a circle. For as a matter of fact an excess in value held by present productive goods over future productive goods can exist only as the result of a variation in the estimation of articles of consumption separated by an interval of time, and now this difference in the evaluations is to be explained, in its turn, by the value relation between present and future productive goods!"

146. As we have already learned from the chapter on value, it is very important, from the point of view of the Austrian School, to know not only the *quantity* of the goods supplied and demanded (the "volume" of supply and demand), but also the *subjective evaluations* of each unit on the part of both parties concerned ("intensity"). Definite prices can only be arrived at as a result of the ratio between these two quantities.

147. *Op. cit.*, p. 538; Böhm-Bawerk therefore admits in this passage that the *capitalists* do not estimate their present goods as higher than future goods.

148. *Op. cit.*, p. 541; the competition among the capitalists as a result of the production credit, is therefore here considered to be the chief cause for the formation of profit.

149. Karl Marx: *Capital*, vol. II, pp. 421, 422; see also, in the same work, the section on Adam Smith's resolving of the exchange value into $v + s$, *op. cit.*, p. 427 *et seq.*

150. *Cf.* for example, the *Positive Theorie*, pp. 541, 542, 543, 544. We are ignoring the arguments concerned with such persons as seek consumption credit, for Böhm-Bawerk ascribes practically no importance to these arguments; see *Positive Theorie*, p. 296, *footnote*.

151. An old, now almost forgotten economist, N. F. Canard, excellently formulated this Marxian thought, at any rate he formulated it at least as well as the much vaunted Rodbertus; see

N. F. Canard: *Principes d'économie politique,* Paris, An X (1801); in this book, which was *couronné par l'Académie,* the author says: "He owes it, therefore, only to his industry and his labour, that there exists such a wide difference between civilised man and natural or wild man" (page 3). "We must therefore distinguish, in the case of man, between the work necessary for self-preservation, and superfluous work" (page 4). "It is only by accumulating a quantity of superfluous labour that man has been able to emerge from the savage state and to create for himself, in succession, all the arts, all the machines, and all the means of multiplying the product of labour by simplifying the labour" (p. 5).

152. The destruction of capitalism, which has already been achieved in Russia, and is beginning all over Europe, is now assigning the objective physical quality of the product to a rôle of principal importance and relegating to the background the product considered as value; of course, from the point of view of capitalism, this is only another phase of the "abnormality" of the situation.

153. This article was originally written as a contribution to the Marxian Journal *Prosvyeschenye* ("enlightenment"); it contains an analysis of the eclectic theory of the principle of coalition as applied to the theory of value. It is therefore an appropriate appendix to our present book. Of course, certain passages in this essay, which have no direct bearing at all on the logical side of the theory of Tugan-Baranovsky, which is now out of date, have been outdistanced by the facts. Yet we are leaving the entire article in its original form, the more since certain predictions in the article have been literally fulfilled. Thus, for example, Mr. Bulgakov has taken the veil, while Tugan-Baranovsky has succeeded in becoming a minister in the counter-revolutionary cabinet. It is also interesting to note that Mr. P. P. Maslov is now attempting to emulate Tugan-Baranovsky's practices.

154. To be more precise, it must be equal at the *margin.*

155. In order to avoid misunderstandings, let us point out expressly that we are for the present not directing our criticism against Tugan-Baranovsky's terminology, and are using the terms "value" and "labour costs", in the same sense as they are found in Tugan-Baranovsky.

156. Tugan-Baranovsky refers here to Sombart's article: "Zur Kritik des ökonomischen Systems von Karl Marx," see *Braun's Archiv,* vol. VII.

157. We are here speaking of the social "costs"; as we shall see below, this designation is very important.

158. *Op. cit.*, p. 70. We shall mention another point, although it has no direct connection with the question; Mr. Tugan-Baranovsky does not understand (pp. 68, 69) the importance of exchange value in Marx; we are therefore glad to elucidate this concept for him. In the course of his analysis, Marx is *occasionally* obliged to *assume* that *the commodity is sold according to its cost of production* (*value*). In this case, costs would be equivalent to exchange value; this means that Marx is not speaking of the *absolute*, but of the *relative* quantity.

158. Tugan-Baranovsky: See page 55.

BIBLIOGRAPHY

Adler, Karl Dr.: *Kapitalzins und Preisbewegung*, München, 1913.

Ammon, Alfred: *Objekt und Grundbegriffe der theoretischen Nationalökonomie*, Vienna, 1911.

Bastiat, Frédéric: *Harmonies économiques*, Brussels, 1850 (*Harmonies of Political Economy*, Edinburgh, 1870).

Bernstein, Eduard: *Zur Theorie und Geschichte des Sozialismus*, Fourth edition, Berlin, 1904.

Böhm-Bawerk, Eugen: *Geschichte und Kritik der Kapitalzins-Theorie*, Second edition, Innsbruck, 1900.

— *Kapital und Kapitalzins* (*Capital and Interest*, London, 1890), II. Abteilung. *Positive Theorie des Kapitals*. Innsbruck, 1912. (*Positive Theory of Capital*, N. Y., 1923.)

— *Grundzüge der Theorie des wirtschaftlichen Güterwerts* (*Jahrbücher für Nationalökonomie und Statistik*), New Series, vol. xiii, Jena, 1886, pp. 1-82, 477-541.

— *Einige strittige Fragen der Kapitaltheorie von Karl Marx*, Vienna, 1900.

— *Zum Abschluss des Marxschen Systems* (*Staatswissenschaftliche Arbeiten. Festgaben für Karl Knies*). Berlin, 1896. (*Karl Marx and the Close of His System*, London, 1898.)

— *Der letzte Massstab des Güterwertes*, "Zeitschrift für Volkswirtschaft, Sozialpolitik und Verwaltung," vol. iii. (*The Ultimate Standard of Value*, Phila., 1894.)

Bortkievitz, Ladislaus von: *Der Kardinalfehler der Böhm-Bawerkschen Zinstheorie* (*Schmoller's Jahrbücher*, vol. xxx).

Boudin, Louis B.: *Das theoretische System von Karl Marx*, Stuttgart, 1909. This is a translation of the author's *The Theoretical System of Karl Marx*, Chicago, 1910.

Bukharin, Nikolai: *Eine Ökonomie ohne Wert*, (*Die Neue Zeit*, 1914, Nr. 22, 23, 46).

Bulgakov, Sergey: *Philosophy of Economy* (In Russian).

Canard, N. F.: *Principes d'économie politique*, Paris, 1810.

Carver, Thomas Nixon: *The Distribution of Wealth*, N. Y., 1904.

Cassel, Gustav: *Die Produktionskostentheorie Ricardos, etc.* (*Zeitschrift für die gesamte Staatswissenschaft*, vol. 57).

Charasoff, Georg: *Das System des Marxismus*, Berlin, 1910.

Chuprov, A. A.: *Contributions to the Theory of Statistics*. (In Russian.)

Clark, John Bates: The Distribution of Wealth, N. Y., 1908.

Condillac, Etienne Bonnot de: *Le Commerce et le gouvernement, considérés relativement l'un à l'autre*, Paris, An III (1795).

Cossa, Luigi: *Introduzione allo studio dell'economia politica*, Milan, 1892. (*Introduction of the Study of Political Economy*, London, 1893.)

Diehl, Karl: *Sozialwissenschaftliche Erläuterungen zu David Ricardos Grundgesetzen der Volkswirtschaft und Besteuerung*, Part II, Leipzig, 1905.

Dietzel, Heinrich: *Theoretische Sozialökonomik.*

—*Zur klassischen Wert- und Preisstheorie* (*Conrad's Jahrbücher, Third Series*, vol. i).

Eckstein, Gustav: *Zur Methode der politischen Ökonomie* (*Die Neue Zeit*, vol. xxviii, First Half).

—*Die vierfache Wurzel des Satzes vom unzureichenden Grunde der Grenznutzentheorie* (*Die Neue Zeit*, vol. xxii, Second Half).

Engels, Friedrich: *Ludwig Feuerbach und der Ausgang der klassischen deutschen Philosophie*, Stuttgart, 1888. (*Feuerbach, the Roots of the Socialist Philosophy*, Chicago, 1906).

—*Hernn Eugen Dührings Umwälzung der Wissenschaft.* Third edition, Stuttgart, 1894. (*Landmarks of Scientific Socialism*, Chicago, 1907.)

Frank, S.: The Marxian Theory of Value and its Significance (In Russian).

Gide, Charles: Précis du cours d'économie politique, 1878. (*Political Economy*, London, 1914.)

Gossen, Hermann: *Entwicklung der Gesetze des menschlichen Verkehrs und daraus fliessender Regeln für menschliches Handeln*, 1854.

Hilferding, Rudolph: *Das Finanzkapital. Eine Studie über die jüngste Entwicklung des Kapitalismus*, Second edition, Vienna, 1920.

—*Böhm-Bawerks Marx-Kritik.*

Jevons, W. Stanley: *The Theory of Political Economy*, London, 1871.

Kaulla, J. R.: *Die geschichtliche Entwicklung der modernen Werttheorien*, Tübingen, 1906.

Kautsky, K.: Preface to Louis B. Boudin: *Das theoretische System von Karl Marx*, Stuttgart, 1909.

Keynes, John: *The Scope and Method of Political Economy*, London, 1891. (Bukharin quotes from Manuilov's Russian translation, Moscow, 1899.)

Knies, Karl: *Die politische Ökonomie vom geschichtlichen Standpunkte*, 1883.

Lassalle, Ferdinand: *Herr Bastiat-Schulze von Delitzsch, der ökonomische Julian, oder Kapital und Arbeit*, in Ferdinand Lassalle's *Reden und Schriften.* Neue Gesamt-Ausgabe. Herausgegeben von Eduard Bernstein, vol. iii. Berlin, 1913.

Lewin, David: *Der Arbeitslohn und die soziale Entwicklung.*

Lexis, W.: *Allgemeine Volkswirtschaftlehre*, 1910.

Liefmann, Robert: *Über Objek, Wesen und Aufgabe der Wirtschaftswissenschaft* (*Jahrbücher für Nationalökonomie und Statistik*, vol. cvi; Third Series, vol. li; Jena 1916, pp. 193-249).

Lifschitz, F.: *Zur Kritik der Böhm-Bawerkschen Werttheorie*, Leipzig, 1908.

List, Friedrich: *Das nationale System der politischen Ökonomie*, 1841. (*National System of Political Economy*, Phila., 1856.)

Manuilov, A.: *The Concept of Value according to the Doctrine of the Economists of the Classical School.* (In Russian.)

Marx, Karl: *Theorien über den Mehrwert*, 4 vols., Berlin, edited by Karl Kautsky.

—*Das Kapital*, 3 vols. Seventh edition, Otto Meissner's Verlag, Hamburg, 1914, 1919. (Our quotations are from the Kerr edition, Chicago, 1909-1915.)

—*La Misère de la philosophie*, Paris, Giard & Brière, 1907. (*The Poverty of Philosophy*, Chicago, 1910.)

—*Zur Kritik der politischen Ökonomie*, Stuttgart, 1907. (*A Contribution to the Critique of Political Economy*, Chicago, 1913.)

Menger, Karl: *Die Irrtümer des Historismus in der deutschen Nationalökonomie.* Vienna, 1884.

—*Grundsätze der Volkswirtschaftslehre*, Vienna, 1871.

—*Untersuchungen über die Methoden der Sozialwissenschaften und der politischen Ökonomie insbesondere*, 1883.

Miklashevsky, A.: *The History of Political Economy*, Dorpat, 1909. (In Russian.)

Mill, John Stuart: *Foundations of Political Economy.* 2 vols., London, 1848; (author quotes Soetbeer's German translation. Third edition, 1869, vol. ii).

Mises, Ludwig: *Theorie des Geldes und der Umlaufsmittel.*

Neumann, F.: *Naturgesetz und Wirtschaftgesetz* (*Zeitschrift für die gesamte Sozialwissenschaft.* Edited by Artur Schäffle).

— *Wirtschaftliche Grundbegriffe* (*Handbuch der politischen Ökonomie*, edited by Schönberg).
Oncken, August: *Geschichte der Nationalökonomie*, Leipzig, 1902.
Oppenheimer, Franz: *Die soziale Frage und der Sozialismus*, Jena, 1912
Pareto, Vilfredo: *Cours d'économie politique*, Lausanne, 1896.
Parvus: *Der Staat, die Industrie und der Sozialismus*, Kaden, Dresden.
— *Ökonomische Taschenspielerei* (*Die Neue Zeit*, Vol. X, under the nom de plume of J. H.).
Pribram, Karl: *Die Idee des Gleichgewichtes in der älteren nationalökonomischen Theorie* (*Zeitschrift für Volkswirtschaft, Sozialpolitik und Verwaltung*, vol. 17).
Ricardo, David: *Principles of Political Economy and Taxation*, 1817. (Author uses Eduard Baumstark's German translation: *Grundgesetze der Volkswirtschaft und Besteuerung*, Leipzig, 1877.)
Rodbertus-Jagetzow, Karl: *Das Kapital*, Vierter sozialer Brief an von Kirchmann. Berlin, 1884.
Sax, Emil: *Das Wesen und die Aufgaben der Nationalökonomie*, Vienna, 1884.
Scharling, Wilhelm: *Grenznutzentheorie- und Grenznutzenlehre. Conrad's Jahrbücher*, Third Series, vol. 27 (1904).
Shaposhnikov, N.: *The Theory of Value and of Distribution*. Moscow, 1912. (In Russian.)
Schatz, Albert: L'individualisme économique et social, 1904.
Schmoller, Gustav: *Grundriss der allgemeine Volkswirtschaftslehre*, Leipzig, 1908.
— *Über einige Grundfragen der Sozialpolitik und der Volkswirtschaftslehre*. Leipzig, 1898.
Schor, Albert: *Kritik der Grenznutzentheorie, Conrad's Jahrbücher*.
Schumpeter, Josef: "Die neue Wirtschaftstheorie in den Vereinigten Staaten," *Jahrbücher für Gesetzgebung, Verwaltung und Volkswirtschaft*. Edited by Gustav Schmoller, vol. 34.
— *Das Wesen und der Hauptinhalt der theoretischen Nationalökonomie*, Leipzig, 1908.
— "Bemerkungen über das Zurechnungsproblem," *Zeitschrift für Volkswirtschaft, Sozialpolitik und Verwaltung*, 1909.
Smith, Adam: *Wealth of Nations*, London, 1895.
Sombart, Werner: "Zur Kritik des ökonomischen Systems von Karl Marx" (*Archiv für soziale Gesetzgebung und Statistik*, vol. vii, Berlin, 1894, pp. 555-594).

— *Der Bourgeois*, 1913.
— *Luxus und Kapitalismus*, 1913.
Spitz, Philipp: *Das Problem der allgemeinen Grundrente bei Ricardo, Rodbertus und Marx* (*Jahrbücher für Nationalökonomie und Statistik*, vol. 106, Third Series, vol. 51, Jena 1916, pp. 492-524, 593-629).
Stolzmann, R.: *Der Zweck in der Volkswirtschaftslehre*, 1909.
— *Zur Kritik der Grundbegriffe der politischen Ökonomie*. A paper in the periodical "Zhizn".
Struve, Peter: *Economy and Price*, Moscow, 1913. (In Russian.)
Torrens, Robert: *An Essay on the Production of Wealth*, London, 1821.
Tugan-Baranovsky: *Fundamentals of Political Economy*. (In Russian.)
Verri, Comte de: *Economie politique ou considérations sur la valeur de l'argent et les moyens d'en faire baisser les intérêts*, etc. Paris.
Wagner, A.: *Grundlegung der politischen Ökonomie*.
Walras, Auguste: *De la nature de la richesse et de l'origine de la valeur*, 1831.
Walras, Léon: *Etudes d'économie sociale. Théorie de la répartition de la richesse sociale*, Lausanne-Paris, 1898.
— *Théorie mathématique de la richesse sociale*, Lausanne, 1883.
— "Principe d'une théorie mathématique de l'échange," *Journal des Economistes*, 1874.
Wieser, Friedrich von: *Uber den Ursprung und die Hauptgesetze des Wirtschaflichen Wertes*, Vienna, 1884.
— *Der natürliche Wert*, Vienna, 1889. (*Natural Wealth*, London, 1893.)
Wicksell, Knut: *Zur Verteidigung der Grenznutzenlehre*.
Zheleznov, V.: *Fundamentals of Political Economy*, Moscow, 1912. (In Russian.)

INDEX

Printed in the USA
CPSIA information can be obtained
at www.ICGtesting.com
JSHW021410250624
65368JS00002B/105